Passionate Uprisings

Passionate Uprisings

Iran's Sexual Revolution

Pardis Mahdavi

Stanford University Press
Stanford, California

Stanford University Press
Stanford, California

Printed in the United States of America on acid-free, archival-quality paper

Library of Congress Cataloging-in-Publication Data

Mahdavi, Pardis, 1978-
  Passionate uprisings : Iran's sexual revolution / Pardis Mahdavi.
    p. cm.
  Includes bibliographical references and index.
  ISBN 978-0-8047-5856-7 (cloth : alk. paper)--ISBN 978-0-8047-5857-4 (pbk. : alk. paper)
  1. Youth--Sexual behavior--Iran--Tehran. 2. Sexual freedom--Iran. 3. Sex--Political
aspects--Iran. 4. Sex--Religious aspects--Islam. 5. Iran--Social conditions--1997- 6. Iran--
Politics and government--1997- I. Title.
  HQ27.M32 2008
  306.70835'0955--dc22   2008027906

Designed by Bruce Lundquist
Typeset at Stanford University Press in 11/15 Bell MT

For my grandmother Ghamarjoon

Contents

Prologue

In Iran, all things related to sex had a door, a closed one. Now we, this generation, are opening them one by one. Masturbation? Open it. Teenage sexual feelings? Open that door. Pregnancy outside of marriage? Open it. Now the youth are trying to figure out what to do with all these opening doors.

Khodi, male, age twenty-three

Over the past several decades, so it is said, a sexual revolution has occurred, and revolutionary hopes have been pinned to sexuality by many thinkers for whom it represents a potential realm of freedom, unsullied by the limits of present day civilization.[1]

A S THE DOOR of the Iran Air jet plane opened, I could feel my heart beating anxiously. As I began to descend the staircase to the tarmac, a gust of wind from the plane's engine blew away my headscarf, leaving me to chase the tiny piece of silk down the runway while the other passengers gasped and scolded me. "Don't push!" yelled one woman, as I lunged to follow my headscarf and dropped all my baggage on the stairs. "What are you doing, sister?" yelled an angry man, attempting to avert his eyes from my now uncovered head. I finally caught my scarf and wrapped it tightly around my head and hair. In reality, it took only a minute to get my scarf back, but it seemed like an eternity.

It was the summer of 2000, three years after President Mohammad Khatami, Iran's first reformist Islamic president, was elected. It was also my first trip to Iran. For more than two decades I had watched the events of the country my parents called home unfold from halfway across the world. As Iran endured a bloody revolution, a prolonged war with its neighbor, mass political executions, and major political protests, I pieced together a story from media reports, monthly phone calls to relatives I had never met, and accounts from my friends who had traveled there and came back with vivid stories about parties, love, and poetry readings, contrary to the images I had seen on television.

In the 1990s, following the death of Ayatollah Khomeini and the end of the Iran-Iraq war, many refugees and political exiles living in the Iranian diaspora began to return to Iran to visit or repatriate; their desire for reunification with the home country had increased due to political changes that occurred during the Rafsanjani and Khatami presidencies. Although the Iranian community in California, where I grew up, had become strong and vibrant, many of my parents' friends had dreams of returning to Iran, and thus began exploring this option by visiting there during those first few summers when Iran began experiencing an "opening up."[2] My family, tarnished by memories of violence and extremism, was still fearful about visiting; my father explicitly forbade my mother to take us should she decide to go herself. During the summer of 1998, however, many of my friends went to Iran with their parents, and came back with stories that caught my attention. Two of my friends were exposed to their first dating and sexual experiences while visiting Tehran that summer. They told stories of sexual experimentation and mating rituals that I had never thought would take place in my imagined Iran, which included only women clad in black chādors wailing and whipping themselves, and black-bearded men with heavy hearts and souls. When I had thought about relationships in Iran, I had foolishly thought that marriages were arranged, and that dating and sex before marriage were heavily regulated and limited, and I was reminded of Iranian films that featured arranged marriages and conjugal debt.

My friends' romantic tales of a change in sexual and social discourse caught me by surprise and sparked my interest. I was curious to understand how young Iranians in Iran interact with one another as well as with the regime, and thus I was determined to visit Iran soon. In May of 2000, having been encouraged to write feature stories on the Iranian women's movement as a stringer for the *Los Angeles Times Magazine*, I finally opened a door into the world I was so desperate to experience.

The night I stepped off the airplane in Tehran's Mehrabad International Airport is forever etched in my memory. Fearful that I might be caught without a headscarf again, this scene dominated my nightmares. For years to come I would dream that I had left the house in Tehran naked, without my proper Islamic dress, and was being chased by the infamous *komite* (the Iranian morality police). However, amid these nightmares and in my transition to being an Iranian American in Iran, I began to hear and feel the changes in sexual discourse that friends and informants[3] described as a sexual or sociocultural revolution—*enghelāb-e-jensi* and *enghelāb-e-farhangi*, respectively. By the time I'd been in Tehran for a few months, I had experienced firsthand this sexual and social world in both the public and private spheres. I had begun to see the insatiable hunger for change, progress, cosmopolitanism, and modernity that many of my Tehrani friends linked to sex. As I listened to their stories, which were both romantic and pragmatic, I heard them speak of embodying rebellion and resistance, and I began to realize that these were important narratives about the project of modernity in Iran. I began to see the construction of a young Tehrani identity in a changing sociopolitical sphere, and started to see the push for social change that they were enacting and embodying.

Little did I know that night when I chased my headscarf down the runway that I would spend the next seven years regularly walking off planes at that airport. That summer was a turning point in my life. When I returned from Tehran I began my graduate studies, and decided to pursue a course of study that would enable me to further investigate the changing sexual and social culture of young Iranians. I maintained my contact with friends and informants I had met in 2000, and returned to Iran in the summer of 2002. In 2004 I officially embarked on the ethnographic fieldwork that forms the basis of this book, although I had been conducting informal fieldwork since 2000. In 2005 and 2007 I made my final data-collecting visits to Tehran and have since been in touch with my friends and informants there through regular phone calls and daily visits to Iran's blogosphere—the cyberspace that thousands of young

Iranians now inhabit through their daily Weblogs, or blogs. The tide is changing in Iran and the young people are increasingly facing new challenges—challenges that they are eager to accept.

When looking at a changing Iran it is important to focus on the majority of Iran's population—the restless urban youth—and the ways in which their self-defined and self-termed sexual revolution has caused a discourse shift and a change in the state apparatus of the Islamic Republic of Iran. Following are two anecdotes—one from the very early stages of my fieldwork in 2000 and one from my most recent field visit in the summer of 2007—that help to illustrate this shift.

July 2, 2000

I spent last night in my friend Diar's car, parked outside his parents' apartment. It wasn't comfortable, but I consider myself lucky. The evening had started out innocently, with Diar suggesting that we go visit a friend of ours, Mahmoud, who was hosting a scholar of the famous Iranian poet Hafez. Mahmoud had promised a lengthy discussion of sexuality within Hafez's poetry, but more importantly he said we would be talking about the sexual revolution, enghelāb-e-jensi, with which I was now so fascinated. A few other friends were meeting us there, and we were going to have a quiet evening, good food, and good wine that they had managed to purchase illegally from their alcohol dealer that afternoon. When we showed up, about fifteen young people were there, chatting and laughing and drinking wine, with British rock band Pink Floyd humming in the background. As we entered, I took off my Islamic clothing—a black headscarf, or *hejāb*, and matching black, loose-fitted *mānto*.[4] Mahmoud brought me a glass of wine that smelled delicious. Just as I relaxed into a worn-out old couch near the window, there was a knock at the door. I didn't think anything of it and was about to take a nice long gulp of wine, but everyone else froze. "We aren't expecting anyone else, are we?" was all Diar managed to get out before the door was forcefully opened by members of the komite. Almost automatically, the women (myself included) grabbed the nearest headscarf and coat, threw out their glasses of wine, and headed for the windows. Diar and I were sitting close to a window, so he grabbed my hand and led me out to the balcony. "Jump," he said, "I'll be right behind you." "Jump?" I asked incredulously, looking at the bushes below. "Just do it, before they come get us; I'll be right behind you." All I managed to hear before I jumped was members of the komite yelling at Mahmoud and breaking various belongings. Diar and I jumped and then ran top speed to his car. He started the engine and looked in the rearview mirror. "We're being followed," he said, motioning toward two uniformed men on motorbikes. "Get down, lay down under the backseat," Diar commanded, and I obeyed. The komite continued to follow us, and when we got to a stoplight, they pulled up next to us and got off their motorbikes. They walked up to our car and one of them spat angrily on Diar's face. Diar was silent. "What were you doing driving away from that apartment so fast?" they asked him. He remained silent; I could sense his fear. One of the officers reached over and slapped Diar in the face while the other began attempting to drag him out of the car. Other cars drove past us; their drivers saw the scene and the dire straits we were in but looked the other way and just continued driving. Just then Diar snapped out of his shock, pulled away from the officers and back into the car, and sped away, driving expertly down alleys and side streets until we eventually lost them. "Given the way this evening ended up unfolding, I don't think I have it in me to take you home; it's just too much tonight," he said. "But you can't sleep in my house because my mother's aunt is visiting from Mashad; she is very religious and would *lowe medan* [rat us out], so you're going to have to sleep in the car, OK?" he said. Neither of us thought to use the logical option of calling a taxi for me, we were that distraught. I nodded silently at Diar's request, suddenly aware that I had soaked myself in sweat and tears out of the fear that the evening's events had inspired.

Seven years later. . . .

June 2, 2007
Last night I witnessed an event that assured me things have changed, and as if witnessing it wasn't enough, it made the morning papers! The morning papers! Meaning that the Islamic Republic is openly admitting that something is going on, that the calm façade of the public secret is being broken. As we were driving home at about eleven o'clock

last night we saw a usual sight in Tehran's busy city streets: a traffic jam. But this one was different. People had abandoned their cars and were all running toward an intersection where there was a parked car. Ever curious, my friend Laleh and I got out of her car and started running toward the commotion. When we got there, the scene I saw inspired both hope and laughter. A woman was standing on top of the hood of her car, taking off her clothes. "You accuse me of the crime of bad hejāb just because it slid a few centimeters back; I'll *show* you bad hejāb!!" she screamed, taking off first her hejāb and mānto and then her shirt, bra, and belt. As the two komite officers who had tried to arrest her made their way to her car to grab her, other people ran out of their cars and attacked the officers. Thirty men outnumbered each komite member, with women standing on the sidelines cheering and yelling insults at the officers. Laleh and I took in the scene for a few minutes before heading back to our car. On our way home Laleh was very excited, so she began driving quickly and carelessly. In an attempt to speed past two more komite officers on motorcycles, she accidentally bumped into them and almost knocked the back officer off his bike. Instantly they used their sirens and pulled us over. "Shoot," I said, suddenly afraid of being caught. "You should have been more careful; I'm not in the mood to deal with the authorities right now." "Relax," she said, smiling as she looked at the officers in her rearview mirror. "These guys are young and cute; I bet all they're looking for is a date or to flirt with us for a bit," she said, pushing back her red mānto to reveal her thighs. I looked at her in shock. "What are you doing?!" I asked. "Don't worry, the season of *begir begir* [harassment] is over. That was last month; now we're back to doing what we want," she whispered. I had to remind myself that in recent years harassment apparently came only in seasons.

The officers came over and smiled at us. "Why did you hit me?" asked one of them playfully. "It was a love tap," said Laleh with a big grin while batting her eyelashes. I sat in silence, muted by confusion as Laleh continued to flirt with them. "How come your little friend is so quiet? Is she a mute?" asked the officer, nodding his head toward me. "No, she's just from the other side of the water (*un taraf-e āb*)," she explained to them as I shifted in my seat. In all my time doing fieldwork, I always tried to conceal, especially from the komite, who would only harass me more for it, the fact that I was from the United States. "Oh, are you *khāreji* [an outsider]?" asked the officer. I looked at him and nodded, expecting a smart-aleck comment to ensue. Instead he just smiled at me and said, "Well, welcome, pretty lady. You ladies free for dinner?" The irony of a flirtatious morality policeman.

What had happened in these seven years? This is a major point of inquiry in this book. In the summer of 2000 I went to Iran to study urban young Iranians' views about the government, the Iranian women's movement, and changes that had taken place since the election of reformist president Khatami. What I ended up researching that summer, and for the next seven years, was the emerging young adult culture in Tehran. I described and analyzed the meaning and significance of young Tehranis' changing sexual and social behavior in relation to Iran's sociopolitical climate. As friends, relatives, and informants began to tell me about and show me the underground world of the self-defined sexual revolution taking place in Tehran and other urban centers throughout the country, the focus of my study became the intersection of sexuality and politics in postrevolutionary Iran and, what I am particularly interested in now, the resultant changes in public discourse that this intersection has caused. Young men and women alike from varying socioeconomic groups told me of their numerous premarital and extramarital partners, relationships that they had formed against the backdrop of a theocratic regime that exacted heavy punishment on those who violated laws against premarital and extramarital sex. Informants asked me for help and for information about reproductive health. Friends took me to elaborate parties inside and outside of Tehran. Runaway women with whom I spent many evenings told me about their sexual escapades. Music, dancing, alcohol, and premarital sex—all punishable offenses according to the Islamic Republic's strict moral policies—were taking place in an almost hedonistic fashion in Tehran on a daily basis. Still other informants asked me to accompany them as they sought out illegal, black-market abortion procedures and potions.[5] For seven years I followed the status and tone of this sexual revolution, paying close attention to the ways in which the state began to adjust, however clumsily, to its changing youth.

I watched women from both uptown and downtown[6] walk the streets of Tehran wearing more and more makeup and dressing less and less Islamic in style. Shrinking and colorful headscarves replaced long, black, loose-fitting and conservative hejāb, and form-fitted overcoats replaced looser, more conservative mānto. All the while these women explained to me that what I was witnessing was a sexual and social revolution, intended to have political reverberations. What seemed to other people to be fashion choices or responses to peer pressure actually had an intellectual architecture (for some of the youth), and some of these choices of self-presentation had a political stance behind them. I realized then that it was important to look at the ways in which the sexual revolution enacted by the young people has brought about changes in the social, economic, and political spheres of Iran.

It is important to focus on the youth (aged fifteen to thirty) in Iran, not only because they make up the majority of the population and are the future of the country, but also because, as Roxanne Varzi notes, "they were the target of the Islamization project that hinged on the war; now they are supposed to be an index for the success of the Islamic Republic."[7] Specifically, the Islamic state sought to formulate ideological subjects through enforcement of proper "Islamic being," hoping that "the ability to make people act out, to write and discipline bodies (through public laws, for example) is precisely what is said to make people believe."[8] The Islamic Republic relies on the performance of proper Islamic rituals to produce believing Islamic citizens, and thus continues to attempt to enforce such rituals of Islamic ideology as proper Islamic dress and comportment. In response, many young Tehranis are subverting those rituals in an attempt to reclaim them, as well as their own agency and citizenship, vis-à-vis the state. Many young adults argue that they are now using their bodies and their sexualities to speak out against what they view as a repressive regime. In other words, because the Islamist[9] regime exercises much of its power through a fabric of morality (by legislating the body, comportment, and proper behavior), the young people indicate that in the absence of an option for overt dissent, regardless of how peaceful, they are attacking the regime by seeking to create a state of *fitna*, or moral chaos, to undermine the regime's moral fabric. I argue that consequently a new sexual culture is emerging among Iranian young adults that has captured the attention of the state.

Urban young adults, who compose almost two-thirds of Iran's population,[10] are highly mobile, highly educated (84 percent of young Tehranis are currently enrolled in university or are university graduates; 65 percent of these graduates are women),[11] and underemployed (the unemployment rate among this age group is 35 percent).[12] Many are also highly dissatisfied with the current regime. Through in-depth research that looks at often-overlooked elements such as style,[13] daily lives, sexual practices, and health and education infrastructure, it may be possible to illuminate the ways in which young people in Tehran interact with their social, political, and economic environment in order to express their dissatisfaction with their current situation. The demographic shift in favour of young people who are now educated (due to the Islamic Republic's free education policies) but underemployed and highly dissatisfied with the regime has combined with a lot of free time and exposure to other young adults who are dissatisfied with their environment.

This book aims to unpack and assess the sexual and social revolution that young Tehranis claim to be enacting. Throughout my time in Iran I heard hundreds of young people use the phrase *sexual revolution* in reference to changes taking place in Tehran. Key informants reminded me that wearing tight māntos and headscarves that revealed highlighted hair was often more than a fashion statement and more than being part of a global youth culture. They emphasized that changes in style were about codes and speaking to a regime that would hear only these signals. Their style and their attempts to embody a sexual revolution, they told me, were their ways of speaking back to the regime, to the morality police who had made them suffer for so long, and to other potential members of the quiet revolution.

I do not claim to provide here a comprehensive picture of youth culture in Iran. I recognize that it is impossible to make generalizations about the majority of a nation's population, especially given the ethnographic nature of the study as well as my small sample size. My goal instead is to explore the emergence of a new youth culture against the backdrop of a changing religious and political sphere. I want to assess the changes in sexual and social thought and dialogue taking place among certain groups of young adults in Tehran, and simultaneously to understand the potential risk factors and health outcomes in which this shift in youth culture has resulted. I hope that by bringing the voices of my informants to the reader, using their own words, I can begin to understand and map out some of the changes taking place in Iran today from the perspective of the nation's youth.

1   Welcome to Tehran

May 18, 2005

I feel the rumble of the engine under my seat and the harmony
of honking horns. Beeeep! Beep! Beep! Beeeeeeep! Sitting in the
passenger seat of my friend's old Paykan (a popular old car in Iran),
I can smell exhaust, though I don't know whether it's coming from
our car or from any of the seemingly thousands of cars that are
sitting, stuck in traffic, on Mollasadra freeway. I watch the heat rise
as women use the bottom portions of their headscarves to cover their
noses and mouths, an unsuccessful attempt at blocking out the smell
of the traffic, melting asphalt, and smog that settles on Tehran in
the summertime. It's hot. I feel beads of sweat trickling down my
neck and back, and as they make their way to the seat beneath me, I
realize that I have been sitting on a poster of the latest Iranian film,
Mārmulak ("Lizard"), which has been outlawed in Iran for its mockery
of Iranian clerics, but become popular among the youth, who buy, sell,
and trade it on the black market. I pull the poster out from underneath
me, careful not to tear it as I try to make sure that the dampness of
my sweat has not already damaged it. I hold up the poster and begin
to read out loud the actors' names. My friend Shadi turns up the
latest hit from Shahram Shabpareh, a popular Iranian singer living
in Los Angeles who now has a large fan base in Iran. A few years ago
she would have been listening to American pop music, but this new
trend toward popular diasporic music is interesting, and as I try to
understand its significance I am distracted by a young man in the
car next to us who is leaning out the window to talk to me. "I love

that song," he says as Shadi turns down the music to flirt with him. A few months ago I would have been surprised at this open display of heterosexual sociability and potential mating; now I see that it is part of daily life for some people as they sit in their cars on the winding freeways and streets of Tehran, waiting to get to their destinations. I look over at my friend, who is smiling and batting her mascara-coated eyelashes at the young man next to us. In a stroke of luck, traffic starts to move. Who would have thought that in Tehran traffic is worse than in Los Angeles or New York? Amazing. Shadi shifts gears as we start to move. "Come to my place," the young man across the way shouts, swerving across the road to come closer to us while not hitting the now moving traffic. I shake my head. We are going to a shelter for runaways, I remind her. "No thanks," she says halfheartedly. "I have good movies to show you on my DVD player," he offers. She is unimpressed. Finally, the young man writes his phone number on a piece of paper and almost causes an accident as he pulls his car, a Kia Pride, close to ours and passes his phone number to me to give to Shadi. She smiles. It's always an adventure on the streets of Tehran.

May 18, 2007

I'm riding in Shadi's new car, a Peugeot, and we are driving past Evin Prison (for political prisoners). My stomach begins to churn as I stare out the window and am reminded of the recent arrests of fifty-two Iranian Americans, most prominently Haleh Esfandiari, an Iranian-American academic who conducts research on women and gender in Iran. At this point several of my friends and colleagues have been arrested, and I have been told that if I don't leave the country soon I will be next. I look at Evin Prison and fear grips me as I tell Shadi to pull over because I think I'm going to throw up. "You think you might be next to go in there?" she asks me, motioning toward Evin. "Look, I don't know, but I don't want to wait around to find out," I tell her.

There is silence as Shadi pulls over the car and we get out to sit on a small patch of green grass that is near the highway. Then Shadi puts into words what I have been dreading for the last seven years as I have been doing my research: "You may not ever be able to return once you leave," she tells me. I nod. I know this but have been putting

it out of my head for a long time. "I guess it comes with the territory,"
I respond. "I should have known better than to do an ethnographic
study of sex in Iran," I add, taking a deep breath and sitting down on
the grass as hundreds of cars whiz by us. "Well, how are you going to
remember Tehran?" she asks.

I look at her and start thinking about things to remember if I
don't ever come back. I look at the cars passing by and tell myself
to remember the traffic: to think about *artiste bāzi,* driving "like an
artist," swerving between cars and showing off bravery and talent on
the road; about how each and every driver is a talented artist when it
comes to navigating the roads and traffic of Tehran; about the boys
dancing in the car next to us as they pass by. I tell myself to think
about Hamid Askari and Reza Sadeghi, Iranian singers approved by
the Islamic Republic who have become the rage in Tehran, and how
their popularity is so different from that of Shahram Shabpareh, the
Los Angeles–based pop star who was popular in 2005 and in 2000
and 2004, when *khāreji* (foreign) music was still popular. I think about
how I need to remember the improved cell phones and cell phone
services, and about how people rely on those little pieces of technology
that transmit fifty thousand text messages per day and that are young
people's lifelines. I reflect on the air quality, which actually has gotten
better in the southern parts of town, where there is now less traffic
thanks to the use of *tarh-e terāfik* (special driving permits) that allow
drivers who purchase them to enter sectioned-off parts of town. I take
a deep breath and tell myself to remember the smell of freshly cut
grass in the air—the odor of freshness mixed with burning fuels and
dirt. I think about the burning corn, the *goje sabz* (green plums), the
fasl-e mivehā (fruit seasons). I think about the crowded public taxis,
in which three strangers, men and women together, are crammed
into the back seat of a Paykan, limbs touching and odors emanating;
I wonder how it happens that in a country where social interaction
between men and women is limited it is appropriate and even common
for men and women to sit almost on top of one another, whether in
a taxi or on the back of a motorbike. Scenes flash before me from
the past few years: a woman's chādor getting caught in the door of
a taxicab as it speeds off, leaving her uncovered; two men riding on

the highway on a motorbike, holding their helmets in their hands rather than wearing them lest their freshly gelled hair get ruined. I think about my friends here and how we all read the newspaper and every morning try desperately to get online to see what the news has to say about Iran. I think about the significance that reading the papers takes on in Tehran, a place where you have to be aware of your surroundings because of their effect on your life. I remind myself to remember how everyone is always looking over their shoulder, in every move they make, to see who is watching. I think about the morality police in their green suits, harassing people, women especially, even in their cars. I tell myself I will remember the conspiracy theories that everyone has about the U.S. government, about the Islamist regime, and even about their own neighbors.[1] I declare I will never forget the snowcapped peaks that can be seen from almost every part of the city, and that I will remember the wine flowing at uptown parties, and the crack being passed around at downtown gatherings in the park. I tell myself to go home and remember the parks with their flowing streams and flowers in bloom during most seasons of the year. I reflect on the juxtaposition of a mural telling us about how the nation's youth are important or showing a martyr, next to a billboard advertising Dior and Prada sunglasses. I think about how frustrating it is to sit in traffic, yet exciting at the same time because we never know what we are going to see. I will remember going out for *āb-miveh* (juice) from a juice stand, something I'd never thought of as recreation until my informants showed me its popularity and significance. I feel my stomach churn, and tell myself to remember that living in a police state means having a constant feeling of unease, of wondering what's going to happen next, what the newest rules will be. I will recall honking horns, angry shouts from angry cab drivers, the smell of fumes emanating from the bus next to me or from my informants who chain-smoke. I will remember going to parties and coming home with my hair and my clothes reeking of smoke; and pulling my headscarf back on my head, covering my nose with it so that the fumes of Tehran's pollution don't get to me. I will think of the sounds of music, and the sounds of the call to prayer; cell phones that cut off, and cell phone calls that don't go through; staying inside the house because I didn't want to deal with the stresses going on outside. I will remember the hedonism of some of my informants, who live each day as though it might be their last; I will recall the cocaine on the coffee table, the alcohol bar fully stocked. I will hear the beat of the music we danced to so many nights.

I feel the tears coming into my eyes as my head fills with memories. Shadi sits down beside me and asks if I am OK. "I'm not okay," I tell her. "Tehran has changed me, and I will never again be okay."

In 2006, when I began writing this book, I struggled with where in Iran's long history to begin in order to historicize the current Iran that my informants now inhabit. I wondered if I should begin by describing the first prodemocratic constitutional revolution, of 1906, when important advances were made toward the emancipation of women and the creation of modern institutions, but it seemed too far removed from a young Tehrani's experiences. I then thought to begin by describing the events of 1953, when Prime Minister Mohammad Mossadegh's democratically elected government was overthrown by a joint British-American CIA coup in 1953, setting the stage for the anti-Western sentiment that eventually toppled the regime of Mohammad Reza Shah Pahlavi in the late 1970s. I resolved, however, that because this is a story about the children of the revolution, it is appropriate to begin in the late 1970s and early 1980s, when most of them were born into what became the Islamic Republic of Iran.

After the British-American coup of 1953, some of Iran's younger generation, who had witnessed the elimination of nonviolent dissidents, chose the path of armed rebellion against the dictatorial monarchy (the Shah's regime). Then, throughout the 1960s and 1970s, many people became disillusioned with the Shah's rule of Iran, specifically his ties with the West. Many Iranians began to feel that the Shah no longer represented Iranian interests but rather had sold out to Western cultural and capitalist influences. A strong movement of "Iran for Iranians" began to emerge to reclaim Iranian heritage and culture, and to reject Western capitalist influences. Interestingly, many of the anti-Shah, anti-West discussions began taking place in the mosques, because these were seen as the only safe spaces away from the surveillance of the SAVAK, the Shah's secret police. Numerous women involved in this movement began to don hejâb in an effort to reclaim their Iranian and Islamic heritage by covering their bodies to hide them from the outside gaze. (This is discussed further in the next chapter.) Although many factions of revolt—some secular, some leftist, some religious, and a significant number who saw themselves as Islamic Marxists—originated during this time, the movement led by Ayatollah Khomeini began to emerge as the loudest voice. In 1979 this movement gained enough momentum to stage a revolution that ousted the monarchy. In the aftermath, the clergy took control of the state, introducing the Islamic system of law called *sharia*. This clerical rule has fundamentally changed the worlds of everyone remaining in Iran, making everyday life largely centered on Islam and increasing state monitoring of and control over individual lives.[2]

The 1980s were marked by a period of economic decline, which continues to this day as the reverberations of global economic sanctions are felt throughout the country; unrest and conflict, including the Iran-Iraq war, which resulted in a high mortality of young men between the ages of fourteen and forty; and the arrests and executions of political prisoners by the Islamist regime. As one young Iranian woman notes in her blog *Khabarnâme* (newsletter), "We had a revolution so that a regime that from 1957 to 1975 had at most killed hundreds of Iranians . . . could be overthrown, and we brought in a regime that would kill thousands during its first days alone . . . let alone its first years."[3] In September of 1980, shortly after the Islamic revolution and a mere year and a half after Khomeini's return to Iran, Iraq invaded Iran, and the eight-year Iran-Iraq war began. This war eventually had a significant effect on the parents (or more accurately, the fathers) of the children of the revolution. The 1980s are also often referred to as a period of cultural revolution whereby members of the newly installed Islamist regime sought to bring back what they considered to be Islamic culture by installing mandatory Islamic legal dress codes, by shutting down universities to re-create an Islamic curriculum and purge the universities of any and all professors who did not comply with these changes, and by attempting to marginalize women in the labor force through policies preventing them from working in certain fields (such as prohibiting them from becoming judges) and by placing quotas on women's enrollment in certain programs of study at universities.[4] During this time commonly referred to as "Islamification," the government also encouraged pronatalist policies to repopulate the Islamic republic with nationalist Muslims.

The early 1990s (after the death of Ayatollah Khomeini) were a time of transition from one Islamist authority to another. As conservative and reform parties vied for power, the social and political environment oscillated between restrictive and progressive directions. In 1997, much of this changed as President Khatami, who is often described as the voice of young people, women, and reform, was democratically elected by 75 percent of the population and came to power shortly thereafter. The election of President Khatami, however, did not diminish and still has not diminished the authority of the Ayatollah Khamenei, the spiritual ruler of the Islamic Republic of Iran, who still controls the army, the komite, and much of the magistrate.[5] With the election in 2005 of conservative, hardliner President Mahmoud Ahmadinejad, the extent of religious control over daily life has tightened; the current president aims to increase the powers of the komite, who have already begun their raids on private homes, beauty salons, gyms, popular restaurants, and café hangout spots for young people. Many scholars argue that the target of the Islamists has always been the secular elite, and Iranian elites living in Iran note that this attack has only worsened since the election of President Ahmadinejad.[6] The future of religious and state control over personal lives is uncertain; nevertheless, Iran's current religious leaders continue to influence legislation on health, education, morality, comportment, and other issues that confront their young adult population.

Today the Islamic Republic of Iran is a country in transition. This transition is as much political and socioeconomic as it is demographic. Iran is theoretically an Islamic republic governed by Islamic law, or sharia, which, as interpreted by the clerics in power, mandates among other things that women and men should interact minimally before marriage and that women should be covered in "proper" Islamic dress (ideally a cloak from head to toe, hiding any body shape). Much of Islamic law also seeks to legislate social, sexual, and familial behaviors through the language of morality. Ideas about heterosexual relationships sanctioned by religion (*mahram*)—such as mother to son, husband to wife, and so on—and those that are not (*nāmahram*)—such as men and women who are not married or related by blood—are now part of state rhetoric and have been discussed in religious spaces, at public gatherings, and in private settings such as the home.[7] Some of the religious and moral rhetoric coming from the state is also reproduced by families (in the case of young people whose families are religious) while other families (mostly the nonreligious middle class) often contradict the harsh rules imposed by sharia. In accordance with sharia, heterosocial interactions between unmarried and unrelated men and women are forbidden and punishable by lashings and imprisonment; sex before marriage and extramarital sex can also result in harsh punishment, such as lashings, imprisonment, and for the crime of adultery, death. The morality police often patrol the streets of Iran looking for people who are in violation of these Islamic moral values to arrest and punish.[8]

In the outwardly religious and conservative world of the Islamic Republic of Iran, significant numbers of urban young people are skeptical of, disaffected from, or openly hostile toward the values underpinning the Islamic revolution. The regime has effectively stifled political opposition, and attempts by young people to express their aspirations and criticisms have been met with suppression, social control, and violence. Due to young people's experience with overt political activism being violently punished, there is little appetite among some urban young Iranians for engaging in overt political activism or rebellion. Scarred by the traumas of revolution, an eight-year war with Iraq, and decades of clerical rule, Iranians, it could be argued, no longer wish to risk bloodshed to achieve the changes they desire. Young Tehranis with whom I spoke indicated that for their generation social behaviors seem to have become expressive of experiments with and aspirations toward political and sociocultural reform—a more quiet, less overt form of rebellion. More than half of my informants specifically characterized their behavior as part of a larger sexual and social revolution.

The Islamic authorities demand sexual and social modesty, and dedication to living an Islamic lifestyle. This lifestyle entails the strict enforcement of Islamic performative rituals, including prayer three to five times a day, Koran recitation, and observance of the holy months of *Ramadan*[9] and *Muharram*,[10] as well as refraining from alcohol consumption, contact with members of the opposite sex prior to marriage, music, and dancing.

"They tell us 'go pray, five times a day, go visit the shrine of the prophets, observe your fasts,'" noted one twenty-three-year-old man from Tehran, "but they don't tell us why. They teach us how to prepare for prayer, over and over, how to enter the bathroom with the right foot or the left, but never for practical daily interactions! Why?" Many urban young adults throughout the social landscape of Tehran increasingly reject Islamist social restrictions because they feel that religion has been forced on them without their choice, and they see their social behavior (including style of dress, sociability, and interactions) as political statements to bring about social change. The rebellion of some young people—most of them from the secular middle and upper classes—represents resistance and alternatives to ideas about sexual purity, the good Islamic body, and gender segregation that have been in effect since the revolution.

Iranian young adults are growing up in a clerical environment, under a regime that challenges their notions of agency and citizenship and their right to their own bodies. They are also faced with issues of gender segregation and a regime that openly favors men over women. For example, according to current sharia, a woman's testimony in court is worth half that of a man, and the blood money, or *diye* (payment due to a family after the murder or accidental death of a family member), due to a woman's family is exactly half that owed to a man's family. It is important to recognize, however, the positive changes in women's involvement in the workforce and in higher learning that the Islamic Republic's gender-neutral education policies have brought about. Women now have increasing opportunities in higher education, which leads to increased employment opportunities—a significant change.

The behavior of many young Tehranis is understood and described by my informants as rebellious or dissident. Such behavior is seemingly found, although on a lesser scale, in young adult cultures in many countries. It is vital to look at the many layers of what young Iranian people are challenging, including what they perceive as tradition relative to their perceptions of modernity, of their parents, and of the authorities, sharia, and the regime. By employing an analytical framework that notes that modernity is increasingly expressed in the transformation of gender relations[11] or in the transformation of intimacy in modernizing societies,[12] some young Iranians seem to find it easier to negotiate their everyday interactions and intimate relations than to negotiate changes in the state. For some of these young people, gender and social relations are contexts in which to talk about citizenship. Many of them may be reacting to questions related to citizenship through intimacy and intimate relations. In this way, young people perceive themselves as acting out a sexual and social revolution in their daily lives on the streets of Iran.

The Ayatollah Khomeini, the leader of the Islamic revolution, famously said, "The Islamic revolution is not about fun, it is about morality; in fact, there is no fun to be had in the Islamic Republic."[13] This quote is found on posters and walls in many parts of Tehran, where one can also find young adults spray painting over it, talking and laughing, and defiantly wearing "bad" Islamic clothing (for women, form-fitting overcoats, open-toed shoes, rolled-up pants revealing ankles, and loose head coverings with strands of hair flowing from beneath them; for men, collarless T-shirts, shorts, and hair gel on long locks of hair). The young people often smile at these Islamist slogans that dot the busy Tehran streets on their way to parties where they drink alcohol and dance to the background noise of satellite TV; to sex parties; to one of the many popular dance classes, although dancing is strictly illegal; or to an underground store where they can purchase many of the CDs and movies outlawed by the Islamic Republic. Perhaps some observers would see this behavior as a movement toward consumerism, but most young Tehranis with whom I spoke talked about the importance of the black market as a symbol of social change. These young people, as well as their parents, also emphasized that the fact that young people can now purchase goods on the black market and are seen in the streets wearing makeup, nail polish, or fancy imported sneakers is an important indicator of changes that have taken place vis-à-vis the state, which now allows young people to walk the streets with more relative freedom and access to black market goods than they had in the past.

Iran's economy today has been hit hard by global sanctions forced on the Islamic Republic. Unemployment is rising and the economy is in a downward spiralling depression. Because a large portion of the young adult population are either students at one of the universities or graduates who are either unemployed or employed only part-time, young people in Tehran have a lot of free time to spend roaming the streets and attending social gatherings. Even those young adults who do work full-time manage to find time to gather in public squares, malls, or coffee shops, thereby demonstrating the changes taking place in the Islamic Republic.

During the first decade following Islamification (the 1980s) and partially into the 1990s, young people had few public spaces in which to congregate and gather socially. Post-Khomeini, after the Iran-Iraq war, and then more prominently during the Khatami era, young adults in Tehran began to carve out more recreation spaces for themselves in the public sphere. Popular Tehran mayor Gholam-Hossein Karbaschi put considerable effort and resources into creating many of these public spaces (such as parks and outdoor recreation areas) and has been credited with many of the positive changes that took place in Tehran in the late 1990s.[14] Parks and malls became increasingly popular hang-out spots, and since 2000 many coffee shops, pizza parlors, cafeterias, and food courts, where young people can get together, meet, mingle, and potentially date, have opened. These spaces, and the fact that young people can gather in these spaces without arrest and harassment, indicate some of the changes that have taken place in the Islamic Republic, due partially to the negotiations between the youth and the state, and partially to members of the regime who are sympathetic to changes desired by many of the youth. Daily lives that would otherwise be monotonous and filled with the frustration of seeking employment or, for many young people, being employed in a field that is not related to their course of study or interest (for example, many engineers are now taxi drivers and many computer scientists now work in construction) are instead filled with group activities such as hiking, playing sports, attending dance classes, going to beauty salons, spending time with friends at coffee shops or Internet cafes, joining clubs and organizations, or sometimes just walking or driving through the busy Tehran streets looking for potential partners. In the evenings, the young adults keep themselves occupied with a myriad of activities, including attending elaborate parties (for young people in the north) or small gatherings at the homes of friends or family members (specifically, parents who are opposed to the Islamic ideology of the state permit social gatherings in their homes while parents who are more allied with the Islamists' ideology forbid such gatherings, forcing their children to attend parties in other homes without their knowledge), talking with friends, studying, or perfecting a hobby (such as painting, photography, or writing). Other young people in the southern (lower-class) parts of town often work in the evenings or spend time in parks or outside of mosques or the main bāzār in town. Still other informants indicated that they spend their evenings in the company of their partners or potential partners.

In Iran, the punishment for premarital sex ranges from social and familial estrangement to imprisonment and lashings; drinking and dancing could call for detainment, accompanied by up to seventy lashings. More than three-quarters of my informants talked about experiences of being detained and punished by the morality police; many young adults noted that being arrested is a regular occurrence. In recent years, however, young people are held overnight and intimidated rather than physically punished—again, another sign of the changes taking place in the last decade that are important to examine in this context. An unmarried or unrelated young man and woman, if caught in the company of one another, even in a car or public park, might receive up to eighty-four lashings each, although even this has become rare. Young Tehranis often go on dates and spend significant time alone in cars, in parks, and at restaurants, and many of the young adults I spoke with were unapologetic, even brash, about their behavior. "We know that if we get caught we could go to jail," began one eighteen-year-old woman. "We recognize the consequences of our partying, but we do it anyway. It's sort of an F-you to the system, if you know what I mean; it's our way of protesting." She calls her partying a kind of *laj*, a word that can be loosely translated "playful rebellion." "That's half the reason we party so hard and engage in such sneaky and risky behavior," she added. Perhaps there is no place in the world where the stakes and implications of partying are so high. However, it is of no small significance that young people are now able to gather, to wear increasingly revealing "Islamic" clothing, and to engage in social relations with less punishment than before, which is evidence that the state is trying, however clumsily, to adjust to its youth and their behavior.

Tehran's landscape has changed dramatically since the revolution. The city's population has nearly doubled, and urban sprawl has led to the creation of new neighborhoods and, since the 1990s, a new kind of vibrant consumer culture in direct opposition to Islamic values. (During the 1980s and well into the 1990s, the Islamic morality police kept much of the consumer culture at bay.) Today, fast-food restaurants, cafes resembling Starbucks (where young Iranians meet to date), spas, beauty salons, and gyms that have alternating male-female workout days line the busy city streets. By 2004, former Tehranis such as my parents found themselves lost in the city in which they had grown up, surprised by the explosion of consumer culture that surpassed that of their world before the revolution. Sprawling and congested highways, *hookah* (water pipe used for smoking tobacco or opiates) cafes, video rental stores, and ATM machines make the physical attributes of the city totally different from the image that Islamists and the Western media project about Tehran.

Becoming the Sex Doctor

July 3, 2005

I am tired. I am exhausted. I haven't slept in five nights because I want to make sure I get the research methods right. My days are filled with interviews with teachers, counselors, parents, and doctors. My nights are consumed by the youth. I have breakfast with parents who are worried about their children's future. I have lunch with counselors at drop-in centers who want to give young people the support they need to maintain mental and physical health. In the evenings I go either to a party uptown with rich or middle-class kids or to an abandoned warehouse downtown to see how young people with fewer monetary resources indulge in the sexual revolution. Sometimes these parties are raided and everyone ends up spending the night in jail; other evenings I go to a local shelter to meet runaway youth and spend the night trying to understand their world. Last night I slept on the street, underneath a bridge called Pol-e-Gisha, with a group of commercial sex workers. They hadn't welcomed me at first, had said they didn't trust me and wouldn't talk to me about their lives; but week after week I returned to the streets and walked with them, sat with them, and stayed with them until dawn. Last night they finally welcomed me, offered me some of their food, and let me stay with them in their hiding spot under the bridge. It has been six days since I slept more than a few hours per night. I must be awake during the day to talk to the "adults," but I must also be a night owl to spend time with the youth, some of whom don't emerge from their homes until the cloak of night rolls in to conceal them. I don't know if I'm making sense of this anymore.

Most of my interviews took place during my time in Iran in the summers of 2000, 2002, 2004, 2005, and 2007. My first two visits were more journalistic than the others and served to secure access into the world of the youth I continued to study throughout my research on broader aspects of cultural change in Iran. The bulk of my data were collected during 2004, 2005, and 2007. My research in Iran focused on participant observation, focus groups, and in-depth interviews. I observed and talked with people at Internet cafes, public parks, shopping malls, parties, gyms, dance classes, runaway shelters, sex worker venues, private homes, and local squares where young people tended to gather. Additionally, I volunteered at two drop-in centers and one needle exchange, gave seminars at Tehran University, joined the advisory board of an anthropology journal at the university, and conducted archival work at the Ministry of Health, the Ministry of Education, and a number of nongovernmental organizations. I also continued to do online research about young adult culture on a weekly basis by reading Iranian blogs, spending time in chat rooms, engaging in instant messaging with informants in Iran, and closely monitoring the newest in Iranian pop and underground culture, including music, videos, and online publications.

My research in Iran consisted of conducting 105 face-to-face in-depth qualitative interviews with urban youth (aged eighteen to twenty-five) of Tehran, both men and women, of varying socioeconomic classes.[15] All names and biographical information throughout the book have been fictionalized to protect my informants. Additionally, although many of the interviews I conducted were recorded and later transcribed, several interviews were not taped (either due to the venue and situation in which the interview was conducted or at the request of the interviewee), and thus their utterings have been reconstructed from memory. In addition, because much is lost in translation from Persian to English, I have chosen to translate the quotes of my informants in such a way as to convey their demeanor, and thus the quotes may not always read like Persian phrasing or idioms.

In addition to in-depth face-to-face interviews, I also carried out forty-three online interviews with students from Tehran University (in the form of e-mails and instant messages). I also collected thirty-five sexual history surveys, which I designed with the help of an anthropologist and a psychologist from Tehran University and distributed among a random sample of university students across three universities in Tehran. In addition, I ran six focus groups of from six to eight young men and women. In the summer of 2007 I interviewed twenty-eight parents of young adults about their views on the changing youth culture, and I interviewed and observed twenty professionals, including doctors (mostly gynecologists), nurses, counselors, and teachers, throughout my time in Iran.

It is important to reiterate that the young people described throughout this book come from or have spent extensive amounts of time in Tehran, and thus are all urban young adults; most are lower-middle, middle, and upper-middle class and literate, and for the most part would consider themselves secular.[16] Throughout my time in Iran, however, I did interview and spend a significant amount of time with many young people from lower-class parts of town. This book focuses on young Tehranis who are apparently secular and middle class because they seem to have become the trendsetters for young people of all classes throughout the city and the country. Although this ethnographic study focuses on only 105 young people in Tehran, these particular people have played an integral role in constructing the contemporary ideological and intellectual narrative about sexuality, social interaction, and the present moment in Tehran. The young people I describe are an important group to study, follow, refer to, and gauge change by because they have been at the heart of changes taking place in behavior, outlooks, and ideas. In other words, when these young people have decided to enact changes in what is considered acceptable in social, cultural, or sexual behavior, the effects and reverberations have been felt throughout the country.[17] When, for example, members of the secular middle class have decided that certain types of clothing or Islamic dress are in fashion, it has taken no more than a few months for many young people throughout Tehran and in other major cities such as Mashad, Shiraz, and Esfahan to begin to emulate their styles. Similarly, when fashionable youth have initiated changes in intellectual or sociocultural trends, they have been quickly adopted by youth in other socioeconomic groups throughout the country. Social movements and shifts in ideas often begin within a small group of people in an urban area and then spread throughout the country.[18] Secular middle-class youth in Tehran are part of a group whose members identify themselves (and are described by other young people in Tehran, Mashad, and Shiraz) as trendsetters for changes taking place among youth throughout the country.

Many lower-class young adults in Tehran and other urban areas emulate the styles and behaviors of the young people in fashion and find themselves drawn to parts of town where they can seek out and observe these stylish and popular young adults. One twenty-three-year-old taxi driver named Houman, who lived in a lower-class part of town, told me he liked to work uptown so he could be around *bache maruf* (cool youth or famous kids) and know what was in fashion so he could keep up with his friends who also worked uptown but lived downtown.[19] "It's like you gotta try hard to look a certain way," he began.

If you don't, they [other young people] think there is something wrong with you. Like if one day I don't gel my hair right or wear sunglasses that aren't in fashion anymore, my friends will say, Why are you so *javãd* [unfashionable or conservative in style]? That boy has no *perestizhe* [Iranian pronunciation of *prestige*]; he doesn't know who he is; he shouldn't be our friend. And women, well, they will talk to you only if they deem you appropriate, like if you are carrying the right cell phone and have like a nice car or something.

Conversely, some of the young adults who make up this admired group (mostly young men, although I spoke with five women who admitted to doing this) find themselves frequenting lower-class neighborhoods in search of anonymous sexual partners. They consider this activity a form of sexual "slumming," which also occurred during the prerevolutionary period when young men would visit *shahr-e-no* (a part of southern Tehran near the railroad tracks that is colloquially referred to as Tehran's red-light district) to seek sexual favors for money; today gifts are given more often than money in exchange for sexual favors.

There is much mobility among the youth of Tehran, with young people frequenting neighborhoods other than those they are from, and a lot of interaction between socioeconomic groups. In fact, during all

Figure 1.1. Downtown girls spend time in uptown Tehran's busy
streets. © 2006 by Nader Davoodi. Used by permission.

my visits to Iran I found it very difficult to discern the socioeconomic status of my informants. When I spent significant amounts of time in lower-class neighborhoods, I still saw young women in brightly colored headscarves wearing makeup and carrying designer handbags (which I was later told were fake or stolen). "It's getting really difficult to tell who is wealthy and who is not here in this city," said Sahar, a twenty-year-old student at Azad University in Rudehen.[20] "I look at them, I mean really look at the women, and they could all be wealthy. No one 'looks' poor; how are you supposed to know who is from *pāyin shahr* [downtown]?" she asked her friend.[21] "The shoes help," her friend responded. "Sometimes it's only the quality of the shoes, whether they were made in Iran or abroad, that will tell you the difference." Sahar told me, "Plus, so many people who were pāyin shahri now live uptown near my parents; they even come to our parties! We can't really figure out who is who anymore," she sighed. The next evening, as I was on my way to a friendly gathering in Niavaran, a wealthy neighborhood in one of the northernmost parts of town, almost in the mountains, the taxi driver reiterated Sahar's points. "*Khānum* [Madam]," he began, looking at me in his rearview mirror to make sure I was listening. "People are all mixed up now; the rich are now poor—that's what happened to me—and the poor are now rich," he lamented, hanging his head and wiping beads of sweat from his brow. He explained that before the revolution he had owned multiple nice cars from all over the world, but now he was relegated to one Paykan without air conditioning. "The people who used to live in Shush [an area south of the bāzār and close to the railroad tracks that is a lower-class part of town] now live in Shemrun [an area in the north known for large homes, gardens, and relatively clean air] and the people who used to live in Shemrun are now in Shush! It's a mess, and it's hard to figure out who is who!" So, just as it is difficult for Iranians living in Tehran to identify one another's socioeconomic status with accuracy, I also found it an enormous challenge to report the social class of my informants with absolute certainty.

However, the interest in sociopolitical change, the desire to push for more social freedoms, and the embodiment of the sexual revolution are now becoming increasingly widespread. One young woman, a popular blogger who calls herself Borderline, posted an interesting blog entry that referred to the fact that young people in rural parts of the country are now becoming more like the young Tehranis with whom she grew up.

At last it's over. I've spent the last five years in the nasty hellhole of Meybod [a small desert town]. But it's over. . . . I've packed my things and moved back home [to Tehran]. I remember when I started my course at that so-called university . . . we must have been the first group of single women entering that God-forsaken place and setting up on our own . . . so many times coming home and washing the spit of passers-by off my clothes. They just could not tolerate our shameful headscarves. . . . Without exception, then, all the native women used to wear chãdors. They say that things are changing and extremists are getting more tolerant. A friend of mine even thinks we started a revolution here.

It's been just five years but the same shopkeepers who would refuse to serve us if we were not wearing a chãdor now have teenage daughters who dress more provocatively than we ever dared to. . . . Looking around this tiny town only five years later, you see that many of the local young women have shed their black chãdors.

Our allegedly reformist president did not bring about a more tolerant society. . . . Societies evolve and change, and it's the ordinary people (us) who change them. . . . Seventy percent of our population is under thirty and many just don't want to live like their parents used to. Eventually they will have to not just tolerate us . . . but also live by our rules.[22]

This young woman is a popular blogger and her posting received a lot of response from other bloggers who agreed with her. Many other bloggers wrote of similar experiences living in towns outside of Tehran and noted that "the [cultural] revolution is spreading."[23] I also witnessed changes in attitudes and style of dress in Mashad, where I routinely visited for one to two weeks each of the years I was in Iran. In 2000, most Mashadi women were wearing chãdors, and even young women were encouraged to wear long, loose mãntos and tightly wrapped dark headscarves. In 2002, when Tehrani women were moving from short mãntos to tight ones and to open-toed shoes, some young Mashadi women had just made the transition from chãdors and long mãntos to shorter ones with lighter-colored headscarves. In 2004, some Mashadi women had caught up to the fad of wearing open-toed shoes and short, tight, brightly colored mãntos, but Mashadis were still not wearing as much makeup as Tehrani women were. By 2005 many young women in Mashad looked exactly like young Tehrani women, with layers of lipstick, shrinking shawls used as headscarves, and increasing amounts of plastic surgery. This is not to say, however, that no Mashadi women were wearing chãdor, but rather to highlight that the majority of young women I observed dressed more like secular middle-class youth from Tehran, and my observations were affirmed by ten informants in Mashad. In 2007, when I made my last visit to Mashad, all the women I spent time with talked about their boyfriends and their sexual escapades—topics I had not heard these young women discuss during the previous seven years I had known them. The shift in what is considered acceptable conversation could be felt. Even in Mashad, the holiest and one of the more conservative of Iranian cities, young women were embodying and enacting the social and sexual changes emanating from Tehran; and more important, these changes in comportment were taking place with the effective assent of the state. The women were walking the streets of Mashad, Tehran, Shiraz, and Esfahan in makeup, tight coats or mãntos, and brightly colored headscarves with a lot of hair showing, and not getting arrested. This behavior demonstrates that changes in interaction between the state and youth, both inside and outside of Tehran, as well as changes in behavior and sociability that were previously reserved for private and "underground" spaces, are now taking place "above ground," where they can be observed by the state.

Much of this book focuses on young Tehranis who are or seek to be part of or to emulate the young adults I am calling secular or nonreligious middle-class youth. There is, however, much diversity of opinion among members of this group, as well as in how they interact with members of the regime, who themselves also represent a range of viewpoints. At times I refer to the opinions of the majority of my sample or of a majority of the regime. These comments are intended not as generalizations that homogenize the diversity of opinions and viewpoints, but rather as reference points for analyzing changes in the sociocultural and political climate. Many of the broad generalizations made in this chapter are elaborated on and teased apart in the chapters that follow. It is my hope that the complicated and heterogeneous behaviors and opinions of both youth and members of the regime are apparent throughout the book.

It is also important to reiterate that changes in fashion are not simply superficial (although some young people wear certain clothes in response to peer pressure or just to look good) but rather have deep social and political significance, and indicate a shift in ways of thinking about how people should dress as well as changes in culture. It is crucial to emphasize that not all young people who wear makeup or have highlights in their hair are focused only on their appearance (many have political and economic aspirations and their appearance is only part of their identity) or spend all day roaming the streets or preparing to attend parties; many of my informants work long hours as lawyers, doctors, engineers, teachers, and artists and in a number of other professions. It is important to remember that these shifts in ideas are not universal; several of my informants did not agree with the lifestyles and choices of the fashion-conscious youth and were highly critical of their behaviors. It is interesting to note and to question, however, why this group of young people is rebelling as hard as it is and in this particular way, and why the government is so interested in and yet threatened by them. During the last election, it was this group of young people that presidential candidate and former president Rafsanjani appealed to for help in running his campaign. He solicited young people—specifically members of this subculture who drove expensive cars and dressed fashionably using designer accessories—to advocate for him. Additionally, he set up outdoor disco-style music venues for the young people in hopes of gaining their support. Whether this group is appealed to by the Islamists or by other young people throughout the city and country who are looking to imitate them, they are an interesting group with its own style of sexual, social, and cultural politics whose members may be trendsetters for youth throughout the nation.

Reflections

Throughout my time in Iran I was acutely aware that the researcher herself can often become the subject of inquiry both for her informants and for herself. My interactions and interviews with urban Iranian young adults were framed by my experiences as an Iranian American struggling to define my own identity and to learn more about my own culture. Simultaneously, my position as an Iranian-American researcher enrolled in an elite Ivy League institution affected how my informants viewed me, and thus how they responded to me.

My friends and family, both in Iran and in the United States, often call me "child of the revolution." Conceived in Iran in 1978, at the beginning of the revolution, I was born in the United States after my mother, eight months pregnant, boarded one of the last direct flights from Tehran to the United States. I was born and raised in an Iranian community and Persian was my first language, but I did not see Iran until the summer of 2000, shortly before my twenty-second birthday. Since then I have been returning regularly to my parents' native country, although I am aware that I cannot call Iran home. My brothers and I were raised in Southern California, which is home to hundreds of thousands of Iranians and Iranian Americans, and thus many people often say that I adopted the California brand of Iranian culture. During my first trip to Iran, my cousins and friends made fun of my Americanized Persian (*Farsi mesle Armani ha sohbat mikoni*, "You talk Persian like an Armenian"), which many young Iranian Americans now refer to as "kitchen Persian." Over the years since then, however, I have been able to train myself to speak Persian with an urban Tehrani accent. I have worked hard to learn the vernacular of my target population, and have attempted to keep up with the slang. When I am in Tehran, however, most people comment that they can tell that I was raised in the West because of how I walk, how I look people in the eyes, or the lifestyle I adopted while living in Tehran (I lived and traveled alone, which was uncommon for young unmarried women). My age and my background as an Iranian who had grown up in the West often served as points of fascination for my informants. Some of them were suspicious of me because of my Western background, but most said they found it easier to be open with me because they assumed I would be open-minded because I come from un taraf-e āb, "the other side of the water."

Additionally, many of my interview subjects wanted to ask me more questions than they would allow me to ask them. After bombarding me with questions about myself, my upbringing, my relationship status, and the amount of money I make, they would sometimes ask me about

Western icons such as Britney Spears, Madonna, Justin Timberlake, or the cast of *Friends*. Others who knew my educational background (I introduced myself as a medical anthropologist) would spend hours asking me about sexual and reproductive health, HIV, and other health concerns—questions they had always been too afraid to ask parents, friends, or teachers. Some of the young people affectionately took to calling me the "sex doctor," asking me to resolve their sexual and relationship issues; or the "condom-lady," because I gave them condoms if they asked for some during an interview.

As an Iranian American, I represented many things to these young people, including a window to the West, a glimpse of what their lives might have been like had their parents made the decision to migrate, and a mirror in which to see themselves. I noticed that my experience in Tehran changed me on a daily basis. Spending time with my key informants, who were also my closest friends, changed my perspective on many things. For example, when I first arrived in Tehran, I felt that the women wore too much makeup, used too much platinum blond hair dye, and at parties dressed in clothing that may have been construed as overly revealing. It took me months of spending time with these women, hanging out at beauty salons for days and sometimes weeks, to understand the symbolic meaning of their appearance. In my first few weeks I judged them for being too superficial; some of my earliest notes indicated my disapproval as I referred to them as "Iranian Stepford Wives" and accused them of all looking alike, of having used the same plastic surgeon to sculpt their identical noses and of using the same makeup. However, the more time I spent with them, the more I realized that their appearance wasn't about the superficiality, peer pressure, or consumption as much as it was about their image of modernization. Some of my female informants told me that spending hours on their appearance made them feel good and strong, and that for them wearing red lipstick symbolized defiance while for others it was a form of artwork. It was not until I started feeling the need to spend time in salons myself—getting highlights, my hair straightened, my eyebrows threaded, and my nails done—that I started to understand what they meant. By the end of 2004 I had gotten to a point where I was able to appreciate the amount of time and work they put into themselves; I had begun to see the subtleties in their differing styles of makeup as art. By the time I returned to the United States I had gotten so used to the Tehrani "painted dolls" that I found myself staring at women in New York, wondering how they could have left the house wearing so little makeup. Participating at a conference shortly after my return in 2004, I was shocked not only to find that I was upset at the other women for coming to a conference without looking well put together, but also to realize when I looked in the mirror that I was the most made-up woman in the room. It took several months for me to get back to my usual style of wearing a minimal amount of makeup.

In Iran I was also angered by women who wore too much clothing. I used to get upset with my cousins who refused to adopt the more stylish way of wearing hejāb—wearing a shawl over one's hair and then loosely slinging one end of the shawl over the neck, a la Marilyn Monroe or Isadora Duncan. Most of the urban young women had adopted this type of headdress, but some of my cousins insisted on the old way of wearing a headscarf by tying it under the chin, or they wore *maghna'e*, a form of head covering that shows *gerdi-e surat*, that is, the face from forehead hairline to neck. Sometimes I would ask them, if one day the government told you it was OK to take off your head covering, would you do it? They would respond negatively. They would tell me that Iranian men weren't ready for that, and they were scared they would be *dorosteh mikhordan* ("eaten alive") if they left the house without proper covering. For the first month I was in Iran, I would become intensely angry upon hearing this. I would yell at my cousins and tell them they were weak for putting men above themselves. I would tell them it was people like them who stunted the social revolution. My position changed, however, as I slowly began to understand what they meant. Each day more and more men would harass me as I walked down the street. When I entered the bāzār dressed fashionably, men would follow me, make comments, and pinch my upper legs until they were black and blue. After a few visits I learned that if I didn't want to spend the afternoon hitting men with my handbag, making a scene, and fighting them off, I would have to dress more modestly. If my coat was tight and slightly unbuttoned, a man would walk past me and make a snide comment such as *dar e yakhjal baz eh* ("the refrigerator door is open"), or another would nudge his buddy and then loudly announce, *bebin khatt-e Emām tā kojā bāz e* ("Oh look how wide the Imam's mouth is") while giving me a dirty look or a pat on the bottom as I walked by.

One day as I was horseback riding with my female informant-friends, the harassment was taken to a new level. Often when we went horseback riding without men, other men on the streets who passed us in their cars or motorbikes would stop and stare. Some would volunteer comments such as "Hey, look at that horse between her legs; I wish I were that horse," or "Women can't ride horses," or my personal favorite, "Look at me baby, I'm hung like a horse; why don't you come and ride me?" The man often accompanied his gesture with foolishly jumping up and down on the grass while grabbing his pants. I would try not to let these comments get to me, but usually they would. One day it was too much, however, as two men on motorcycles decided to surround me and my horse as they shouted comments. The horse, like me, became agitated, and as I tried to ease her into a canter to take me away from the men, she twisted her neck and threw me. I hit the ground hard, my headscarf and coat came rolling off, and the men howled with laughter. "I told you, women can't ride horses!" one said to the other. "Oh, and look at the girl's mane. Nice hair, honey. Wow, you are hot! Why don't you come ride me home and I'll just lose myself in that hair of yours!" That did it; I got up, jumped back on my horse, and started screaming every Persian profanity I had ever learned at the two men. They were startled and drove away in confusion. After they left I cried. That afternoon I was harassed by two men on the street not only because my mānto was form-fitting but also because it had dirt on it. "Hey, you want to roll around with me honey?" one of the men asked me. As he reached to pinch my leg I slapped him, and walked away with more tears in my eyes. That evening when I got home I called the cousins I had yelled at just a few months earlier. "You were right," I told them, "these men can be animals, and I now understand why you sometimes feel the need to dress conservatively. Forgive me for judging you but I'm still adjusting to all this." On the other end of the phone I heard my cousin smile. "Don't worry honey," she said. "Nothing in Iran is as simple as it seems."

The line between informants and friends was blurred regularly. My key informants were people I spent a lot of time with, and they became my best friends. Many ethnographers have discussed power relations between anthropologists and their informants, noting that it may be a parasitic relationship because the anthropologist is using the informant for information but the informant doesn't receive anything in return. I tried to give informants my friendship, and found myself reliant on theirs as well. Being in a complex setting such as Iran is not easy and can get very lonely. Without friends, the experience is almost impossible to bear. The ambiguous nature of the relationship can also affect the interviews the informants give and the level of honesty with which they answer questions. I spent large amounts of time with some of my informants before interviewing them. It was only by immersing myself in their social groups that I could get them to trust me enough to be willing to share their stories with me. In the process of my immersion, however, my informants would often learn about me (given that we spent so much time together, it was inevitable that I would reveal some personal details) and come to have a certain understanding (whether correct or incorrect, I will never know), and this may have affected their responses to my questions. Some may have been afraid to tell me the truth, some may have embellished their answers, and others may have withheld information. In an effort to reduce these biases, and more important, to protect the research and the informants, I did my best to keep details about myself and the nature of my research to a minimum. Summarily, my friendship with my informants shaped the information I received in complex and difficult-to-discern ways. This is an issue I recognize and continue to grapple with.

Iran's Sexual Revolution?

Iran is at a crucial moment in its history. More young people populate the nation than ever before. These young adults, children of the revolution, are highly educated, underemployed, and highly dissatisfied. The sheer numbers of youth who face the same issues is staggering. These young people are coming together in search of their own voices, in search of agency, in an effort to reclaim their bodies, and are enacting a sexual revolution right now. The changes in sexual and social culture described by many of my informants are not centred solely on casual sex, multiple partners, or group sex. Rather, the sexual revolution they believe they are engaging in is also about changing what can be said about sex; it is about pushing the limits of restrictions on social behaviors and attacking the fabric of morality under which the regime seeks to govern its citizens.

During my time in Iran I struggled with whether changes in fashion (which were the external indicators of the sexual revolution, according to my informants) and sexuality could be revolutionary. I wondered if wearing a Gucci headscarf, drinking a martini, and having lots of boyfriends was about opposing the Islamic Republic or about wanting to be like the women on *Sex and the City*. Certainly some of my informants purchased and wore designer wear in order to fit in with their friends or because they saw themselves as part of an affluent and stylish elite. Several informants told me they wore makeup or highlighted their hair because they liked how it made them look; they emphasized that it made them more desirable. Other friends and informants wondered whether, if regime change were to occur, young people would continue their behavior and whether it would still be revolutionary. Most of my informants repeatedly told me as they applied their makeup in the school restroom before going to class in order to outwit the morality police, who would insist on wiping down their faces before they entered school grounds, that wearing makeup or certain types of Islamic clothing was about making a statement.

Many of the goods that young Tehranis demanded were sold on the black market, which made them desirable. If these goods were openly sold and easily accessible, they would no longer be seen as symbolic of a changing young-adult culture. One informant said that because running shoes like Nike or Reebok were sold only on the black market, they were among the most desirable shoes. She emphasized that these sneakers were more eye catching to the morality police than the plain tennis shoes sold in bāzārs across the city. "But," she added, "I don't think they look that nice. Once they become copied and available everywhere, no one will want them." Thus the black market itself creates a certain economy that is folded into the young people's social revolution.

Throughout my time in Iran I struggled to understand the changes in sexual and social behavior and their significance. After several years it became apparent that the changes taking place among young Tehranis are not ephemeral and have meaning and significance to informants and to the members of the regime and the morality police who obsessively patrol, police, and punish those behaviors. Many key informants reminded me that because wearing a DKNY headscarf or being in a car with a boyfriend could get them arrested, the headscarf was more than a label and the boyfriend was more than a passing amusement; instead these behaviors are a threat to the social and moral order affecting all aspects of the Islamic Republic.

My research raises a lot of questions: Is this actually a sexual revolution? How far reaching are its effects? Would the young people continue to behave the way they do if regime change occurred? How do others perceive the young adult social movement taking place in Iran? I continue to struggle with the impact, meaning, and future of sexual revolution in Iran. The changes taking place among urban young adults and the relationship of these changes to the Iranian state are many. The young people seem to be using their bodies to make social and political statements against what they view as a repressive regime. However, although the young adults have made great strides in attaining greater social freedoms and more attention and respect from authorities, the battle between the young Tehranis and members of the Islamist regime still rages. Unfortunately, due to the risks that accompany their social behaviors, most of the casualties will be among the youth if education and information are not quickly disseminated to them.

2   Life in the Islamic Republic of Iran

I T IS ESTIMATED that two-thirds of the thirteen million people who reside in Tehran are under the age of
thirty. Of the young adults who are eligible for and desire employment,
roughly half are officially unemployed and many more are employed only
occasionally.[1] The daily routines, experiences, and encounters of many
of these young Tehranis illuminate the social context of the changes in
young adult sexual and social culture that this book describes. The ways
in which they go about their daily activities and interact with the surrounding environment vary from person to person, but they have many
things in common, and these daily experiences are the basis of this book's
analysis of the sexual revolution. In this chapter I explore the daily lives
of young Tehranis by following them through their daily routines—to
school, to their recreational activities, and to parties.

Although many of my informants were drawn from different social
circles, socioeconomic groups, and venues, a significant number of them
have similar characteristics, such as being secular, holding antiregime
sentiments, and being educated. Although there is certainly some hetero-
geneity in the familial, educational, personal, and professional backgrounds
of my informants, I want to reemphasize that they were a small group
and were not selected randomly. My intention here is not to claim that
all young people behave the way my informants do, but rather to illuminate the daily lives of a group of urban young adults and illustrate how
their behavior has had far-reaching effects on the state, on other young
people, and on many people throughout the Islamic Republic who now
see a social movement making waves around them.

Stories from the Heart

I have chosen to focus on seven of the informants with whom I became close during my times in Iran and who represent a variety of social, economic, educational, and political circles. I met these key informants through friends and relatives in Tehran who knew about my research and introduced me to people they thought were key players in the sexual revolution. All of these informants were eager to talk to me and became quite vested in my work. During the long months that separated my trips to Iran, I relied on weekly correspondence with these seven people, who all wanted to help in any way they could.

Diar is a twenty-four-year-old photographer who still lives with his parents. He was the first young man I met in Tehran, the first to speak of the sexual revolution, and a key player in changes taking place among Tehran's youth through his involvement in youth media and his own blog. Asana is a twenty-one-year-old university student who can speak to the rhythms and routines of being a female student in Tehran. Amir Ali, twenty-four, and Nina, twenty-three, are a brother and sister pair who work full-time in somewhat lucrative businesses. They come from a working-class background but have now attained middle-class status. They are somewhat representative of the many young adults who work full-time and don't have large amounts of time on their hands but have a vested interest in being a part of the social and sexual changes taking place in Tehran. Mojdeh, twenty-five, works full-time running her father's construction business and is also a housewife and mother. The way she negotiates these various positions is a very delicate process and speaks to the issues faced by many women who work full-time, are parents full-time, and yet see themselves as part of the youth movement. Finally Laleh, twenty-five, and Alaleh, twenty-four, are two unemployed young women who spend their days in luxury. Laleh is married and the mother of a six-year-old boy. Some would call her a housewife, but she self-identifies as a dance teacher because she teaches all her friends to dance in weekly dance classes held in her basement. These two women did not finish high school, and they are now extremely wealthy due to the success of their families and husbands in the postrevolutionary economic reshuffle. They are part of a larger group of young women who have a lot of time on their hands as well as access to money, which puts them in a position to engage in a lot of partying as well as recreational use of drugs and alcohol. They represent *allāfi*, or being idle, which is a major factor in the new youth culture. Many Iranians define allāfi as a state of not having anything to do—"no work, no studies, no concrete goals or ambitions," explained a nineteen-year-old male university student. According to him, allāfi leads to a "cultural fixation on outer appearances and social relations, and is almost encouraged by the government, which seeks to encourage this by making it hard to pursue goals and ambitions and meaningful activity by creating *dargiri* [troubles, red tape] or unnecessary troubles in daily life." This description echoes a sentiment that is popular among many of my informants.

My seven key informants represent different types of people in the emerging sexual culture of Tehran, although they are all members of the nonreligious lower-middle, middle, and upper classes. I routinely followed each of them through their daily activities, spending days following them from morning until night, in order to get a sense of what their lives were like. I became a fixture in their lives, and they in mine. On the eve of my departure to the United States in 2005, all seven of them were at my apartment. For some of them it was the first time they met each other. Several of them had seen each other before at parties but had not formally conversed. They were all aware of one another's existence, and I have heard that since my departure they have all become friends, even though they come from different social circles, and from time to time they gather together to call me.

Diar: "Life in the Islamic Republic Isn't Bad—If You're a Man!"
Diar, a twenty-five-year-old man, is unemployed despite repeated attempts to find a job in the photography and film industries. He is an avid consumer and fan of Iranian films, especially documentaries on various aspects of Iranian culture. He has long, curly black hair and a goatee and wears black-rimmed glasses. He says his idol is Martin Scorsese, but he wants to look like Jim Morrison. Diar was the first young man I met, other than relatives, on my first trip to Tehran in 2000. He is also a self-proclaimed Iranian nationalist who also identifies himself as a feminist. "I love women, and I love that our Iranian women are so strong," he has often said to me. "I am in complete support of the women's movement."

During the first summer that I visited Tehran, I spent a lot of time with a young woman named Golnaz. Born and raised in Iran, she was then living in Canada, but because her parents still lived in Iran, Golnaz spent all of her summers with them in Tehran. I had met her on one of her visits to California when we were younger, and we had maintained our friendship. Her stories about summers in Iran had been among the reasons I so desperately wanted to visit and study my mother's homeland. One night during the summer of 2000, she invited me to a party at her cousin's house. When we arrived at the party, she introduced me to the host. "This is my cousin, Diar. He is wonderful!" she said, kissing him on both cheeks. I stuck out my hand to shake his, but instead he hugged me and gave me two kisses, one on each cheek. (This form of greeting between young people was new to me at that time.) That night Diar and I became instant friends. He showed me his collection of films in an effort to convince me of the wonders that Iran holds. "Iran is the best country in the world," he told me that night and again and again for the next seven years. "There is no other country in the world as beautiful, as rich in resources, and as warm in terms of culture," he described while showing me footage of a small town in the North called Masouleh. "This country, my country and yours, Pardis, holds lots of possibility and secrets. I'm going to take it upon myself to show it to you," he said proudly.

Over the next few weeks, Diar took me on numerous hiking trips with a number of his friends who were also artists and photographers. It was during this time that I was introduced to the sexual revolution taking place in Tehran. Diar and his friends talked about the changes in social and sexual spaces, and introduced me to a series of other self-proclaimed revolutionaries. Diar and his friends frequently went to the mountains outside of Tehran to be away from watchful eyes (such as those of his parents, with whom Diar was living while struggling to find employment) and to talk openly. One afternoon as we were hiking there, Diar began to speak to me about Tehran's sexual revolution. He told me that in his view the time for Iran's sexual revolution had come. "We are ready for changes in the way people view our bodies. We are ready to claim our bodies and our sexualities," he said as we hiked higher and higher into the hills. "Why shouldn't we have a sexual revolution? We need some kind of revolution, and this seems the best way to achieve change," he explained as his friends nodded in agreement. From that moment on, Diar and I talked repeatedly about the status of the sexual revolution, and he has continued to keep me informed of changes and gains. "Come back to Tehran. Women are wearing sandals. The new headscarves are much better. Sex is talked about more openly. Come soon," wrote Diar in an e-mail during the spring of 2002. Ever the photographer, he takes lots of pictures of young people enacting changes in fashion and the party scene and bravely sends them to me, being careful to blur all faces. From the outset Diar was, and remains to this day, an important connection for me in taking the pulse of young Tehranis.

By the time I arrived in Tehran in 2005, Diar had gotten a job as assistant photographer for a local magazine. Earlier that year he had purchased and was living in a small apartment that he also used for doing freelance photography work. He invited me to spend an afternoon with him viewing his latest photographs and told me that he had procured a few documentaries that would be of interest to me. When I walked into his apartment-office, I smiled. It was beautiful and covered in posters of films by Martin Scorsese and other prominent Western filmmakers. The office portion of the apartment was filled with photographs he had just developed, and his closet had been turned into a darkroom for developing film. In one corner of the apartment several couches had been pushed together to create Diar's makeshift bedroom. As he escorted me into the office area and offered me some tea, I couldn't help but grin widely at Diar's success. I knew that he had overcome many obstacles to achieve these gains.

"I'm really proud of you, Diar. You did it. You made it. And I know it wasn't easy," I said, acknowledging the challenges all young people face in attaining employment in postrevolutionary Iran. Diar sat down next to me, lit a cigarette, and drew in a deep breath. "It hasn't been easy for me," he said, "and you know that. I spent five years looking for a job with absolutely no success, living with my parents and worrying about my next meal. But I did it. And I'm a stronger man for it."

"I think what you have done is amazing," I said. He shook his head and patted my hand. "Actually, what you are doing is amazing too," he told me. "I remember when I first told you about the sexual revolution here, you were skeptical. Now look at you! You are writing a book on it and you have found out more about our revolution than we have! I'm so glad that you have taken an interest in it." He put out his cigarette and turned on the television. "Now, I want to show you some films I have collected for you that will help you in your research. Documentaries on sex workers, runaway women, and my favorite, a film on Valentine's Day in Iran. You know it's the second most popular holiday in Iran?" He fast-forwarded through some footage to show me clips of young Tehranis making heart-shaped cookies. "Whoever said that modernization isn't happening should see this!" Diar exclaimed. "We have taken a Western holiday, made it our own, and popularized it. This is living proof of the sexual revolution!" Diar's excitement was palpable. I spent the rest of the afternoon and evening in his apartment watching films and clips that spoke to the Tehrani sexual revolution. Throughout, many of Diar's friends came and went, and we had many discussions about the progress of the sexual revolution. At the end of the evening, Diar drove me home.

"See, this too is proof of the gains we have made," Diar said, reaching over me to start playing a CD of rap music he had recently downloaded from the Internet. "What do you mean?" I asked. "Well," he replied, "remember the first days when we used to hang out? How *tan e-moun milarzid* [our bones were shaking] when I drove you home late at night, afraid that we would be caught? We didn't dare listen to music; we drove home in silence. I always thought you were praying we wouldn't get caught that whole time." We both laughed and let out a sigh of relief as he turned up the music. "Now we can drive around, listen to music, and do a lot of things we never could do before. Things are changing in the Islamic Republic, I'm telling you. Things really aren't so bad here. We have fun, we listen to music, we party, we have our 'sexy time,'" he said, using the English phrase to which I had by then become accustomed. "Things are pretty good here," he said, and then paused and looked at me sternly for a moment. He then touched my headscarf and added solemnly, "Well, I guess things are better here if you are a man." We drove the rest of the way home in silence.

Asana: "School Is Fun, But What's the Point?"
Asana is a twenty-one-year-old urban-planning major at Azad University in Tehran. She is from Shahrak-e Gharb ("little town in the West"), a "better" neighborhood in the western part of Tehran. She comes from

a family that would have been called *bāzāri*,[2] or merchant class, before and during the revolution. Her father, who owned a carpet stand at the bāzār, married Asana's mother when she was only thirteen and still in middle school. Asana's mother gave birth to her at the age of 16 and promptly decided to drop out of school. Asana is the first woman in her family to attend university, and although her mother is supportive of her education, she cautions Asana against too much ambition, often telling her that a higher education may not produce many employment opportunities and may hinder her prospects for marriage. Asana's mother believes that Iranian men are not interested in marrying educated women, and thus she is concerned about her daughter while being proud of her at the same time.

Asana and I often discussed her relationship with her parents. "My mother tells me, 'Asana, don't get too wrapped up in ideas of grandeur. You will graduate, but probably not be able to get a job. Then you will have to focus on finding a husband,'" she told me one afternoon as we sat in a coffee shop near her house. She looked at me with an exasperated expression on her face, then took a sip of her chocolate milkshake, which had just arrived. We were hanging out at one of the newest and brightest coffee shops in the western portion of Tehran. It was lined with yellow and blue tiles and florescent lighting. Coffee shops have become one of the most popular places for young people to spend time and meet other young people. Some are dimly lit and filled with couples; others play loud music, have bright lights, and serve a variety of fast-food snacks; still others provide Internet services for youth who do not have access to the Internet at home or who prefer to surf and chat away from the watchful eyes of their parents. These coffee shops were not around during the first decade and a half of the Islamic Republic and are a symbol of how Iranian youth have reshaped public space. At these coffee shops one can hear music that is illegal (because of its dancelike qualities), see women and men who defy the rules of Islamic dress, and witness unmarried, unaccompanied young men and women exchanging amorous sentiments, glances, and whispers. Overheard conversations might include discussions about fashion, politics, or changes in music trends favoring trendy underground Iranian bands over imported American music.

Figure 2.1. Ladies relaxing in a coffee shop in Northern Tehran.
Note the exaggerated layers of makeup and the loose headscarves
that conceal very little, accompanied by tight, colorful māntos.
© 2007 by Nader Davoodi. Used by permission.

After looking around the crowded coffee shop, Asana sighed and continued. "I get so frustrated, you know? Who wants to study hard when
you know your degree isn't going to get you anywhere? That's why we
study enough to get by, but our main focus is on fun," she said, flashing
a smile at a young man sitting behind us. A few strands of highlighted
hair fell into her face and she brushed them aside, giving her purple
mascara-coated eyelashes a flutter. Asana was born a few years after
the revolution, when her father elevated his status from being a bāzāri,
or owner of a carpet stand, to being a *tājer*, or businessman. Many informants with whom I spoke, as well as Iranians in the diaspora, have
commented that the bāzār gained status during the period of Islamification in the 1980s when many of the members of the regime who had
been supported by the bāzāris elevated their status by subsidizing their
businesses and appointing them to higher positions (in trade or, as in the
case of Asana's father, by making them commission agents). This development is important to consider when looking at shifting class dynamics

because it is an indication of ways in which the flow of capital changed hands after the revolution and once the Islamists gained power. It also points to potential tensions in class dynamics, because people who had been wealthy (and potentially monarchy supporters) were stripped of their assets and had trouble interacting with former members of the lower class, specifically bāzāris, who had suddenly gained power and to whom former members of the upper middle and upper classes now had to appeal for economic support.

The year Asana was born her father bought their apartment in the Shahrak-e Gharb. Although they had become middle or upper-middle class due to her father's status as a tājer, in terms of *farhang* (a Persian term that refers to culture, tradition, and level of education; similar to our notions of cultural capital), they would still be seen as working class, especially given her parents' lack of education. Asana has described her father as very traditional and very strict. On more than one occasion I have heard her say, "Sometimes I just want to get married to get away from my dad!" She says that he forbids her to wear much makeup or to go out with male friends. Her mother, whom Asana describes as a bit more understanding and as seeing herself as more "modern," often defends her daughter against Asana's father and helps her daughter find creative ways of avoiding his strict rules. Sometimes she accompanies Asana to parties or outings (which presents a bit of a problem in that her mother is watching her every move, which can dampen the mood of a youthful party, but Asana says it is better than not getting to go to the party at all), and she often helps her daughter put on her layers of makeup and change into her party attire before leaving the house. During the day, when Asana's father is out of the house, her mother is more lenient with her, which affords Asana the ability to maintain her social activities. I often wondered why Asana's mother and father hold such different views about what their children should and should not do. In fact, many of my informants' parents were open to the social changes taking place among the youth. They often hosted parties for their children or bribed members of the morality police to have their children released from custody or to prevent their arrest altogether. These parents were mostly against the ideology of the Islamic Republic and therefore approved of the subversive behaviors of their children. More often than not, both parents were open to their children's behaviors and permissive of their desires to socialize and dress stylishly. I was curious about why in Asana's case only her mother supported her behavior. When I asked Asana about this, she told me it was because her mother had come from a different socioeconomic background than her father had. She described her mother's family as educated middle class, and although her mother hadn't been educated herself, her mother's father was an engineer who held open-minded views about equality for men and women. When Asana's grandfather died, her grandmother was left with a lot of debt and thought it best to marry off her daughters in the hope that her newly acquired sons-in-law would help her pay off these debts. Asana's mother had hoped to attend college, but her husband forbade her to do so; thus she was determined to send her daughters to university, despite her fears that it would weaken their chances of marrying. "She did it for my grandfather," Asana told me when I asked her why her mother had been so adamant that she attend university when she was so worried about her marriageability. "I guess she did it for his memory. He was a great believer that women and men should both be educated."

One day I arrived at Asana's house early in the morning to spend the day with her. After eating breakfast with her family, we walked to the bus stop and boarded the bus bound for the Damavand campus of Azad University.[3] On the way there I asked her what her daily life was usually like. "Well, each day you end up doing something, something fun, it doesn't matter, whatever. You come home, like especially us, us university students. We go to class, what? Maximum four hours per day, right? Something like that, and then we don't even have class every day, so that is on top of that. So there you go; we are in class until maybe 4 P.M. and then we come home and we call our friends to see what is going on." She turned around in her seat to take a note passed to her from one of the young men on the bus. "Oh yeah, and relationships," she added. "Relationships are a form of activity here in Tehran, a form of *tafrih* [fun and extracurricular activity]. I go out with boys, different boys; that helps me pass the time too." She scribbled a response on the back of the note and passed it back to the young man, who winked at us. Although we were on our way to the university, a space where proper Islamic attire and comportment were mandatory prerequisites for entry, Asana occupied herself on the bus by applying yet another layer of makeup and lipstick. Similar to other female university students I interviewed, she told me that the extra layers assure her a defense against the guards who may or may not be outside the main gate of the campus with damp face towelettes.[4] "If they are there, well, then I will wipe a layer of this stuff off, then reapply my lipstick as I go into class. If they aren't there, well, then better for me, I will look stunning in class," she said, offering me some of her lip gloss.

On this particular day there were no guards standing outside the gate, and the young men and women rushed into class, giggling and passing notes to one another the whole way in. The atmosphere in the university was relaxed and happy. The students casually strolled down the halls, talking to members of the opposite sex in packs of three or four. The professors smiled as they passed us on their way to class. After Asana's class ended, we met up with a few of her friends to go for pizza at one of their favorite pizza joints in Tehran. When we walked in, the brightly lit, multicolored restaurant was packed with young people, in couples and groups, all sharing pizza and exchanging subversive glances. I was reminded of the pizza parlors in the United States where young people gather after school to play video games, chat, dance, and meet other young people. In Tehran I noticed that there is so much that is not said but rather shown through body language. I am reminded that unless one learns the subtle body language of seduction, one can make several mistakes easily. For example, the wrong kind of smile can project the image that you are ready to go home with the young man across the way. Asana taught me to be more scrupulous with my smiles. At the pizza parlor I decided to keep my head down and not smile at anyone. Each time I looked up there were young men looking in our direction, casually running their fingers through their hair to show off newly acquired wristwatches or bracelets. These young people were clearly interested in one another.

After eating our pizza, we took a subway and then shared a public taxi back to Asana's house.[5] Once we were in the safe space of the home, we took off our headscarves and mãntos as quickly as possible and hung them on a rack provided for guests next to the door.[6] I pulled off my linen coat after wiping my brow with my silk headscarf. Even though young women have modified Islamic clothing so that it is more fashion-able, the heat of the summer can often frustrate those who look forward to entering their homes or the homes of friends and family members without wearing hejāb. I too was grateful to enter a house where I could take off my Islamic wraps and cool down. I had learned to wear more stylish māntos and headscarves, but I was still not comfortable in them, especially not in ninety-eight-degree weather.

At Asana's house we drank cool watermelon juice prepared for us by her mother to, she said, *jigaretun ra khonak konin*, that is, "cool our liv-ers." We then retired to Asana's room. After we had spent less than an hour on her homework, her cell phone rang. It was a friend asking her to come to the public pool nearby or go for a stroll in the park. A few minutes later one of her boyfriends called to announce that his parents had left for the afternoon and that she should come over and take advan-tage of the situation. Asana was delighted at the choices of social activi-ties and was about to announce to me what she would like to do when her mother came in to announce that a friend of Asana's had called the house asking if it was OK to come over. Her mother had taken the lib-erty of saying yes and was now informing Asana of her decision. When her mother left the room, Asana rolled her eyes. "She sometimes thinks she's in charge of my social life. It's so frustrating. I totally wanted to go to my boyfriend's house; I'm kind of horny, you know? But now I have to stay here," she said, pulling her long, thick brown hair back into a ponytail and tying it up into a bun held in place with two pencils. She grabbed her book bag and fished out a pack of cigarettes.

When I asked whether her mother knew about her boyfriends, she shook her head. "No way! Are you kidding? I mean she knows I have boyfriends, but she thinks they are just friends. She doesn't know I go over there and give them blow jobs, you know?" she said matter-of-factly. She opened her pink and white flowered notebook to show me a picture of one of her boyfriends that she had pasted inside the cover. "He's *nāz* [cute]," I said. When I asked how she kept him a secret, she smiled and said, "I lie. I lie about a lot of things. I tell her I'm going to my friend's house, but then I go to his house. It's bad to lie, but it's worth it." She put out her cigarette and sprayed the room with perfume to mask the scent of smoke. I took it that her mom also didn't know she smoked.

When her friend came over we went to a coffee shop for a milkshake and then a walk in the park. That evening we went to a mutual friend's house where we made spaghetti and I taught them how to make garlic bread. As we sat down to eat our delicious Italian-inspired meal, our host made an announcement. "I have a special treat for us tonight!" she said. "What is it?" asked Asana. Our friend opened up a closet and pulled out three large blue and red cans with Russian writing across them. "Beer!" announced our host triumphantly. She poured us each a glass of warm, imported Russian beer. After we finished our meal and managed to acquire a bit of an alcohol buzz, our host pulled out her small boom box while Asana produced a mixed tape of Iranian pop music from her purse. We put on the "illegal" music (recorded by Iranian exile singers in Los Angeles), which Asana had purchased from a "music dealer" in the Tajrish bāzār, located in the northern part of the city, and danced all night, singing songs and practicing new dance moves with one another. Toward the end of the night, Asana's mom picked her up from the gathering. In the car she had brought a more modest mānto, makeup remover, and cucumbers to take away the smell of alcohol from her daughter's breath. Asana sighed and turned to me. "See what I have to go through? If it's not the morality police I'm trying to escape, it's my father."

Amir Ali and Nina: "Reaching Goals and Having Fun"
Amir Ali, a twenty-four-year-old man, and Nina, a twenty-three-year-old woman, are the model of a perfect sibling relationship. They are best friends, work at the same company (in network marketing), and have the same group of friends. Together, by their hard work, they have brought so much additional wealth to their family that they have moved from a working-class neighborhood to Sa'ādat ābād, a middle-class part of town. The week before I left Tehran in 2005, they purchased two new cars, one for their parents and one for the two of them to share.

Amir Ali and Nina were born during the revolution (Amir Ali in 1979 and Nina in 1980). As do many of my informants, they refer to themselves as children of the revolution. Their parents were members of the upper middle class before the revolution. Their mother is still a university professor. Their father, who came from a wealthy family that had had ties to the Shah and supported the monarchy, worked in the family business until the revolution, during which much of the family's wealth was taken away. Most of their father's assets were lost because he had not invested his money and thus found himself in a more vulnerable position than his siblings. Directly opposite to what happened to Asana's parents, Amir Ali and Nina's parents were forced to move into low-income housing when their mother lost her job at the college when all of the universities were shut down in the 1980s during the period of Islamification. She was not able to regain employment at the university until 1995. For most of their childhood, the family struggled with money while some of their cousins, whose parents had made wiser business investments, lived in the lap of luxury. "I remember in the 1980s," Amir Ali began, "when we were little, our mom would take us to our cousins' country houses to play once a week. They had so many toys, everything they ever wanted, and they were mean to us because they said we looked like beggars." Nina elaborated on her brother's recollection. "As we were growing up, it didn't get much better. They [our cousins] always had it so much better than us; everything came so easily to them. They could pay to have all these fancy tutors, and their parents paid their way through college. Not us, though; we've had to work hard since day one," she said. Her brother picked up where she left off. "The worst part was that we had to hang out with them all the time and go to their fancy parties. But I guess it was educational," he added. It was interesting to me to hear them talk this way of their past because when I met them in 2000 they seemed to be middle or even upper middle class. Later I found out that they were just good at pretending to be of a certain class. Nina wore her cousins' hand-me-down fancy māntos and headscarves while Amir Ali purchased fake jewelry and sewed designer labels into nondesigner clothes. Eventually they actually acquired enough money to be considered middle or upper middle class—a transition they say took place between 2003 and 2005.

Amir Ali, a slender and shy young man with wavy brown hair and glasses, had majored in business and engineering at Amir Kabir University. He was very modest about his achievements and I often had difficulty getting him to talk about himself. "You don't want to hear about that," he would say when I asked him for details about his life. It took him several months to open up to me, but once he did I learned that he had led a difficult life yet had always been optimistic, hard working, and goal oriented. Throughout his studies he went to school part-time and worked part-time. He even worked throughout the obligatory military-service period after university, attending military training in the morning and working odd jobs to earn extra money in the afternoon. When his friends and other young people his age complained about the poor economic state of the country, Amir Ali was always optimistic. He never let the political situation cloud his hope for his economic future. One of the first things he said to me reflected that optimism:

Well, here, whatever goal you want to reach you can reach, but it all depends on how you go about it. You can have your wits about you and be smart and be the type of person who doesn't give in, if you are like this. You've got to pay attention. Wherever you live, everywhere, it doesn't make a difference, in the world. Everything has its difficulties; if things were so easy to get, then you wouldn't enjoy having them as much. It's those times when you become really satisfied with yourself.

Amir Ali proudly told me this back in 2000, when I first met him while he was still at university. He had decided he was going to be successful and make a lot of money so he could give his family the life his cousins had had while they were growing up. By 2005 he had reached many of his goals and had bought his parents an apartment and a car.

Nina often told me that her enthusiasm and ambition were inspired by her brother. In all the time I spent with the two of them, I never once saw them fight or argue. Brother and sister adored each other and supported each other throughout many of their obstacles. Nina was a graphic design major at Tehran University when I first met her in 2000. She didn't work through college but instead helped with the housework while her mother was working. She would often rush home after school, finish her homework, prepare a meal for the family, clean the house, and then go out with her friends. When I asked her how she managed to do it all, she would say, "I don't have a choice; I love my family, I want to help, and so I do it. But I also love my friends. I'm trying to create balance." Upon her graduation from college, she followed her brother's career trajectory and joined the company he was working at as a graphic designer. Today the two of them work together and make enough money to support the whole family.

I began spending a lot of time with Amir Ali and Nina in 2000. At the time, although they frequented some of the venues popular among young Tehranis and knew many people in the various circles in which I traveled, they never struck me as typical young members of the social movement taking place in Tehran. They both dressed modestly, and although they enjoyed evenings out with their friends, going to parks, cafes, and movies, they were not the frequent-partying, type, nor did either of them have a boyfriend or girlfriend. I remember asking them in 2003 about their romantic relationships. Both of them turned red and told me they didn't see themselves having these kinds of relationships anytime soon.

By 2005, many aspects of their personalities had changed, and perhaps this can be linked to the changes in their socioeconomic status, although they attribute it to the changes taking place in the youth culture throughout Tehran. "It finally hit us! The enghelāb-e-jensi! We finally understood why everyone was doing the things they were doing," explained Nina one afternoon. "It's not because we suddenly had money like them, but it's like I woke up one day and realized, oh! These things are happening for larger reasons than we think. Fashion means something. There's a sexual revolution going on and we have to be a part of it!" As I looked at her that day, I hardly recognized her. She had changed so much, and she reiterated that these changes had occurred because she was no longer afraid to change. Inspired by the success of the social movement that young people around her had been enacting, she no longer feared the morality police or the state, and she wanted to assert herself.

In 2005, although Amir Ali and Nina still had the same sibling relationship and the same ambition, everything else had changed. Nina had gotten a nose job, thinned out her eyebrows (which had formed a thick unibrow the year before), and had gold highlights added to her hair. When I first saw her that summer, I was shocked. She had replaced her loose black mānto with a white fitted one, and her conservative headscarf, which she used to tie under her chin, was now a pink Christian Dior shawl. Her Gucci sunglasses were strategically placed on the top of her head. When she fished cigarettes out of her purse and started talking about her newest boyfriends, I nearly passed out. "Yeah, Pardis, I'm totally dating two new guys at the moment, but I can't decide between the two of them," she said to me at the coffee shop one afternoon. "What?" I said, still not able to believe neither my eyes nor my ears. "Yeah, I don't know what to do, but I'll take you to a few parties so you can meet them; maybe you will have some insight." I was dumbfounded.

When Amir Ali drove up in a new car with his hair slicked back and wearing tight jeans and sunglasses that would catch many a female eye, I was even more surprised. He ran up to us and gave me a hug before taking off his Prada sunglasses. For the first few years I had been friends with him, he had been too shy even to shake my hand; it was only in 2004 that he had accepted my hand, but a hug was a big step. He had often told me that women made him nervous and he hoped I was OK with his awkwardness around me—awkwardness that had been shed like snakeskin. "Things are going well," he began. "We've moved into Sa'ādat ābād [a western part of town known for being a nice, middle-class neighborhood], and I have a new car on the way. I'm dating a new girl; she's cute and smart and, well, we'll see what happens." Again I had to double-check that the pair I was having coffee with was the same Amir Ali and Nina that I had befriended in 2000.

The next day, both of them went to work from 8 A.M. until 6 P.M. At 7 P.M. they picked me up and took me to the park to meet some of their friends. We strolled around the park as they told me about network marketing, the future of Iran, and the sexual and social revolution taking place in the country. "We are living in exciting times," Nina told me as we took a seat in the cool shade of a tree. "It's great; we can voice our discontent with the regime by what we do, how we look, and what we do for fun. Do you know any other country like this?" she asked as everyone nodded and indicated their agreement. It seemed as though the change taking place in these two siblings was directly related to their decision to join the social and sexual revolution. Their new look and style could be partially attributed to their newfound wealth and to the wealthy neighborhood into which they had moved, but it seemed (by how they talked) that this was a way for them to engage in the sociopolitical scene in which many other young Tehranis were involved.

After our stroll in the park we went to a nice restaurant atop the hills for dinner. The view was breathtaking; the glittering lights of Tehran were complemented by the trees and flowers that surrounded each table. There we continued our conversations. After a few cocktails with eight or nine other young people who worked at the same company, we decided it was time to go home. The evening had been filled with discussions about the regime, the upcoming election, and presidential candidate Rafsanjani's most recent attempts to attract young adult voters. Amir Ali and Nina both indicated that they felt the changes taking place on Tehran's city streets were leading to changes in the regime. As we were discussing these and other issues, Amir Ali caught the eye of a waiter. "We should probably leave," he said, motioning to the waiter. "Walls have ears here, and we can continue our conversation in the car." We all gathered our belongings, paid the check, and left.

"Your parents don't mind that you go out until late like this?" I asked them on our way home. "No way!" Nina quickly responded. "First of all, they trust us; they know we are good kids, and as long as we are together it's not a big deal." "Also, we support them," Amir Ali said. "Financially, I mean. And you know, it's not like we aren't working either. We have our fun but we get our stuff done too. We have created the perfect work–life balance. We are happy, and they are happy that we are happy. Can you imagine anything better than that?" I nodded in agreement.

During the summer of 2007, when I visited Nina and Amir Ali, they were both still working at the same company and still upbeat about their lives and environment. I had been having a particularly difficult visit due to entanglements with the authorities, who were arresting many Iranian-American scholars, and thus I was feeling very pessimistic about the country and found their optimism somewhat frustrating. "You really think that things in Iran are moving forward?" I asked them. "Yes! Absolutely!" said Amir Ali. "What you see now is just the typical cycle that we go through here, with the regime cracking down for a few months, then they'll let up again," said Nina. Amir Ali chimed in once again. "Yeah, I mean it's not perfect right now, like I mean today when I was on my way to work, the morality police stopped me because I like to wear a necktie to work. They said neckties are too Western and fined me thirty-thousand tomans [U.S.$33]. But that's fine. That's today. Tomorrow we will do what we want." "But that must be frustrating," I said, "to not get to wear what you want?" Nina stepped back in to clarify their point:

Look, for us, this is life here; we don't think it's strange; only you who come from outside think it's strange. Just like, you know, when you go to your parents' house you speak Persian and wear proper clothes, and when you go out with your friends, there you speak English and wear sexy clothes, right? Well, for us it's the same; it's like drinking water. We dress and act a certain way on the street and a different way in the home; if it wasn't like this we would find it strange.

"But does it ever weigh heavily on you that you have this *zāher/bāten* [outer self/inner self] divide? Does that affect your mental health?" I asked. Nina and Amir Ali both shook their heads as Nina elaborated:

No, it doesn't, first of all because the zāher and bāten are becoming closer to one another, that is to say, I can wear makeup outside and inside, and I can hang out with my friends at coffee shops and at parks as well as at parties. But the other thing is that we have been taught how to live like this since we were little. Just like you were taught to walk, bicycle, or eat certain foods, it's a part of your life, right? Well, this is our life and we are used to it.

"Shift that research lens of yours," Amir Ali told me. I nodded and took note.

Mojdeh: "There Is More to People Than Meets the Eye, Especially in Tehran"

The first time I met Mojdeh, in a coffee shop in the northern part of Tehran, I thought she was just another one of "those" ladies of leisure from northern Tehran who spent all her time on her appearance and could converse only about designer wear and plastic surgery. She had clearly had a nose job, cheek implants, and collagen lip implants, and she had peroxide blonde hair coming out of her bright orange head shawl, with bright orange toe and nail polish to match. She sat down, her bracelets clanking on the table, took off her Channel sunglasses, and began fanning herself. When my friend Laleh introduced me to Mojdeh, I had to take a deep breath and stop myself from passing judgment. Part of me didn't want to speak to her or listen to anything she had to

say. She seemed like she would be a shallow person, and at that point I
felt saturated by women like this, frustrated at their lack of willingness
to engage with me in conversation because I didn't look a certain way
(meaning that I refused to wear a lot of makeup and was still fearful of
wearing revealing coats and headscarves). Three months after that day
I considered her one of my best friends in Tehran. I realized that she
had so much more to say about the layers of the sexual revolution than
I could possibly have imagined.

Barely five feet tall with bleached blond hair, Mojdeh is a twenty-five-
year-old factory supervisor who is also the mother of two little girls. She
says that she is asked to wear many hats at once but wears none of them
well. Mojdeh was born outside of Tehran, in Tabriz, a city located in the
northwestern part of the country. The first of ten children, by age six she
was asked to help with the housework and child rearing. She says she la-
ments the loss of her childhood and now strives to give her daughters the
childhood she never had. Her mother gave birth to her at fifteen, when
her father was twenty-eight. Although her father never received formal
schooling, he was a hard worker and fast learner and quickly became the
head of a local textile factory in Tabriz. Within a few years he had saved
enough to buy the factory, and after the revolution, textile manufacturers
and those who worked in and dealt with the bāzār doubled their wealth
almost overnight.[7] Soon Mojdeh's father had earned enough money to
purchase several factories and a construction company, and the family
moved to Zafar, one of the wealthier parts of Tehran when Mojdeh was
twelve years old. Four years later, Mojdeh was married off to her first
cousin on her father's side, and two years after that, at the age of eighteen, she had the first of her two daughters. She was a virgin when she
married but, according to her, she got caught up in numbers of sexual
partners *after* her marriage. By the age of twenty she had begun her first
extramarital affair, a practice that she continues to this day.

Being that she was the eldest and, according to her mother, the favorite child of her father, she was handpicked to learn how to run the
businesses when her father decided he wanted to retire. A few years after
her second daughter was born, Mojdeh began working part-time overseeing her father's company in the southern part of Tehran. Her husband
also works in one of her father's textile factories and was supportive of

his wife's decision to get involved. They hired a part-time nanny, and Mojdeh began working every day.

Now, from 8 A.M. until 5 P.M. Mojdeh oversees one of the major factory sites near *meydun-e-Shush*. Because she didn't finish high school, she says, she has a difficult time with the details of the company's finances, but her husband and father both told me that she is a fast learner and an excellent manager. "I know that the workers look at me funny 'cause I look like one of those typical northern Tehrani women, but I've worked hard to prove them wrong," she said, touching up her mascara and pursing her lips. "It's true that I don't look like the typical textile worker, but I have some good ideas too, and I love being involved in the family business. Plus, I work only during the day, then I get to go home and play with my girls, and some nights come and hang out with you lovely ladies," she said, referring to our monthly gatherings.

Each day at 5 P.M., Mojdeh rushes home to feed her daughters and help them with their homework. She prepares the house and dinner for her husband and then after dinner often calls up one of her friends or lovers and goes out. According to Mojdeh, her husband is too wrapped up in his own work and family to take notice of her personal affairs, but she thanks God that he is not jealous and does not wish to regulate her social activities like some of her friends' husbands. The afternoons I spent with her we usually took her daughters for a swim and then prepared dinner. After dinner we would go to a coffee shop or to the home of one of her friends for a party. Rarely did she invite her husband to join us. She would often meet her lovers at these parties, and then I would make my way home. The next day she would always call to make sure I had enjoyed myself and then tell me of her sexual exploits. I remember her on more than one occasion grinning deviously and saying, "I didn't have the exact childhood I wanted, but believe me, I'm making up for it now!"

Alaleh and Laleh: "We Are Ladies of Luxury, and You Could Say We Are in Style"

Alaleh, twenty-four, and Laleh, twenty-five, were both born in Tehran. They are cousins who grew up across the street from each other near the southern part of town, close to the main bāzār. Now that they are older and have children, they still live across the street from each other, but today they live in a middle-class neighborhood in the northwestern part of the city. Before the revolution, their families struggled to make ends meet, as did the families of many of the young people I met in Tehran. Their fathers were both merchants involved with the bāzār. Laleh's father sold construction materials and Alaleh's father was involved in fabrics. Neither of their mothers finished high school and both were married by the age of fifteen. Laleh was born when her mother was sixteen, Alaleh when her mother was seventeen. Neither Alaleh (who is now divorced) nor Laleh (who is still married) attended university. Today they are not employed, but they do not consider themselves housewives.

Alaleh was born the year of the revolution to parents who were hopeful about the changes the new regime would bring. A few years after she was born, her father became wealthier because, like Asana's father, he was appointed to be a tājer. Thus the family's status was elevated during the 1980s. They moved out of their working-class neighborhood and purchased a home (which is uncommon in Tehran because even the wealthiest people often live in apartments) in *Shahrak-e Gharb*.[8] They had three more children after that, and Alaleh was married off by the time she was seventeen. Her father, hailing from a "traditional" family, often told me that he does not believe women should be educated; thus he wanted to marry his daughters off as quickly as possible because that was their "destiny." At nineteen Alaleh had her first and only child, a daughter named Rhana. At twenty-one Alaleh was divorced and moved back into her parents' home. Although her father was unhappy about the divorce, he supported his daughter out of his love for his new grandchild.

"It wasn't easy for me to get a divorce, but I hated my husband," Alaleh often told me. "I mean I really hated him; he disgusted me. I didn't really know I would hate him, and at first things were good with us. He didn't mind that I wasn't a virgin at marriage, and I didn't mind that he was really into his opium. It seemed like a good situation," she said between gulps of her vodka martini. We were sitting on her balcony, which faced the inner courtyard of the house; shielded from her neighbors' eyes, we were able to enjoy the afternoon sun without headscarves or māntos, and we relished these afternoons. Alaleh and her friends often started drinking at 4 P.M., and they would continue the festivities until midnight or later. They would leave their children with nannies and spend most of their days shopping, at the beauty salon, lunching with one another or with their latest boyfriends, and then gathering at each other's homes in the evening to hang out and have fun. They often told me that they loved the lives they had created for themselves in the Islamic Republic, and they firmly believed that they were carving out a social space for themselves that suited their interests. "We have fun here in the Islamic Republic, believe it or not," Alaleh once whispered in my ear at an evening party she was hosting. "Maybe the women don't have as much fun as the men, but we are changing all of that." She smiled, parting her full, lipstick-lined lips to reveal a large toothy smile before puffing on a marijuana-and-hashish joint that had been handed to her.

On most occasions when Alaleh started drinking or smoking, she brought up the topic of her ex-husband and the details of her sex life with him. "I didn't like living with him though, you know?" She pulled her shoulder-length black hair back into a loose ponytail with a light blue rubber band. As she leaned over to take a sip of her cocktail, a few strands of hair fell around her face. She tucked them behind her ear before continuing.

I didn't even like having sex with him. Can you imagine? Me? Not wanting to have sex with a hunk of a man? Which, believe me, my husband was. But I didn't like it. He liked me though. Some afternoons I would be cooking or washing dishes, two activities that really don't become me, can you imagine? Me? Cooking? Anyways, he would come up behind me and have sex with me while I was doing housework. I wouldn't even get into it. I would yawn and continue with my housework. Like when I was washing the dishes he would come up behind me—and mind you this was usually in the summertime, so it was hot and I wouldn't bother wearing panties 'cause it was just too much trouble. Well, you know, that gave him easy access. He'd come over, I'd even have my dishwashing gloves on, and he'd come up behind me and then one, two, three, he would do me.

Alaleh made gyrating motions to imitate her husband and fell to the floor laughing. "When he finished I would go into the bathroom and clean myself up and go on about my daily work." Shifting to a more serious tone, she said, "I really hated him."

Alaleh also frequently talked openly of the details of her divorce—a process that, her mother told me, had been surprisingly easy given that Alaleh's husband had decided not to keep custody of their daughter. Alaleh told me she felt freer now and enjoyed her life so much more as a divorcee than she ever had as a married woman. "People sometimes ask me if I'm lonely now that I'm not married at my age, but that's the last thing I feel!" she said, taking Laleh's hand and giving her a loving look. "I have lots of boyfriends to keep me entertained, plus I have wonderful women in my life, like my cousin here. She is the first person I talk to in the morning when I wake up, and the last person I speak to at night before I go to sleep," she said, winking at her cousin. Laleh responded by blowing her a kiss. "*Aāsheghetam*, I love you," she said to Alaleh and kissed her hand. These women, like many of my other informants, were very close and had formed an intimate friendship. They were also often physically intimate (hugging, holding hands, and kissing), but they saw this as an extension of their friendship rather than as a form of sexual relationship.

Laleh's family history and life trajectory were similar to her cousin's. Her father experienced a similar economic boom in the years following the revolution (he too became a tājer) and moved the family into a duplex apartment in *Shahrak-e Gharb* so that the kids would not be far from their cousins. Never falling behind her cousin, Laleh was married off at the age of seventeen to their neighbor, a man twenty years her senior who was in the construction business, overseeing the erection of new buildings and businesses. Laleh too had her first and only child, a boy named Sassan, by the time she was nineteen. Laleh is still married, but she too hates her husband. "When I think of him, I want to throw up!" she said making a vomiting gesture with her body and spilling her martini. "He disgusts me, and the worst part is that I was a virgin at marriage. But a few years after we were married I got smart and realized that a married woman has a lot of power."

Laleh and Alaleh as well as several of my unmarried informants regularly reiterated their belief that married women hold more social status in Tehran. They indicated that a married woman is seen by her family and society as more serious, or *sangin* (literally, "heavy," but referring to a person who takes themselves seriously). Unmarried informants often told me that when members of the morality police would find out that a woman was married, they were less likely to harass her about her appearance and behavior and would say they relied on the women's husbands to punish them. There was therefore a general consensus that married women could get away with more because they had fulfilled their duty of marriage and in a way had earned some amount of freedom. Laleh would sometimes wonder aloud if she had taken these freedoms too far or if she was entitled to behave a certain way because she had put up with her husband for so long and even given him a son. "I started taking boyfriends a few years after we were married, like the rest of my married girlfriends, and occupied myself with looking good and having fun. I was bored being a housewife, having nothing to do, nothing to make the days pass more quickly, so I started taking care of myself—dying my hair, exercising, and becoming an expert at applying makeup and being sexy," she said, using the English word *sexy* for effect. "It's amazing how you can distract yourself by becoming skilled at looking good, isn't it?" she asked rhetorically.

I spent many afternoons watching Laleh get ready for her dance class. The memory of one of my first few afternoons with her remains vivid in my head.

July 18, 2003

After applying four layers of makeup, Laleh pulls on a glittering pair of gold short shorts, or hot pants, and a red, white, and blue sparkling sports bra. She ties a small headband around her head to push back her red and pink highlighted hair. She takes a look at herself in the mirror and sighs. "I really am beautiful, aren't I?" she asks me. I nod. "Look how I was wasted on my husband. Don't you make that mistake, Pardis," she tells me, grabbing my hand and rushing us down to the basement of her apartment building. *"Nomre-ye bist-e kelās-o nemikhām!* [I don't want the top of the class]," bellow the six ladies already in Laleh's basement singing along with a hot new Iranian pop song from Iranian-American heartthrobs Kamran and Houman. The women are wearing mismatched leotards, tights, leggings, and shorts with colorful headbands. The first time I attended this makeshift dance class, I was instantly reminded of a Jane Fonda workout video from the 1980s. The young women would walk into the basement in hejāb and promptly remove their Islamic layers to reveal a variety of color and pattern combinations, such as leopard-print leotards with pink tights and purple leg warmers. As we walk through the door on this hot summer afternoon, the women rush toward Laleh and give her a collective hug. "You're late," jokes one of the dancers. "We've been waiting!" adds another. "I see you put on our favorite song," Laleh responds, smiling at the women and sneaking the first of many glances at herself in the mirror-lined wall she has created for this class. As I watch Laleh watching herself, I wonder if the dance class is just an excuse for the women to interact with and look at their bodies in different ways, but I don't have time to finish my thought because Laleh orders all of us to line up behind her. I take my place in the back of the room. I wear loose black pants and a T-shirt, an outfit that has earned me dozens of criticizing lectures from the other dancers, not to mention from Laleh herself, who has made several attempts to lend me her dance outfits, with no success. I am thankful for the seven years of Iranian dance classes that were forced upon me in San Diego by my mother. Never did I think that knowing how to dance well would prove to be so important in my adult life. But at parties and social gatherings throughout my times in Iran, I was given a lot of credit for my ability to gyrate my hips while popping one shoulder at a time or doing a half-backbend while singing along with the hottest Iranian hits. In fact, my dancing skills have now earned me a permanent spot in Laleh's twice-weekly makeshift dance classes, which enables me to observe her and the women who frequent the class. Recently I have been using the convenience of these gatherings to conduct group interviews with five to eight women at a time. Laleh announces that today we are going to work on perfecting our arms and shoulders. She tries to be serious, to teach us dance skills, but as soon as the music comes on it becomes a free-for-all, with all of us dancing in our own styles, trying to outdo one another but laughing, smiling, and joking the whole time. At the end of class the women hug one another and Laleh. As they pull on their outer layers of Islamic clothing, Laleh calls out, "*Tā shambe* [until Saturday]!" She flashes me one of her brilliant toothy smiles. "Without things like dancing, drinking, and going out with the ladies, I think I would have killed myself here," she says hugging me. "Without people like you, my cousin Alaleh, and the dancers to get me through these miserable days, this miserable life, I don't know what I would do. Thank goodness we all have each other. I always say that I have been blessed with my dancing ladies; without them I wouldn't be the fabulous woman you see before you," she proclaims, blowing a kiss to her reflection in the mirror behind me.

I spent a lot of my leisure time with Laleh and Alaleh, going from one activity to the next with them and regularly attending the dance classes. Some mornings Laleh would come and pick me up and, after picking up Alaleh, we would go to the gym to work out. Working out for them consisted mostly of gossiping and sitting in the sauna and Jacuzzi, but nevertheless it was always entertaining. After the gym we would go to Laleh's house, where inevitably her housekeeper would be cooking or cleaning, and doing a poor job of both, according to Laleh.[9] She would routinely yell at her housekeeper, and then we would go into her room. "You see this room?" she would tell me, pulling me by the wrist into her bedroom. "Supposedly I share it with my husband, but like this apartment, it's really mine, and he, well, he's more like a guest here," she would say, throwing open her closet doors to reveal only women's clothing. I often wondered where her husband kept his belongings, but this question was never answered. The next two hours would be spent showering, dressing, and applying makeup. Laleh and Alaleh would literally paint their faces on and then spend anywhere between half an hour and an hour and a half picking out what to wear and deciding what the appropriate mānto-headscarf combination would be. Three hours later we would leave the house for lunch. We would either go to the house of another young woman whose husband was at work or away on business and drink and dance until 5 or 6 P.M., or we would go on a double date to one of Tehran's dimly lit hidden restaurants. The dates I went on with them were uncomfortable for me, but the young (and often not so young) men were flexible and would allow me just to sit and observe their flirtations. The dates usually consisted of the men showering Laleh and Alaleh with compliments, paying for lunch, then offering to repeat the date or to retire to one of their homes. Sometimes the men were married and had wives in other cities; sometimes they had bachelor pads. If this was the case, I would go home and then a few hours later Laleh would pick me up and take me either to the beauty salon, to a coffee shop, or to Alaleh's house, where we would spend time at their private pool. Pool parties at private homes were a regular outing for the ladies, and I spent much of my time interviewing other young women in that relaxed environment.

After a few hours in the sun (the women didn't usually get into the pool, because it would ruin their makeup) we would return once again to Laleh's house. There we would humor her husband for an hour or two, play with her son and with Alaleh's daughter if she was there, and then leave the house again for another gathering or party. At 3 or 4 A.M. the ladies would finally want to go home to bed. At that point, exhausted, I would get into a cab and find my way home. Every now and then I would tell them that they partied so hard I could hardly keep up. "If we don't live like this, we cannot exist in the Islamic Republic," Laleh would tell me. "We hate our government, despise our families, and our husbands make us sick. If we don't look fabulous, smile, laugh, and dance, well then we might as well just go and die."

On Being a Woman in Iran

Through my own experiences, as well through stories told by my informants, I came to understand that the daily interactions and encounters of my informants were heavily shaped by gender. As mentioned in the first chapter, young women have to face the reality that although they compose almost 60 percent of university graduates, they face higher unemployment rates than men. According to the latest figures released by the Iran Statistical Center (which reflects statistics up until 2004), the country's unemployment rate is 12.8 percent (although unemployment among young people ages eighteen to twenty-five is nearer to 40 or 50 percent) and the rate of unemployment among women is 22.4 percent.[10] Although the lowest official double-digit figure for unemployment in early 2004 may not seem problematic, the number is still discomforting because unemployment is especially high at 34 percent for fifteen- to twenty-year-old women, who constitute 25 percent of the labor force.[11] Young women are also repeatedly denied access to positions of power (although there are several women serving in parliament and a number of female deputy ministers) and consistently receive lower wages than men. Additionally, the komite tend to police young Tehrani women's appearance and behavior much more than that of young Tehrani men. Many young women expressed to me their frustration over this aspect of their daily lives and said it made an already difficult struggle even more challenging.

"You know, 97 percent of the problems in the *jomhuri-e eslāmi* [Islamic Republic] are caused by men but fall on the shoulders of women," said Paranaz, a twenty-one-year-old university student, while grinding her teeth. Parts of daily life are much more difficult for women than for men, which I experienced firsthand as a woman, and many of my informants affirmed my experiences. Paranaz noted that although women constitute the majority of university graduates, they are still underemployed and never taken seriously in the workplace. "My mom is a teacher," she told me. "She teaches at the university here, but people are always giving her a hard time. We women have to work twice as hard as the men just to get half the respect they automatically get." Setareh, a colleague who taught at Tehran University while I was there, alluded to Paranaz's comments about not being taken seriously as a professional woman. "You know, women here are very bored and they don't have a lot of ambition. Their entire focus is on what they think they should be doing, which is servicing their men. It's so sad." Setareh and I became good friends during the time I spent at the university in 2004 and 2005. A young woman with two children, she earned a master's degree in anthropology. She now teaches courses on sociocultural anthropology but says she is frustrated at having to avoid topics such as gender, sexuality, and certain world religions due to censorship from the academic board that regulates the content of her courses. Her master's thesis and ongoing research focused on low-income housing outside of Tehran and on the communities that formed in these housing projects. She told me she was interested in questions of gender and sexuality but had always been afraid of conducting this kind of research. She became involved in my project and gave me feedback on numerous pages of my manuscript, as well as providing unique insight into goings-on at the university and among the young people I was studying. Most of our discussions centered on gender-related questions and on how young women's lives are shaped by their environment. Setareh identified herself as a strong Iranian feminist and thus often expressed frustration at the status of women in Tehran—specifically at ways in which young women in the new youth movement were behaving. One morning she told me:

I feel that there were women in our parents' generation who fought hard for women's rights, and now it's like feminism is dead in Iran. It had the beginnings of some kind of life before, but now it's totally dead. All that women here want to do is spend their time looking good to try to catch a husband; that is their main goal. If they are married, their goal is to serve their husbands better. But it's because they don't take us seriously, these men. Women's situation here is bad. Look at me: I was always the type of person to be pursuing *elm* [knowledge], education, and this kind of thing. I didn't want to marry; I wanted to be an anthropologist. Then they told me over and over that there was no future in pursuing knowledge, so I ended up marrying and having a child. They told me that was all I was good for. But you know, thank goodness I have a good husband; without him, well . . . I wouldn't be who I am today. He takes me seriously, believes in me. But no one at that school does.

Setareh was one of the most hard-working and dedicated women I met while in Iran. Despite frustrations about not being taken seriously, she pushed on with her career and received a promotion at Tehran University by the time my research was completed. Her husband, also a professor at Tehran University, in the biology department, was very open-minded and supportive of his wife's decision to pursue education and employment in academia, even after having children. She was one of the few women to achieve a high status in her department, and she demonstrated that with hard work and patience it could be accomplished. Setareh recently moved to France to pursue postdoctoral research at a French university, but she hopes to return to Tehran soon.

Other young women complained about the burden of gender inequality in their social lives. Leila, a twenty-year-old urban-planning student and artist, noted that "life is tough for us women here in the Islamic Republic. You have to be really optimistic, not let things get you down," she emphasized with a serious tone. "People bother us a lot; there is a lot of *gir midan* [harassment]. Women can't travel alone easily; I can't go to a restaurant by myself. I guess with my girlfriends I can, and do, but alone it's not the same. Guys can do more, and with ease. It's just tough here for us." Leila was frustrated because she was watching her brother conduct his life with seemingly fewer complications than she was experiencing. She had been invited to attend and participate in several art exhibitions internationally but had been forced to turn them down because as a single woman she had a hard time receiving a visa for international travel. These additional challenges sometimes frustrated many of the young women to no end.

Homa, a religious studies student originally from Mashad, also expressed her frustration at the challenges women face daily that men do not have to endure. "What I don't like is that guys here do whatever they want; they could probably even kill someone and yet no one would do anything. All they have to do is put a beard on, look messy and unkempt, and they can do whatever they want," she said, pausing for a moment to reflect on her last statement. "It's weird too, you know? With guys, the sloppier and messier they look, the more religious they are considered. We women, on the other hand, have to carry ourselves in a certain way, uptight." She sighed, drew in her breath, straightened her spine, and made a large gesture of crossing her legs properly. "Why doesn't anyone tell these guys who have the power that it doesn't make sense to let the guys look messy and try to get your women to be happy about looking like maids or servants in these chãdors!" She finished by referring to a stereotype that painted women in chãdors as lower class, and therefore as more likely to be servants.

These subtleties in class distinction based on dress came up repeatedly in interviews. Women felt that by wearing fashionable or tight mãntos and headscarves instead of chãdors, they indicated that they were of higher socioeconomic status; thus young women who were members of the lower class would often wear mãntos in order to pretend to be of another socioeconomic stature. When young women who were members of the secular middle class were forced to wear chãdors or maghna'e for a particular reason (for example, when entering certain spaces, such as mosques or other religiously sanctioned areas, or to attend public universities), they felt they were being made to look poor by being forced into a uniform. Women played with the subtleties of even this uniform (such as by wearing more makeup or pushing the maghna'e far back on the forehead) to remind passersby that they were indeed fashionable and not *kolfat* (servants or maids), and that they were not happy about their uniform.

Homa was also angry that the regime and the morality police would constantly comment that how women carried themselves was grounds for arrest, but this same amount of scrutiny was not given to the young men. Although some men felt that there was a high level of policing with regard to their appearance, most of them agreed that women were subject to arrest and harassment far more often. The women were usually held to different standards of comportment and morality then the men. For many members of the morality police, violation of the moral codes by a woman was a much more serious offense than violation by a young man. Women consistently were harassed more often, and faced harsher punishment (such as violence or arrest).

I experienced a great deal of this gender harassment and policing during my visits to Iran. On two separate occasions I was almost arrested for doing "unladylike things" such as "loitering" on the street while waiting for my ride to pick me up, or eating ice cream "provocatively." My clothes were always open to comment because I generally was not dressed "Islamically" enough. When I attempted to go to a hospital or clinic to do volunteer work or to a bank to withdraw money, the male tellers or other workers often refused to serve me. They sometimes accused me of not being properly dressed to enter a public space; other times they said that a woman should not try to withdraw money, that it was a man's job. The security guards at the hospital where I volunteered wouldn't let me inside the hospital gates because of my style of dress or comportment, telling me that my maghna'e was slipping too far back, that my mānto was too tight, or that the hospital was no place for a woman to venture into unaccompanied by a man. I often had to wait at the front door for one of the male attendants to come and escort me to the office in which I had been assigned to work.

That I lived alone throughout large periods of my time in Iran was scandalous. That I traveled alone was even worse. People would often ask me where the man who should speak for me was, and why I was alone. I had to carry with me at all times a letter from my father indicating that he had given me permission to travel to Iran without him. I had to make sure I carried myself "properly" in order to avoid harassment from the morality police or the watchful eyes of male shopkeepers. One afternoon a man at the bāzār refused to sell me some books. "What do you want with these, sister?" he asked me, looking down his glasses at the spectacle of a young woman alone wanting to buy politically charged books. I told him I wanted to practice my reading. "You shouldn't be reading these, sister; go home and cook something for your family," he said sternly, pulling a few books out of my hands. *"Bass e"* [Enough]!" I told him, grabbing the books, thrusting some money at him, and taking the books away.

My brother would often tell me that being a person in Iran was hard enough with all the rules and regulations; there were so many rules that one was bound to break at least one unknowingly, and once you had broken one, it was much easier to break others. But being a female added many levels of frustration. Many of my female informants told me this was the reason it was important for women to push for social change, because although they stood to lose the most, they also had the most to gain.

Fun in the Islamic Republic?

"What do you do for fun" was always one of the first questions I asked each informant or group of informants. Understanding how young people pass their time against the restricted backdrop of the regime illuminates how they are restructuring their relationship to the regime. Daily experiences with fun and recreation reflect the changes taking place in the Islamic Republic. The most common responses to the question "What do you do for fun in the Islamic Republic?" were outdoor and physical activities (such as hiking or going on long walks in the countryside); hanging out with friends; listening to or creating art, music, and poetry; going to the park or coffee shops; or partying. Most of my informants lamented the lack of additional recreational activities (such as bars and clubs) and blamed the regime for taking these away. Many expressed pride at having found ways to have fun despite the strong-arm propaganda put out by members of the regime during Islamification. This propaganda called on young people to be sangin (serious), to pay attention to religious studies, texts, and building the Islamic Republic; there was no room in the rhetoric for recreational activities.

"For fun? Mainly sports and getting together with friends," began Kayvan, a twenty-one-year-old university student at Azad University in Punak who was from the center of town. "I like sports much better than the gatherings we have, much more than partying. I like to hike and play tennis. But getting together with friends is always fun. We get together and go here and there. That's about it for having a good time; we can't do much else." Kayvan said he especially liked to play sports and exercise because in most cases this was a form of recreation that was free. He would talk about going hiking or climbing with his friends, and he added that these kinds of activities were *tafreeh-e-sālem*, or healthy fun, as opposed to unhealthy recreation, which to him included drug and alcohol use and multiple-partner sex.

Another young man echoed Kayvan's sentiments about exercise. "Well, mainly what I do for fun here is exercise," said Kamran, a twenty-year-old taxi driver. "I exercise all the time, go on walks and hikes in the mountains; it's my way of getting out my frustration, of getting rid of all that excess energy, you know? That's why I'm able to control myself, to control my temper and my hormones. That's why I thank God I can exercise to get rid of my hormones, which are dangerous here in the Islamic Republic, you know? I pour it all out on working out and rock climbing instead." He flexed his muscles to show them to me, although this action was unnecessary; his T-shirt was so tight that most of his muscles were revealed.

Many of the young women I interviewed also spent a lot of their free time at the gym, at exercise classes, or on hikes in the mountains with male and female friends. They said it helped them look good and feel better, and they were glad for the opportunity to have a physical outlet. Many women added that exercise provided a fun and safe way to get together with friends away from family and partners. They indicated that the gym and the mountains were good places to get in shape while being open with friends without the hassle of harassment by the morality police. "I love working out," said Golnaz, twenty-two. "I work out hard and I look good and feel great. It makes me want to show off my body, not hide it; that's why I wear such tight fitting māntos," she said, getting up from her seat at the coffee shop and doing a catwalk turn. "I look good, don't I?" she asked rhetorically. I nodded and smiled.

Other extracurricular activities included driving around (especially in the parts of town that play host to wide, café-lined boulevards, such as *khiyābān-e Jordan* or *khiyābān-e Valiasr*) in search of other young people and getting together with friends for walks or for tea or ice cream in the park. The parks and mountain areas surrounding Tehran provide a safe haven for many young couples, not to mention that they are popular recreation areas for families, married couples, and Tehranis of a variety of socioeconomic classes. Fariba Adelkhah has done a significant amount of research about and inside the parks of Tehran and has provided an excellent description of the atmosphere of the parks and outdoor recreation areas:

The new municipal gardens have generated various everyday habits. People visit them in family groups . . . but also in various special groups—of women, young people, retired people, soldiers etc.—who are able to go there independently without arousing curiosity. The parks are thus a factor for social differentiation and autonomous conduct for individuals. The inhabitants of the localities make use of the new public gardens in numerous ways: they go there to rest, to sleep, to have picnics, to look after their children, to chat, to play sports, to follow artistic shows, to revise for their examinations, to read newspapers on display, to watch open air films, to pray, to do shopping, to go after girls, or just to pass by. Most of these ways of making use of the open spaces involve new ways of living . . . the parks are the setting for social innovation, though maybe at the expense of "inventing tradition"; but they do not exclude old habits, which have even acquired some new legitimacy—people play chess and draughts there, they unroll their carpets and pray. For all these reasons the public gardens are the setting both for social reconciliation and for at least potential conflict. They provide—better than the mosques, religious meetings, good-bye parties and birthday parties—for coexistence among different classes of society and their favorite consumption and leisure practices. Next to the young couple tucking into a pizza bought from the fast food dealer at the crossroads is a *sonnati* [traditional, "authentic"] family eating *shami-kabab* prepared at home; and the father will move to one side to pray while his grandchildren play ball games.[12]

Darband, a recreational garden area situated high up in the mountains in the northern part of the city, is a popular hangout spot for young people of all socioeconomic classes. A winding road leads up to the base of this mountain area. Once out of the car you walk twenty to thirty minutes to get into the area. Many cafes are built into the mountainside. These hidden outdoor spots are favorites of the young people because the altitude and natural shield of the mountains keeps them hidden from the watchful eyes of the morality police (or in some cases, from their parents or aunts and uncles), who are often markedly absent from these outdoor areas. The higher up I hiked, the more overt became the public displays of affection. In these cafes surrounded by rocks and breathtaking views, young couples lay on daybeds, held hands, or gazed into each other's eyes. They ordered tea and often a water tobacco pipe (which had recently been outlawed but, like other illegal activities, was still used in the mountains) and then lay back to enjoy the peaceful atmosphere. The mountains and altitude also provided relief from the heat and pollution of the city, and the cafes were generally nice places to relax, undisturbed by other people. "Up here we feel *rāhat hastim* [at ease]," said a young man seated on a daybed near mine one afternoon. "It's more comfortable, and we know the morality police won't bother us all the way up in the mountains, and the people who come up here are *ham aghide hastan* [like-minded to us]." He offered me a glass of tea. Although I am not a tea drinker, I took the offering and continued to listen. "Here no one will bother you, no one and nothing. Plus, look at how magnificent it is, this view, these mountains. Where else in the world could you ever find beauty as majestic and grand as the mountains of Iran? Tell me, lady, do you know?" I shook my head and finished the tea. As I was leaving he asked if he could take a picture of me against the backdrop of the mountains. "Sure," I said, "but make sure I look proper and Islamic."

Some of the other parks, especially those built in higher areas, are similar to Darband and provide other scenery in addition to the mountains. They are well attended to and full of flowers and greenery. Cafes and teahouses are built into the hills and along the pathways of these parks as well, and they play host to many young couples and groups of young men and women of all socioeconomic statures (because this is a free outing), who find it a nice reprieve from the chaos of the city. I was informed by many of the young adults that all of these parks are first- and second-date destinations, as well as relatively safe spots for engaging in sexual encounters in the evenings.

Driving around in cars is also a form of extracurricular activity for many of the young people, who view driving as a skill. Perhaps because everyone in Tehran spends so much time in cars (sitting in traffic, trying to get from one place to another, or deliberately cruising particular streets in town to show off a car or meet other young people in cars), many young people deliberatly attempt to make driving a recreation and a sport. Weaving through cars on crowded streets (known as *mār bāzi*, or playing like a snake or snaking between cars) is thought of as an admirable talent. Additionally, competition to see who drives the best, gets to their destination the fastest, and does the nicest job of driving a nice car is also a large part of driving as a form of recreation. Although it was interesting to spend hours in a car watching young people pass phone numbers between open windows or even purchase and sell drugs or black market movies and music, there were many occasions on which I was terrified by the driving style of my companions, feeling that at any moment an accident would occur and many people would be hurt. Young people often drive fast and without fear, scraping

Figure 2.2. Young people often spend a lot of time driving around in their cars. This is a photograph taken after a victorious Iranian soccer game, when young people poured into the streets in their cars to celebrate. © 2007 by Nader Davoodi. Used by permission.

by other cars, sidewalks, pedestrians, and people on motorbikes. They drive across the painted lanes of traffic so that a four-lane highway in effect has six to eight lanes of cars driven by people who pay no attention to staying in the appropriate lane. Reversing on a highway or down a street at full speed is not uncommon; neither is speeding down a one-way street in the wrong direction if it is a shortcut. Traffic is indeed a problem, and there are now several zoning restrictions whereby only certain cars can enter certain parts of town, and license plates ending in odd or even numbers can enter specific zones only on specified days. However, these zoning laws do not extend to the northern part of town, where sitting in a traffic jam in the afternoon is a regular occurrence. The northern parts of town also play host to the main cruising strips, where young people come to meet, show off, and race. Iran maintains one of the highest car-accident fatality rates in the world,[13] and one is often reminded of this statistic when holding one's breath as another car narrowly scrapes past.

The car has also become a portable private bubble that can be used in the public sphere. In their cars young people can play illegal music, socialize with members of the opposite sex, and consume illegal substances. Although young people, while driving, are moving through the public sphere, the car gives them a sense of agency, a sense of control over their own bubble, or a segment of their lives. Many of them also feel that cars bring them independence and security in that they could speed away from angry parents or morality police in a difficult situation. For these young people, the car has become a sacred space, perhaps one of the only spaces in which they have full autonomy.

"They drive their cars the way they drive their lives—trying to get to their goal as fast as possible with very little care or attention to the dangers and risks in front of them. If it will get them there faster, they will go the wrong way down a one-way street. If it will get a girl material things she wants faster, she is ready to sell herself or become a mistress rather than work hard and earn the money. They put everyone at risk by the way they drive, and they put everyone at risk by the way they live," noted Houman, a twenty-one-year-old taxi driver from the western part of town. "It is frightening, but they don't care. They don't care if they die going the wrong way down this street if they look good doing it; and if there is a chance that it will get them where they are going faster, then they are going to take that risk. It's just how we live our lives here."

IN JANUARY 2005, Persian was officially announced as the fourth most used language in the Internet blogosphere. English was first, Mandarin was second, and Persian and Spanish alternated in third and fourth place. That put Persian ahead of Japanese, French, and German. To this day, whenever I quote this statistic to friends who are not Iranian, I get skeptical responses. I would have shared their disbelief had I not witnessed firsthand the amount of time and energy that young Iranians spend online. Even though the Islamic Republic heavily regulates the Internet and has blocked all pornography sites as well as such popular sites as Victoria's Secret, the popular dating and social sites Friendster and Orkut, and other sites where young people around the world meet and chat, the young Iranians in Tehran have found a way around the faux Intranet created by the regime.[14] Those I have spoken with seem to use the Internet in three major ways. First, some young people use these chat rooms to meet other young Iranians for dating, for cybersex, or for other social activities. Second, many use these sites for blogging, a phenomenon that started in the United States and Europe but has recently taken hold in Iran. In December 2005 there were hundreds of thousands of blogs written in Persian.[15] These blogs are an outlet for young Tehranis to express their frustrations with the regime and a venue for sharing daily experiences. According to several of my informants, some of the most popular bloggers in Tehran have achieved celebrity status. Finally, the Internet is used by young Iranians, as by young people all over the world, as a window onto what's happening in the rest of the world, and to participate in the global youth culture.

The Internet provides a relatively safe venue (less visible and more anonymous than other options) for dating and meeting people, especially members of the opposite sex, within the confines of the Islamist regime. Although a certain amount of stigma is still attached to meeting one's partner online, many of the young people I have spoken with have sought and continue to seek partners in this way. "I met my current girlfriend online, through Orkut, actually," said Pouyan, a twenty-three-old architecture student turned taxi driver. "I don't tell a lot of people that, but that's how we met. First we exchanged a lot of e-mails, then we started chatting, and then dating. It was a much safer way for me to keep up my reputation, what with my family and all," he explained. Pouyan felt that the Internet gave him the anonymity he needed to decide whether a particular girl was worth the risk of going out in public on a date. He often said that his reputation as well as that of his family were important to him and he did not want them tarnished by his being arrested for being caught with a woman to whom he wasn't married. Many of the young people I interviewed appreciate the safety and relative anonymity of the Internet when it comes to sexual, or cybersexual, encounters. "I love that I can be just about anybody when I'm online," said one twenty-year-old female university student. "I can go online and be sexy and slutty and no one will ever know. That's why I have a bunch of screen names. And it's a lot easier than risking everything by going out on the streets to meet guys." Several of my informants see online chatting and cybersex as what they call a "safe" recreational activity. Not all of their online chats end up in dates; in fact, many of the married women I interviewed who were unsatisfied with their husbands preferred cybersex over having an affair. Some of them would secretly chat with their cyberlovers while their husbands were away, and would consider themselves to be safely satisfying their sexual needs in this way. "I know chat is not good. But you know I hate my husband," said Sousan, a twenty-four-year-old housewife who, like my other informants, used the English word *chat*. "But I don't feel like having an actual [physical] affair; it's a lot harder in Tehran than it is in New York! I could land myself in jail! Maybe even get myself beaten to death. But what can I do? I'm sexually unsatisfied, so I have to chat. And yes, I do chat with a lot of men, but I can't help it, it's almost addictive."

Although the government has tried to shut down or prohibit access to many of the online chat rooms and popular sites, young Iranians have found ways around the censorship. When one mating or dating site is shut down or made inaccessible, they come up with another. "It's the best, safest, and healthiest way for men and women to meet in Iran," commented one young computer whiz who was responsible for maintaining one of the major dating Web sites. "We can even do temporary marriage online now! Why *wouldn't* we do it?" he asked me, pulling up a humorous site called sighe.net. *Sighe* is the Persian word for "temporary marriage," a practice found only in Shi'ite Islam.[16] The site (which has since been shut down) showed pop-up pictures of young women in bridal attire standing next to smiling young grooms. On the right side of the page you could e-mail questions about sighe to a cleric.[17] On the left side of the page, in the bottom corner, you could click to have the temporary marriage ceremony performed online. The link would also take you to a page where you could print out a record of the marriage that stipulated the conditions, duration, and transactional exchange of the union. Although none of my informants reported using the site, many of them regularly visited it for a laugh.[18]

The government has been closely watching not only dating and sex Web sites but also many of the blogs that politically active young adults are writing. Some of the more controversial bloggers hide behind the Internet's anonymity, but as recently as February 2005 several bloggers were arrested, tortured publicly, and imprisoned. Nevertheless, the blogging continues. "I used to be really politically active, shouting in the streets and stuff," said a twenty-one-year-old university student who chose to call himself Gypsy. "Then I got caught a bunch, whipped, yeah, the whole deal; so I got smart. I started using the Internet." He opened up his laptop and showed me his Web page. In his blog, Gypsy exposed the regime's treatment of prisoners, and he talked about his own resentment toward the regime. "I guess in a way it's kind of therapeutic for me. I write this stuff and somehow, at the end of the day, I feel better," he told me back in 2004. When I returned to Iran in 2005, I couldn't track him down. His blog continued, but he was nowhere to be found. When I asked some of his friends, they told me rumor had it that Gypsy had moved because he was tired of getting caught and beaten by the morality police, who routinely escorted him to the Ministry of Intelligence, where he was further interrogated and physically intimidated. Apparently Gypsy was one of the people whose blog had been tracked back to him and he had been harassed by the police ever since fall 2004. His friend told me that Gypsy had been arrested four times throughout the winter and by spring 2005 had chosen to move to Rasht, his hometown, to continue writing about his political activities.

Today many blogs written in Persian and many more written in English can be attributed to young people living in Iran.[19] People use these blogs as platforms to talk about their opinions of the regime or as calls to arms. Some use their blogs to attract other like-minded young adults with whom to create group blogs with chat rooms for discussing recent happenings. The blogs that are written in English reach a wider audience than those written in Persian, including diasporic Iranians around the world who can no longer read or write Persian. These blogs bring Iranian youth in the diaspora into conversation with young Iranians in Iran. They have been described by the many young Iranian Americans I have spoken with in California as a necessary window into what is happening in the home country.

While outsiders use the blogs to gain insight into what is happening in Iran, many urban young Iranians use the Internet to gain insight into what is happening outside the country. "We know what you guys do in the United States," began one twenty-year-old man who was sitting next to me at a popular Internet cafe. "The Internet spreads information very quickly, and as a result changes here in Iran are taking place rapidly. We are an advanced culture, and we pick things up very quickly; the Internet has facilitated our progress," he explained. Just like young adults elsewhere in the world, these young people are curious about what is hot and what is not; what is in fashion, recent political hot topics, and trends in popular culture worldwide pique their interest. Even though the regime tries to restrict many of the Web sites (in the process creating an intranet of sorts), a lot of the sharp young people I interviewed had found a way to hack through the Intranet and get to the sites in which they were interested. Many of them regularly logged on to American and British news sites such as the BBC or the *New York Times* to see what journalists in the rest of the world were writing. Many of these young adults relied on Western news accounts to get a different picture of what was happening in their own country. "Well, the American and British news sites are sometimes more honest," said Reza, a twenty-five-year-old documentary filmmaker who confessed to reading BBC and CNN Web sites hourly. Others looked at fashion sites and music-downloading sites in order to keep informed of changes in global popular culture. "Remember that things in Iran have changed," began another young man at the Internet cafe. "Your modernization [that is, ideologies and discourses coming from outside Iran] has made it so that nothing, no youth culture, is growing in isolation. We increasingly have access to Internet, satellite TV, and well, we want to try out the things we see. Unfortunately this intersects badly with the regime. But we love it!" he exclaimed, turning his computer screen so I could see the three music Web sites he had pulled up. He explained to me that his favorite sites were ones where he could download American music. He showed me his collection of more than five hundred CDs he had burned from music downloaded from the Internet. He had music from around the world, but he was most proud of the American selections. "This is what makes me the life of the party!" he said proudly.

ONE INFORMANT, Reraj, a twenty-three-year-old medical student at Shahid Beheshti University, made his extracurricular priorities very clear to me:

Pardis: So, what do you like to do for fun?

Reraj: For fun? Well, of course we like to party!

Pardis: I see, and can you tell me a bit more about these parties?

Reraj: Well, of course. There are parties, and we go to them a lot.

Pardis: Like, can you describe the party scene?

Reraj: Well, like, there are usually between twenty and a hundred people at the parties, you know?

Pardis: And where are these parties?

Reraj: In people's houses or backyards, of course.

Pardis: And what are they like?

Reraj: Well, alcohol, there is sex, there is dancing, there is—it's just fun! It's what we do for fun! You wanna come?

Beyond exercise, parks, coffee shops, and time spent online, the extracurricular activity that more than half of the young people I interviewed cited most was attending, planning, and talking about their underground or private parties. I want to be careful here, however, to note that among the 105 young people with whom I spoke, twenty-five informants indicated their distaste for parties and were emphatic about *not* wanting to party. They said that parties were *tafreeh-e-nasālem* (unhealthy forms of recreation) or they cited fear of their parents or the morality police as reasons not to go. Other young people found large parties with alcohol, drugs, and socializing with members of the opposite sex a turnoff and indicated that they preferred small get-togethers with friends, or book clubs or outdoor recreation, to these parties; and some said they could not afford elaborate parties and thus preferred not to have any parties at all.

However, for a large portion of secular middle-class young Tehranis, partying is a favorite pastime and a party is an event to look forward to. Even young people who do not have their own venues for throwing parties or who come from the lower classes also find creative ways to party. Almost every night of the week in Tehran there is a party going on in some part of the city, though when I was there I usually attended parties in the northern parts of town. As mentioned earlier, young people in the southern parts of town and in the low-income areas either came uptown for these private parties or had small gatherings at abandoned warehouses or in alleyways that were unlikely to be frequented by the morality police Although I did not attend many of these smaller parties, my informants from the lower-income neighborhoods described their experiences at these gatherings, indicating that the desire to party is not limited to members of the middle and upper-middle classes. Although many young people do not have the means to attend or host elaborate parties, they have found creative ways of getting together, playing music, dancing, drinking, and having a good time. Many members of the lower-middle and lower classes also hosted parties outside of Tehran, either in the mountains or in the jungle and forest areas north of Tehran. I attended a few of these parties, and most of them had a ravelike atmosphere, with young people taking advantage of the natural protection of the surroundings to play loud music, indulge in drug use, and meet potential sexual partners. Of the parties I attended in Tehran and the parties most frequently discussed by the majority of my informants, endless amount of time was spent planning them or getting ready to attend them, and then creating stories about them afterward. Out of every ten nights I spent in Tehran, probably three were spent at parties. Most conversations I had with my informants involved stories about parties already attended or looking forward to an upcoming private party. Each party involved great risk for both the hosts and the attendees, because it could be raided at any moment and the attendees and hosts could be dragged off to jail. Yet every party was flawlessly executed and provided its attendees with what they described as a badly needed social outlet.

The fact that these parties occurred with very little interference from the morality police or members of the regime is yet another indication of the success of the youth movement, as well as of the ways in which the regime has been trying to adapt to its changing youth population. Had they transpired during the first decade and a half after the revolution, most of these parties would have been shut down by members of the regime; that they are taking place on such a regular basis in Tehran today is a reflection of how the political and social environment of the city is changing, and the attention paid to these parties by the young people reflects the changing youth culture.

Following are some of my own recountings of experiences planning parties, getting ready for them, and attending them.

Parvaneh and Homayoun's Party

Parvaneh, twenty-three, and her boyfriend, Homayoun, twenty-four, were among my favorite couples with whom to spend time. They had been dating for two years and were discussing getting engaged. Parvaneh is a social worker-in-training and Homayoun works with the bāzār, trading currency. They were known throughout the social circles I moved in for having great parties. Fortunately I was privy to both the planning and the execution of one of their famous parties.

July 5, 2004

It is Thursday morning. I have come to pay a visit to Parvaneh and her boyfriend, Homayoun. In typical northern Tehrani fashion, no one is working today (work hours are very hard to determine), and the conversation is about the next party trip to Dubai. Dubai appears to be the window into the outside world that many of these kids count on. Although parents sometimes discourage their children from leaving the country without them, many manage to do so, and thus plan such weekend getaways with their partners.

As we flip through magazines and snack on the usual breakfast of *nun-o-panir* (bread and cheese), we begin to discuss, as usual, my status and my work—yes, in that order. Am I still single? Yes, I am. There are apparently lots of boys that would be good for me in Tehran; should they take the liberty of having some of them come over? That's very kind of them but I'm trying to work things out on my own. End of conversation on this topic. I've gotten pretty good at turning this into a dead-end discussion. So what do I do? Research. That's so interesting. How much money could I make in a field like that? How much do I make now? Homayoun asks. Not enough, I say. That's OK, he says; perhaps I'll find a man to take care of me right? Well, at least I'm from the United States and pretty; that should help, he tells me. But if I want to stay in Iran, Homayoun says, I'm going to have to find a sexual partner to ease the pain of living here. "But look, sex is the main thing here; it's our drug, it's what makes our lives bearable; that's what makes parties so necessary," he says, shoving another bread and cheese sandwich into his mouth.

"I know, parties are essential here," I respond. "That's it!" says Homayoun excitedly. "It's time to organize a party." "Where?" says Parvaneh. "At your parents' apartment; it's perfect!" he exclaims. She is delighted and leans over to give him a kiss. Homayoun then turns to Parvaneh's mom, who has been trying, unsuccessfully, to clear off the breakfast table. Each time she tries to take the plate of cheese, Homayoun begs her to leave it. Now he begins to concentrate on making another bread and cheese sandwich. He pauses to address his girlfriend's mother and asks, "Can we have a party here? We'll clean up and be good." "Sure" she says, "I encourage it. We'll leave that night, the place is yours, we'll be next door." (Her parent's own the apartment next door but Parvaneh now lives there.) "If the komite turn up, we'll pay them off; but try to keep them from turning up, OK?" she finishes as she clears off the table. "Of course we will," Homayoun responds. "What day is it today? Thursday. Let's have the party on Saturday, a weeknight [in Iran, weekends are Thursday and Friday] so the komite won't be too suspicious, and that way we'll have some control." Parvaneh is excited as well but wants to be practical. "Yes," she says. "But let's not phone people until Saturday afternoon; otherwise, word will get out." (Parvaneh later tells me she is always worried that her parties will be too well attended and that the large crowds will both draw suspicion and put her parents' apartment in a vulnerable position.) Homayoun pats her hand reassuringly. "Of course, and no parking on your street, we'll make sure of it." Although Parvaneh's parents owned their entire floor, there was always the worry that neighbors on different floors of the building or from buildings next door would complain of the noise and register a complaint with authorities.

July 7, 2004

Parvaneh calls me and hurriedly whispers, "Pardis! Tonight, party at my place. You can bring one guest, but no more, and no parking on the street," she emphasizes. "I remember," I tell her. "I was there during party orchestrations." "Of course," she says quickly, "I forgot." "When should I come?" I ask. "After 9 or 10. It'll be good," she exclaims and hangs up the phone, leaving me staring at my closet wondering what to wear. I have learned that one has to pick ensembles for these gatherings very carefully. Too fancy and it will look like you are trying too hard. Not dressed up enough and you offend the hosts and other attendees, who expect a certain formality or sense of fashion in return for being invited. I finally settle on my usual form-fitting black pants and black tank top with fake diamond accessories to match. I figure the black will help me blend into the background.

I turn up at the party around 11:30 because I've learned that this is Tehran style; if you show up before 11 P.M. you will find an empty apartment and hosts who are probably still getting dressed. Appetizers ordered from Tehran's most popular Chinese restaurant, Monsoon, are on the table, the room is filled with a thick cloud of smoke, and techno music is blaring. A butler comes and takes my coat and headscarf. Leave it nearby, I tell him. If the place gets raided I need a quick escape, I remind myself, realizing that I am still more afraid of the morality police than any of my informants. Parvaneh and Homayoun rush over to me. Homayoun gives me a kiss on each cheek and then moves to the next arriving guest. Parvaneh gives me kisses and a big hug. "Is it too loud?" she breathes. She is standing so close to me I can smell the vodka on her breath. "Can you hear noise from downstairs?" she says in English to avoid other people's ears, although it didn't seem like there was anything to be heard over the loud thumping of the techno beat. "No," I say. "Only when I got out of the elevator." She breathes a sigh of relief. "That's OK then; we're under control," she says wiping some lipstick off my cheek from where she or someone else kissed me hello. Suddenly the butler is back: What do I want to drink? I don't know. I ask my hostess, who recommends vodka with mango. "So that is the drink of choice?" I ask, making a mental note. She nods and assures me it's Absolut Vodka, "so it must be good, right?" "It's from your neighborhood," she reminds me—a neighborhood that at the moment feels very far away. The music is blaring and Parvaneh looks slightly nervous, but she is whisked off by Homayoun right after she tells me she knows almost no one at her own party; they are all Homayoun's friends!

Smoke fills the room. "It's hot," I tell a young man whom I have caught staring at me, "and the smoke sure could use a path of escape." He looks at me quizzically and says, "What are you talking about? They can't open any doors or windows because then the noise would waft outside and komite would be here in a second. You're not from here, are you?" he says, lighting a cigarette. I try to make my way to the other side of the room. As my eyes start to tear I try to sigh to brace myself for a hot, smoke-filled night, but the smoke fills my lungs and blocks my airway. People come up to me at various intervals throughout the evening because word has spread that I'm the girl from the United States. "That's so cool," they say, trying to show off their English. Dinner is served after midnight. The women delicately wait for the men to be busy stuffing their mouths before grabbing only a bite or two. Most of them are slender and look like Barbie dolls (in fact, *Barbie* is a Persian slang word for "slim woman"). As the evening wears on I catch pairs of men getting more and more drunk and more physically intimate with each other. They tell each other that they make more money and are better than other men; flattery is everything here, but so is criticism.

People start leaving around 2 A.M. but a core group stays behind. They turn off the music and sing revolutionary songs with political content. Seated in a circle, all in a drunken haze, they talk and try to piece together the political climate of Iran. I am surprised at this moment of political engagement, but Parvaneh's friends remind me that they are children of the revolution who are nostalgic and longing for a cultural memory they never experienced. Homayoun sings a song about wanting a different life, a different Iran, more like the Iran

before the revolution. Although they were all born during or after the
revolution, they have constructed a group memory of what Iran was
like during their parents' youth. "What has become of this country?"
Parvaneh asks me, so drunk that she is hardly able to stand. "What has
become of its youth? Of us?"

Azita and Mazyar's Impromptu Parties

One afternoon a few days before the presidential election of 2005, a
young man named Mazyar called me on my cell phone to invite me to a
party at his home the following night. His parents had gone out of town
for the weekend and he had spontaneously decided to have a party. As I
was trying to piece together where I may have met this young man who
was now so eager to have me come to his home, he stopped midsentence.
"You don't remember me, do you?" he asked. I was silent. "I'm Mazyar,
Azita's friend. We met at that awesome party last week at Roya's house.
Remember how much we danced? Like we were in a nightclub in New
York instead of the Islamic Republic?" All of his statements seemed like
questions; his voice went up at the end of each sentence. The more he
talked, the less I remembered him. When he started giving me directions to his house I stopped him. "Don't worry, my friend, I'll come with
Azita, if I come," I interjected. I had learned that going out in Tehran as
a single female this close to the elections wasn't a good idea given that
the streets were overrun by loud, enthusiastic young people cheering on
their candidates, accompanied by increasing numbers of komite, whose
numbers had been doubled in the weeks before the election. A few of
my friends had told me that members of the morality police had been
stopping women traveling alone, looking for excuses to harass them. I
decided not to give them this excuse. "Fine," Mazyar replied. "It's probably a good idea that you don't come alone, but please do come. I'll be
looking forward to seeing you there," he said and hung up the phone.

I promptly called Azita and made arrangements to meet her at her
house at 10:00 the following evening. When the next evening came
around I pulled on my usual black slacks and tank top, covered them
with my new beige mānto and a black headscarf, and made my way to
Azita's house. She handed me a shot of vodka as I walked through the
front door. "But I haven't eaten anything," I protested. She forced the

drink into my hands and then brought me into her living room. There she introduced me to her brother, Omid, an eighteen-year-old university student at Azad University; her friend Hoda, also a twenty-year-old university student, at Azad University; and Hoda's boyfriend, Kambiz, a twenty-year-old Iranian who had recently moved to Canada and was in Iran only for the summer. Being an Iranian living abroad had elevated his status in Iran simply because it had changed his relationship to the West. The closer one is to all things Western, the higher one sits in the hierarchy of this particular group of young Tehranis. Having Western goods (such as Levi's jeans, Reebok shoes, or MAC makeup) and having experience with and knowledge about the United States and Europe immediately earns a person higher social status. Living in Canada gave Kambiz license to behave in any manner he chose, and made him an instant object of adulation for many young women.

After doing a few shots of *aragh sagi* ("dog" vodka, which is often homemade and has a very strong taste and aroma), we quietly crept downstairs and piled into the car of Azita's friend Kayvan. We arrived at Mazyar's party to find a dimly lit room with pairs and trios of teens speaking in hushed tones and draped on sofas and chairs from wall to wall. The scene was sexy and seductive, but also somewhat awkward. No one was dancing or eating the food that was carefully laid out on the table. Mazyar came over to our group, which by now occupied a corner of the room. "Guys, you gotta help me get this party going. Right now it's turning into a sex party; let's try to get people to dance for a bit first," he begged, turning to Azita. She grabbed her bag and fished out her cigarettes. "What do you have to drink? And it better be strong," she said, blowing smoke in his face. At this Mazyar hurriedly brought over a tray of screwdrivers. Azita took a sip and turned to me with a faux puzzled expression on her face. "What is this? Juice?" she laughed. "I mean is there any alcohol in this at all?" she said loudly. I took a sip and almost spit it out; the drink was quite strong, but in this group the more alcohol you can handle, the higher your status. At Azita's response, Mazyar rushed back to the kitchen and returned with an unlabeled bottle of what I presumed was vodka. "What is this, Mazyar?" Azita asked. "I prefer Absolut, but I guess I'll drink your homemade stuff," she said caustically, pouring a heavy dose of vodka into her already strong screwdriver. "She is so cool," whispered Kayvan in my ear. "I want to marry her someday," he said, trying not to blush.

Mazyar then put on some Persian pop music and begged us to dance. No one in the group I was with even wanted to move. "What's wrong, guys?" I asked them. "We don't like Persian music; we prefer European techno or your hip-hop," Azita informed me. "Persian pop is so passé," added Hoda, making a face.[20] "Mazyar, change the music," Omid yelled across the room, trying desperately to save the situation. "I don't have anything other than Persian," responded Mazyar apologetically. It didn't seem to matter, because many of the young people were busy with their sexual activities and didn't notice the music at all. "We are clearly not staying at this party long," said Hoda, finishing her drink. Azita nodded in agreement, pouring more vodka into her glass. At this point it seemed that Azita, barely five feet tall and weighing less than a hundred pounds, was drinking straight vodka, which didn't seem to affect her at all.

I looked over at Mazyar, who was now sweating bullets. I felt sorry for him because I knew that being the host of a party in Iran was no easy feat. One had to worry about having a good-enough party so that it would be talked about among the different circles and maintain one's status; but one also had to worry about being caught by komite or parents. In Mazyar's case, although his parents were out of town, he was worried that they would return or that nosy neighbors would tell Mazyar's parents about their son's social activities in their absence. It often seemed hardly worthwhile to face all these risks. I decided to help Mazyar out by forcing my group to overcome their coolness issues and dance. "Come on," I said to Azita. "It may not be from un taraf-e āb [the other side of the water] but it's good music. Look, we're at a party; let's make the best of it, let's go and dance." Azita looked at me quizzically. After a bit more begging, she agreed to dance with me, which was the cue to get the entire group dancing. I looked over and saw Mazyar's eyes light up. A few songs later, even some of the young people who had been deeply involved in each other had decided to come up for air and were dancing with us. Mazyar came over and thanked our group.

This apparently was not the correct gesture; Azita, rather than being touched by Mazyar's gratefulness, was instead quite put off by it. She turned to me, put out her cigarette, and said, "This party is *not* cool. In fact, it's lame. And the host is even less cool than the party. We're leaving. Round up the troops," she said, hands on her hips. I was surprised at this decision, and I never figured out what exactly had turned Azita off, but I played along and helped her gather the group. As we said our good-byes, Mazyar looked as though he were about to burst into tears. "Don't worry," I told him. "I had fun, even more fun than clubs in New York," I lied. At this his eyes lit up once again and he thanked me profusely for coming to his party. Before we left, Azita handed each of us a cucumber (the usual ritual in Iran for erasing traces of alcohol on one's breath). "For the ride home," she said. "We don't want to be caught by any komite. I'm just not in the mood tonight." Once we were out of the building, the group started criticizing the party and making fun of Mazyar. They did not appreciate his taste in music; they criticized it for being too old and traditional. It was clear this wasn't going to be one of those parties about which there would be epic stories.

When we got to Azita's house, the whole group came upstairs. "Where are your parents?" I asked. "Away for the night," she said, smiling. "Why do you think I invited Kayvan up? I'm going to snack on him all night tonight," she said, dragging me into her apartment and taking off her mānto and headscarf. I nodded and took off my headscarf and mānto as well and hung it neatly on her coat rack. Azita put on some of her preferred European music and turned off all the lights in the apartment. As I tried to glide toward where she and Kayvan were dancing, I bumped into Hoda and her boyfriend engaged in heavy kissing and petting on one of the chairs. Azita managed to find my hand and pulled me toward her makeshift dance floor. When her brother started dancing very close to me, I became very nervous and in my attempt to dance smoothly out of his reach, I ran smack into a column in the middle of their room and gave myself a nasty nosebleed. At this point I decided it was time to leave. I found another cucumber, called for a cab, and made my way home, exhausted.

Alaleh and the DJ

"What are you doing Saturday night, Pardis? I know it's a work night, but change your plans. Alaleh is having a party, an awesome party, with a DJ [disc jockey, an illegal profession in Iran, where dance music is outlawed], and there will be lots of *hooloos* [that is, desirable men; a popular slang term meaning, literally, "peaches," used only by Iranian youth] there. I'm not bringing my husband. Come alone," said the voice. It was Laleh calling me at 8:30 on a Thursday morning to invite me to her cousin's house for what she seemed to think would be an epic party. She told me to arrive at her house three hours before the party was to start so we could make our preparations. "And don't forget to go get your hair done in the morning. Make sure you blow it out straight. And wear a nice dress, no jeans or pants, you hear me?" she commanded. Laleh was never a fan of my more casual style, and although she had resigned herself to my being, as her friends described me, like Sporty Spice from the Spice Girls,[21] she still wanted me to be presentable.

I hung up the phone and went back to sleep. Thursday was the only day I could sleep in and I was exhausted from being at another party the night before. I had to pinch myself to make sure I wasn't dreaming when I recalled the previous evening's festivities. I remember walking in, admittedly, a bit late, but I had forced my friend Babak to stop for food because I had learned that good Iranian women don't eat in front of other people. The combination of not eating dinner and then drinking hadn't been having a good effect on my note-taking skills. After eating almost an entire pizza, I allowed Babak to take me to the party, which was held in a huge garden with beautiful hanging trees in each corner. As I walked in a bit farther, I noticed a large swimming pool, which had been drained. There seemed to be voices coming from the bottom of the pool. "Welcome to the jungle," a young man said. He stripped me of my Islamic dress (which included my headscarf and mãnto) and led me further into what I was starting to think of as the hanging gardens of Babylon. Babak squeezed my arm. "Take a deep breath, Pardis," he whispered in my ear. As we walked closer to the pool, I realized that a full-blown orgy was taking place inside it. As Babak took off his shirt and started to wade into the group of young people, I decided to walk around the pool and perch myself on the diving board. A million questions raced through my head: *Who are all of these people? Are they married? Are they using protection? It doesn't look like it, so are they worried about disease?* It didn't seem that they were, but I later found out how often many of my informants worried about their health, and how many of them had faced serious problems due to unprotected sex, especially those who engaged in multiple-partner sex. *Does anyone notice me?* It didn't seem like it, so I continued to watch as bodies moved from one trio to another. A group of five men and women huddled together below me. I couldn't tell who was kissing whom, and I couldn't see how much oral or penetrative sex was taking place, but it seemed that most of the people were completely naked, and from the movements I could see, it looked as though half were having some kind of sex. *Is this part of the sexual revolution some people talk about?* I wondered. *Have people always been doing this, or is it more prevalent now because they aren't supposed to?* As I was thinking all of these questions, Babak came over to me, half naked, and asked if I wanted to join. I shook my head no. He took my hand and led me off the diving board. We went inside the house, where a dozen young people were gathered around a table of drinks and a pool table. I sat next to them and then found myself playing pool while Babak made his way back to the pool.

We stayed at the party until 3 A.M., at which point I begged Babak to take me home. I was exhausted, and each time I had gone outside to the pool I could not find him. At 3 a.m. he had come up for air and come into the house looking for me. "There is only so much of this you can watch," I had said to him. He agreed and took me home. The next morning I wondered if it had all been a dream, but I realized it hadn't been when I saw the dress and the new sandals I had been wearing stained by the mud of the garden and reeking of Babak's cigarette smoke. I rolled to the other side of the bed, reached for my cell phone, and dialed his number.

"Did that really happen last night?" I asked him. "Yeah," he said groggily. "Good stuff for your book though, right?" he asked between yawns. I laughed; my friends and informants wanted me to write about every adventure I had. "I'm hanging up now," he said. "I'm hung over and really happy. If you want, we can do it again next week," he added. I told him I had had enough, hung up the phone, and went back to sleep.

Two hours later I was awakened again, this time by two informants I had interviewed by the pool at Alaleh's house. They were panicking because they had just been invited to an "epic party" that was to take place at Alaleh's house on Saturday, and they were beside themselves with anxiety and excitement. "Can we come over to your house, Pardis?"

they pleaded. "We're so excited but we don't know what to wear or how to prepare. Will you help us?" asked Sormeh, a twenty-one-year-old woman who had recently graduated from university and now found herself among the many women who were unemployed. "Oh my God, this is going to be the party of the summer. Did you hear that DJ Omid is going to be there?" she screeched through the phone, emphasizing the DJ's name as though he was a well-known celebrity. I clutched my head and felt it pound at her high-pitched screams. I was exhausted and still trying to make sense of the night before, but I couldn't bear to disappoint the two women. "Sure," I said. "Come on over. Just give me an hour to get dressed and eat," I added, remembering I needed to write down what I remembered from the night before.

An hour later they were at my door. They were nervous about going out so close to the anniversary of a student protest that had been violently shut down some years before. July 6 (18 Tir in the Persian calendar, which follows the solar calendar) is notoriously a bad day in Tehran, and the komite are always on the prowl to catch young people going against Islamic norms. Young people who were raised in Tehran explained to me that it is important to learn the "crack-down seasons," that is, the periods of the year when the morality police are more likely than at other times to harass or arrest young people. They told me that religious holidays (as well as a few days before and a few days after), anniversaries of protests, Khomeini's birthday, and before and after elections, months of mourning, or Ramadan are particularly vulnerable times for young people. "If you are careful during those times and lay low, you will be fine. It's like an unspoken code we have with them. They let us party at certain times of the year really hard, and other times we try to lay low, but even that is changing," my friend Diar explained to me.

"I hate that we have to think about this stuff," said Sormeh, taking off her mānto and headscarf upon arriving at my apartment. "Because of all the difficulty of partying here, I really want to go only to places where I'm really going to have a good time. But it's so difficult to go to these kinds of parties; I really have to do a lot of work. I'm going to have to go and buy a new dress, which has to be gorgeous, and I have to go touch up my highlights and do my hair," she complained. Her friend Minou quickly chimed in as I continued hanging up their coats, "But let me tell

you Pardis, this is why we don't like to go to more than one or two parties a week. Even though we have a lot of free time, it loses that sense of
fun and excitement 'cause it's just so much anxiety—not just about how
we look, but about what might happen to us if we get caught. This takes
its toll on us," she explained, dabbing at the perspiration that had caused
small beads of sweat to form around her temples. It was clear that thinking
about the potential consequences of being caught was upsetting her.

The pair seemed very torn about this party. They knew it was going to be a big party and a lot of fun, but they were nervous because
the bigger a party was, and the more high profile it became, the higher
were the chances of getting caught. "See, here there is this issue of laj,"
began Minou, trying to calm her own anxieties:

Like I have told you before, it's all about *laj bāzi* [playful rebellion]. Here,
when we go to parties, of course our bones are shaking, but we go with shaking bones. And I'm telling you, we are scared. Everyone is. No matter what
they tell you, they are scared, from the moment they leave their homes; and
every time the doorbell rings, *delet mirize* [your heart sinks]. *Could it be?* You
ask yourself. *Could it be them?* It's scary. But you know, we have to do something. Something to get back at them, something to remind ourselves, Hey,
we are alive! Hey! We have a say in our lives!

Minou seemed to be saying this as much for herself as for my sake.
Talking about their fears often proved therapeutic for these young people
who revealed to me that they did not have many outlets or opportunities
to speak their minds for fear of being ratted out or gossiped about.

The next few hours were spent discussing clothing options, making hair appointments, and calming one another. The final decision was
that it was too good of a party to miss, that we should go but be aware
of the possibility that we would be caught—but if we were, the women
told me, it would be worth it.

When Saturday arrived, I made my way to the beauty salon and
emphasized that I had been instructed to blow my hair out straight. I
fished out a black evening gown from my aunt's closet and made my
way to Laleh's house. After watching her take nearly three hours to
prepare (during which I watched her try on at least twenty outfits and
coat her face with at least four layers of makeup), we went to the much-

anticipated party. When we arrived, I saw that Alaleh had hired several caterers and butlers. As I walked in, a white-gloved gentleman removed my headscarf and mānto. Alaleh hurried up to us. "You're here!" she exclaimed. "I'm so excited, I've been bragging to everyone all night about you," she said, kissing me on both cheeks. "My smart, beautiful friend from America. Knowing you makes me so cool. Come, I'll introduce you to lots of cute boys. Like Laleh said, there are lots of hooloo here!" Alaleh grabbed my hand and started introducing me to her friends. I turned around to find Laleh already curling up with a young man I had never seen before. Suddenly someone hugged me from behind and gave me a big kiss on the cheek. I turned to find myself face to face with an old friend from the United States, an American journalist who was covering Iran for the summer. I was delighted to see him, and Alaleh was delighted at his delight and mine. She turned to one of her friends and said, "See, I know all the important people from America. Soon I'll be going there myself. I know New York is just waiting for me." The rest of us laughed and drank a toast to the United States. Alaleh later told me that knowing Westerners (and that was the category in which I was placed) elevated her status in the social hierarchy.

"Look, they have Absolut here tonight, and Tanqueray gin!" exclaimed Laleh, reappearing at my side. I had learned that alcohol labels were almost as important as clothing labels. Absolut seemed to be the Prada of drinks. "Did I tell you this party was going to be high class or what? DJ Omid, Western alcohol, and Western guys? Plus, so many of those American guys adore you. If I were you, I'd take a bite out of one of those peaches," Laleh whispered as she was whisked off to the dance floor by another young man. My American friends asked me to dance with them. Once we got onto the dance floor, Alaleh took us to meet the famous DJ Omid. We were all fascinated that a person could make a living as a DJ in the Islamic Republic. Everything he stood for was against Islamic law, yet he had become a star and was not in the least bit nervous about speaking to American journalists. That he had made a name for himself in this environment was somewhat counterintuitive to all of us, but we applauded him and his calm aura. He did not seem to be worried about potential raids on the party, even though his music was playing quite loudly, and even though, if the party was raided, his expensive equipment (which he told us he had saved for two years to buy) would be confiscated.

"DJ Omid!" Alaleh shouted above the blaring techno beat. "I want you to meet my friends; they are from AMRIKA [the Persian pronunciation of America])!" she yelled excitedly. "You guys tell him what to play; you know what's cool," she said rushing off to greet another guest. "That's the first time I've been thought of as cool," remarked my American friend. We talked to DJ Omid and agreed to set up an interview with him and a few other DJs. After that we started dancing. As the beat sped up, more and more young people crowded into Alaleh's living room, which was serving as the makeshift dance floor. The techno beat pulsed and people moved their bodies, lost in the moment; it felt as though the world was dancing with us. "Not so different from a New York night club, huh?" asked one of my American friends. "You're wrong," said another. "Big difference. Better energy here. It's like a nightclub where everyone knows each other and has nothing to lose. Also, their world could end tomorrow; they could get arrested and it would all be over. It gives new meaning to the idea of 'party like there's no tomorrow.' This places pulses like nothing I've ever experienced," he said. As I danced I thought about what my friend had just said. It was true: for many of these young adults, coming to parties could land them in jail or evoke harsh punishment from unsympathetic parents. It was also an important way for young people to lose themselves in the moment, in music or in dancing; it was an escape from many of the harsh realities of their world. Reflecting on all of the challenges that young people faced daily gave a sort of last-days-of-mankind gravitas to the three and four hours of applying makeup and getting dressed.

Two hours later I was still dancing, although my feet were barely holding me up. I was sweating but smiling ear to ear, as were my party companions. I breathed a sigh of relief as the night went on and the komite didn't turn up. Close to 2 A.M. my American friends noted my exhaustion and offered to take me home. The party was clearly a success. More than two hundred people had showed up and danced the night away. No police had come by, nor had there been any threatening phone calls. The music had been exceptional (thanks to DJ Omid) and the waiters had kept the hors d'oeuvres and alcohol flowing steadily all night. As we drove home through the busy Tehran streets, we all agreed that the party had indeed been "epic" and one of the more exciting evenings any of us had had in a long time. Without a doubt it would end up being one of the most talked-about parties of the summer.

"Welcome to the Jungle":
A Less Elaborate Party with More Partygoers

There is no doubt that the parties I have described here are available mostly to members of the upper-middle and middle classes. However, as mentioned before, variations of these types of parties occur among the lower classes as well. Instead of hosting parties at their homes, they choose abandoned warehouses or outdoor venues. Instead of Absolut vodka, they drink homemade liquor or use cheaper stimulants such as opiates.[22] Instead of hiring a DJ, they use the sound systems from their cars or smaller boom boxes to play homemade tapes. I had the privilege of attending a party in the folds of the hills surrounding Rudehen (just outside Tehran) thrown by a group of young people whose families were religious and lived in the southern part of town.

Figure 2.3. Young Tehranis don't necessarily need to own private homes in order to host a party. Here young people form an impromptu party on the streets. © 2007 by Nader Davoodi. Used by permission.

September 15, 2004

I can hear the sound of the *adhan*, the call to prayer, from a mosque close to Negar's house near *Meydoon-e-Shush*. The sun is setting as I help Negar prepare dinner for her family. There isn't much furniture in the house, so we spread out a tablecloth on the floor and set food and place settings for seven. This family of six shares a one-bedroom house that has two bathrooms. Negar continues to check her watch. "Only a few more hours, then we'll sneak out of here," she tells me. Negar has been looking forward to this evening's festivities for weeks now. She has spent hours perfecting our plan. We will have dinner with her family, then tell her parents that we want to go to the mosque to do our evening prayers. Then we will ride the bus to the agreed-upon spot outside of town and walk or catch a ride to the party spot. A hand-drawn map to the party's location is folded in Negar's pocket, and every now and then she pats her pocket to make sure it's still there. After the party we will be sure to return to Negar's house before the morning prayers (when her parents wake up) and change our clothes to make it look like we are going to the mosque to do our morning prayers as well. Negar says her family is never suspicious when she says she wishes to go out to pray, and this is therefore a good excuse.

After we eat with her family, Negar and I hurriedly wash the dishes before collecting our bags for the evening. Negar has borrowed a short blue dress from a friend of hers, and I have brought all the makeup I could find at my aunt's house. We find a public bathroom in a nearby park in which to change our clothes and apply the makeup, and then slowly make our way to the bus stop. It is 9 P.M. and the night sky is pitch black. The bus is filled with mostly men, many of whom reek of cigarette or opium smoke while others smell of liquor. I clutch my bag firmly, partially to make sure it's still there and partly to calm my nerves. It is a long bus ride to the hills of Rudehen. Finally, after an hour and a half, Negar nudges my shoulder; we are to get off at the next stop. As the bus speeds away, I look around me and shudder. There is no sign of civilization in sight, and the shape of the mountains is barely outlined in the moonlight. I am worried we won't find our way. "Don't worry, I have the map," Negar tells me. Just then we hear some voices. "*Khānum hah* [Ladies]!" they shout. We both freeze.

"Ladies, wait. I think we are probably going to the same place," shouts a young man running up to us. We turn to face seven young men and three young women, all giggling in excitement. "Are you going to the party?" asks a young woman. "Yes, yes we are," says Negar, smiling shyly. "Well, then walk with us," says one of the young men. We nod and begin following them. "Hello, I'm Mohammad Reza and this is my girlfriend, Fatemeh," says one of the young men to me as we walk along the dimly lit road. "Nice to meet you," I say. We begin walking toward the mountains and everyone is talking and getting to know one another. "So, how did you and your girlfriend meet?" I ask Mohammad Reza in an attempt to make conversation. "It's interesting, actually. We had both gone to one of these religious festivals, I think during the holy month of mourning, and we were both pretending to mourn. Well, it was obvious we were both pretending, so I took the opportunity to get her number instead of continuing the charade," he explained. I smile at the thought that many young people use religious gatherings as dating venues.

After about fifteen minutes of walking in the dark, I begin to hear music and see a large bonfire in the distance. About a mile left, I think to myself as I continue walking. When we arrive, I am surprised to find about four hundred young people gathered around several different fire pits. Some are dancing to the hum of the boom box, some are singing, others are passing around opium pipes and heroin, and still others (those who are mostly hidden under tree branches) are flirting, kissing, and hugging. The young women are not as made up as young women from uptown would be, but many are wearing short dresses that look like hand-me-downs or home-sewn outfits. There is no alcohol at this particular party, but the supply of drugs such as opium and heroin flows like water. In the corners of several fire pits I see several young men almost passed out. I can only guess that the drugs are having a strong effect on them.

As I try to fight off a shiver from the cold night air, I suddenly realize that I have lost Negar and I may not be able to find her. I make my way to a nearby fire pit and sit down to bask in its warmth. I hold my hands out, wiggling my fingers to warm them up. Just then a young woman comes over to the fire and sits next to me. "You aren't

Figure 2.4. Some young people say that religion is important
to them but they can be religious while being in style.
© 2007 by Nader Davoodi. Used by permission.

one of us, are you?" she asks me. I'm not even sure what that means
anymore—not Iranian? not of the same class? not of the same mind-
set? I remain silent. "I can tell," she says, scooting closer to me. "I'm
not sure what you mean," I finally say. "I can tell that you aren't poor
like a lot of us," she says, smiling. Again I am silent. "Look at your
hands," she says, grabbing one of my hands from near the fire and
taking it in both of hers. Her hands are cold and I fight another shiver.
"They are soft and perfectly manicured," she says. "Plus, look at your

shoes; those are obviously not from Iran. Look at your shoes, then look at mine," she says, stretching out her feet so that I can see her torn sandals. "They are pretty," I say to her. "Yes, but not like yours; I like them better," she says. I take one look at my shoes and take them off. I hand them to her. "You want to trade?" I ask her. She is so excited and gives me a hug. "I've never met a rich girl like you. Who are you anyways? Most rich girls would never come to a party with us, let alone offer their shoes," she screeches. "Take them," I tell her. "Just give me yours for the walk home," I add. We trade shoes that night, and later we become friends and trade life stories. After about an hour or so, Negar reappears at my shoulder announcing that she has met a young man and wants to go off into the woods with him. Will I be OK taking a nap by the fire? she asks. I nod and try to make myself comfortable. It will be several hours before we leave this party in the countryside to head back to urban Tehran.

Young people from all socioeconomic backgrounds are increasingly seeking to carve out recreational spaces for themselves against the backdrop of a repressive regime. Their unending efforts to create these spaces despite harassment and punishment from parents and the morality police speak to a strong resistance to Islamic ideology. My informants repeatedly told me that they were embodying through their lifestyles the changes in sexual and social culture they would like to see enacted. They reminded me that their sexual and social revolution was not about momentary acts but rather was a way of life that included social gatherings and social behavior that could be viewed as hedonistic but that were a necessary part of constructing a world over which they had control, a world they could live in rather than in the world of the Islamists, who would have them stay home and obey. Many of their utterings on their way to school, to group gatherings, and to illegal dance classes focused on resistance and enacting changes in social, sexual, and political ideas and behaviors. Although much of this chapter has focused on the recreational and social activities of young people, I want to be clear that most of my informants also were politically conscious and not focused solely on fun. The goal in presenting their social lives is to point to a shift in behavior and rhetoric. Their lifestyle choices are evidence that thoughts and discussions about a sexual revolution are not fleeting and indicate real change. Two decades ago, young people were not attending frequent elaborate parties, and the few who did, did so with trepidation and recalled that they could never let loose and dance the night away. Today young people go to parties on the eve of Islamic anniversaries that previously used to be cause for staying home out of fear of being caught by the morality police and accused of being un-Islamic for not grieving the loss of a particular martyr or Islamic ideologue. They are less afraid than they used to be, which also indicates that the state has shifted in order to accommodate its youth in certain ways. This adjustment points to an important interactive process between the youth and the state that is discussed further in the next chapters.

It is also important to analyze young Tehranis' sexual and social behaviors while questioning the deeper reasons behind such seemingly hedonistic behavior. As scholars have hypothesized, "children who come from secular families are, by virtue of a normal life (which may mean avoiding prayer, watching satellite television, or drinking), transgressing the state's definition of acceptable social norms and laws."[23] By default they seek to form communities of like-minded youth to make the experience less isolating. These social gatherings, which take place for a variety of reasons (including to seek companionship and like-minded peers or to make a statement), do have potential consequences, both social and emotional, most prominently in regard to physical and mental health.

At times when I attended a party or spent time in Northern Tehran I would think, *If it wasn't for the hejāb, this could be Los Angeles*, because of the heavy emphasis on style, beauty, and luxurious recreation. But I would quickly remind myself that it *wasn't* Los Angeles, because the social, political, and economic environment was so different, and the social, physical, and mental consequences of many behaviors were much more serious. Among many Iranians in West Los Angeles there are high pressures to conform to certain standards of beauty and consumerism, and much of this could be attributed to culture; but life for young people in Tehran is vastly different than life for young Iranians in Los Angeles. Although young Iranians in Los Angeles do worry about social pressures and the potential of gossip to ruin reputations, they do not have to face potential arrest or harassment from members of the morality police, and their lives are not shaped by the same socioeconomic and political forces. Young Tehranis have to face the harsh realities of unemployment and restricted access to social freedoms, education, and resources (such as contraceptives or other harm-reduction materials) that could assist in minimizing the risk of some of their behaviors. They also often speak about the mental health consequences of growing up in a politically charged and volatile country, in an atmosphere that leads many of them to seek out drugs and alcohol and to engage in other potentially high-risk behaviors because of the pressures they feel in their daily lives. Therefore, while on the surface it may seem that some of these behaviors and some aspects of the lives of my informants could be comparable to Iranians in Los Angeles or throughout the diaspora, it is important, I feel, to emphasize that consequences are as different as are intentions behind behaviors; that is, putting on style as a symbol of resistance is different than doing it just to bow to peer pressure or to be in fashion and thus socially accepted by peers. Some Iranian young people feel they are placing themselves at risk, but they do so willingly because they feel that these behaviors are necessary steps toward fulfilling their desires for social and political reform.

3   Tehran Chic

"I speak through my clothes."
Umberto Eco[1]

"SISTER, TUCK YOUR HAIR IN, it's coming out the front and the back of your hejāb! Do you want me to call the authorities?" yelled the airport morality attendant, pressing her face to within inches of mine.[2] "Darling, why are you covering so much hair? Let it out. Your hejāb is too far forward; you look like those traditional, backward women. Stop it!" said my cousin as she pulled back my headscarf and carefully pulled three locks of my hair forward. "Cousin, put on your chādor, it's time to go to mosque. Wipe off your lipstick, cover yourself. We must be modest now," whispered another cousin, handing me a tentlike sheet to cover my entire body as we made our way to a mosque in Mashad. "*Khoshgel* [pretty girl], why are you wearing such a loose mānto? You have a great body! Let it show!" said my date as he rolled up in his new Kia Pride.[3] "Pardis, for Allah's sake, go put on some makeup. We are here, act like you care," bellowed my friend and key informant Mahnaz, attacking me with her newest shade of pink lipstick.

June 22, 2004
Last night was one of those particularly hot nights, made even hotter by my blushing every few seconds in embarrassment at my unfashionable headscarf and mānto. As we walked into Jām-e Jam cafeteria, a popular hangout spot for Northern Tehranis, a swirl of colors engulfed me and I looked down at my own loose-fitting black mānto and navy blue

headscarf with embarrassment. A young woman wearing yellow stiletto heels, khaki capri pants, and a lime green mānto adjusted her fuchsia headscarf to ensure that her Gucci glasses sat neatly on her highlighted hair without pushing the headscarf too far forward or backward. It was perfect. As she ordered and ate her pizza, her headscarf did not move (the way mine always did when I did anything), and her elaborate makeup—which included pink, yellow, and green eye shadow to match her outfit; dark eyeliner; fake eyelashes; and bright red lipstick—also stayed intact despite the sweltering heat of the un-air-conditioned food court. Her friends' mānto and headscarf combinations in reds, fluorescent blues, and shades of green complemented hers. They too wore perfectly applied makeup, stiletto heels and sandals, and translucent headscarves strategically placed to complement their hair (by allowing their coiffed styles to show through) and faces. Their headscarves were not tied under their chins (as mine was) but rather were casually slung over their shoulders to create a perfectly color-coordinated shawl-scarf-headdress combination. They were enveloped in a cloud of perfume and cigarette smoke, which perfected the image. When I walked over to talk to them about their fashion choices, they took one look at me in my unfashionable and highly outdated black mānto and navy blue headscarf and ignored me. "Um, excuse me but could I talk to you ladies for a moment?" I nervously asked, reminded of my awkward middle school days when I had so desperately wanted to sit with the cool kids in the cafeteria. The young woman in the yellow stilettos looked me up and down, took a deep inhale of her cigarette, and then blew a large puff of smoke in my face. I took it as a no and returned to my table, which by now was surrounded by my cousin and her friends clutching their bellies in laughter.

I spent a lot of my time in Iran not only worrying about how I looked but also trying to observe the young people around me to see how I *should* look given my age and the persona I was trying to convey. At first I thought it best to dress inconspicuously because I did not want to call attention to myself. Before my first visit to Iran in 2000, I had purchased a few baggy māntos and some plain black headscarves. I soon realized that the look I had thought would make me less visible actually attracted more attention than when I dressed the way my research subjects did. People saw me as conservative, traditional, close-minded, and often plain unapproachable because of how I dressed. I soon realized that style of dress and bodily comportment was a form of communication among young Tehranis. Many members of the Islamic clergy have referred to the act of wearing makeup and attractive clothes as bringing about a state of fitna, or moral chaos. It is exactly this chaos that some of the young people on the streets of Tehran are trying to create through their appearance. As Roxanne Varzi astutely points out, "the aim of the revolution was not to create faithful Muslims, but to create good Islamic citizens. The difference is that instead of concentrating on faith (which is expected to exist a priori) and intention, the regime concentrated on appearance and ideology—practice was emphasized over inner faith."[4] It is this outward comportment and appearance that some youth are trying to subvert, and style is a language that young people are using to communicate with one another, with members of the regime (in an effort to bring down social restrictions on dress and behavior), and with the world. In this chapter I explore different ways in which style has become a form of expression, paying careful attention to the differences in style as well as to differences in opinion and to the various reasons that young people point to when discussing their outward appearance.

It is important to note that only a decade ago, young women's hejāb was heavily regulated by members of the morality police as women entered the gates of universities throughout Tehran.[5] Today, "Iranian women nonchalantly pass through the gates, despite their heavily applied makeup and revealing hejāb—a sign of changing social order." Many changes have taken place on the streets of Tehran, and rules and regulations about mandatory Islamic dress and prohibition of makeup have been pushed aside at universities and in coffee shops, cafeterias, and public parks. Women in Tehran now wear relaxed Islamic dress along with layers of mascara, eye shadow, and lipstick. Their sense of self (which for some is gained when they enter college) is manifested on the street; in their own words, "makeup is our political resistance."[6] One young woman, a twenty-year-old houseworker from downtown Tehran who worked for a family uptown described her application of layers of makeup as a "way of getting attention, looking good, and being heard. If we are made up and look good, we are going to get more attention, and then we can get what we need taken care of more quickly," she noted. When I asked for a more specific example, she carefully pulled out a few more strands of peroxide-blond hair from underneath her floral-print headscarf before continuing. "For example, if there is a long line at the store and I look good the way I do now, well, I just flutter my eyelashes at the guy behind the counter and he takes care of me first, do you see? This helps me in my daily life," she added. So their sense of style, comportment, and outward appearance is linked to their agency, resistance, and sense of self and citizenship, according to many youth with whom I spoke. Because the outward appearance of these young people frustrates members of the regime, parents, and college administrators alike, such appearance is an act of resistance. By not punishing young people as they used to, the regime has effectively shown their assent to these new styles, and this new development shows both the success of the young people in achieving social gains and the internal changes the state is now making to address its youth population. Many of the young people with whom I spoke saw these changes as markers of success in their self-proclaimed social movement.

For many years scholars have been studying elements of style as forms of communication, political statement, and revolt.[7] In Iran the politics and poetics of dress deserve special attention because style has historically had political and social significance. In the years leading up to the revolution, young people (especially women) who were critical of the Shah's relationship with the West (he was accused of importing Western imperialism) and who supported overthrowing the monarchy showed their political stance by dressing more conservatively. In a move to reclaim Iran for Iranians, many women who opposed the Shah began to don hejāb and later chādor to support an overthrow of the monarchic regime. As Val Moghaddam notes when describing the political climate of Iran in the months leading up to the revolution, "the large street demonstrations included huge contingents of women wearing the veil as a symbol of opposition to Pahlavi bourgeoisie or Western decadence."[8] During the revolution, young women in miniskirts who wore too much makeup were chastised and told to wear Islamic dress and support the revolution. Women's bodies and comportment began to take on increased significance as symbols of Iranian cultural values and traditions. The idea that women's bodies needed to be shielded from the Western gaze in order to restore Iranian honor became increasingly popularized. "The idea that women had 'lost honor' during the Pahlavi era was a widespread one. Anti-Shah oppositionists decried the overly made-up 'bourgeois dolls'—television announcers, singers, upper class women, professionals—of the Pahlavi era."[9] Interestingly, it was these women who became the major targets both during and immediately after the revolution. "The Islamists in Iran felt that 'genuine cultural identity' had been distorted by Westernization, or what they called *gharb-zadagi*.[10] The unveiled, publicly visible woman was both a reflection of Western attacks on indigenous culture and the medium by which they were affected."[11] Therefore many women and men who supported the revolution advocated the veil as a political symbol; however, the majority of the women who wore the veil during those protests did not expect veiling to become mandatory. After the revolution, when strict Islamic dress codes were enforced, many people regretted their prerevolutionary insistence on wearing chādors.

In the early 1980s when Khomeini began making calls for modest Islamic dress, many women—especially middle class and leftist women who disagreed with compulsory veiling—were outraged and began staging protests against these new decrees. In 1981, however, with the defeat of the leftists and liberals, veiling was made compulsory, and Islamic dress codes began to be strictly enforced. Over time, as many people (especially young people) became increasingly disillusioned with a regime that seemed overly focused on maintaining Islamic dress codes, they started to wear more revealing clothes and began to push the limits of mandatory Islamic dress. These changes became visible mostly after the death of Khomeini in 1989, and then took more significant effect after the election of Reformist President Khatami in 1997. In particular, young adults who were born and raised under the current regime and who envision themselves as part of the sexual and social revolution found themselves rebelling the way their parents, who may have been revolution supporters, did: through their clothes. This time, however, they rebelled by becoming less conservative, by taking off the chādors and wearing un-Islamic clothes such as blue jeans and tennis shoes, and adding makeup and hair highlights. They pushed back, speaking to the regime in the very language the Islamists were using to oppress them, using their comportment to assert their agency.

Although strict Islamic dress codes are encouraged today and were at one time enforced by the morality police, young Tehranis now assert individual and fashionable styles. Many Tehranis, young and old alike, indicate that young Tehranis increasingly use style as a way to play with their identity, to seem more or less conservative or religious, or to give the illusion of wealth and modernity. The changing fashions and new, more revealing ways of wearing hejāb, which started in Tehran among upper- and middle-class secular youth (self-identified leaders of the sexual revolution), have spread to working-class young adults in Tehran and other parts of the country as well and are indicators of the spread of the social movement. Bloggers and journalists writing about young people in Iran describe the visual changes in young adult styles of Islamic dress that are spreading across the country. One young woman, a popular blogger who grew up in Tehran, repeatedly writes about her experiences in small towns across the country where young people have caught up to the styles of young Tehranis.

At one time women and their parents in these smaller towns used to laugh at us and call us names like slut or prostitute because we wore lipstick and overcoats that actually fit. Now, today, these women have not only caught up to us, but dress more provocatively than we ever did . . . and their parents, the shopkeepers who used to turn us away, have now finally welcomed us.[12]

For many young people, style of dress signifies political position and social values, and communicates a desire to be part of the young adult movement. More than half of my informants indicated that the way people dress signifies their feelings about the Islamic Republic and their dedication to the new sexual and social revolution they feel will overthrow the regime, or at least create more social freedoms for its citizens. Although it is true that some of my informants cited peer pressure and the desire to look fashionable as major reasons for wearing certain styles, many also added that being in style communicated identity and desire to potential partners or friends. Some young Tehranis put on a stylish appearance in order to draw attention to themselves and to respond to peer pressure, but for most of these young people, style, makeup, and hair are all deliberate statements of the desire for social and political change.

Although it is difficult to discern whether urban young Iranians are actually constructing a new sexual and social culture or are simply part of a subculture within Iran, it is useful to look at literature describing the creation of subcultures, as well as at frameworks for understanding and describing emerging sexual cultures. *Subculture* has been referred to as a set of people whose behaviors and beliefs are distinct from those of the larger culture of which they are a part. The members of the subculture may be distinguished by their common age, race, ethnicity, gender, class, or ideology; by their aesthetic, religious, political, or sexual qualities; or by a combination of these factors. Subcultures are often defined by their opposition to the values of the larger culture to which they belong, although this definition is not universally agreed on by theorists.[13] Many Iranian young people appear to be experimenting with some of the characteristics that defined various subcultures in the West in the 1960s and 1970s—specifically, rebellion, resistance, and the desire to be separated from the Islamic ideology that members of the regime have sought to inject into society. Many urban young Iranians are also seeking to make social and political statements through their style.

Dressing "Islamic"

Islamic law, or sharia, as enforced by the regime in Iran, mandates different styles for men and women. As noted earlier, in 1981, the Ayatollah Khomeini instated compulsory veiling and encouraged all Iranian citizens to wear modest, Islamic dress. According to Islamists in Iran, women should be covered from head to toe to hide their body shape and curves. Women are also told not to wear makeup, nail polish, open-toed shoes, or bright colors. Anything that may attract the attention of passersby is frowned upon. Sharia, as interpreted by clerics in power, also suggests that men should wear long pants and collared shirts so that most of their skin will be covered. Shorts and T-shirts are highly frowned upon, as is hair gel, long hair, and clean-shaven faces (because beards cover men's faces). Pictures and signs throughout Tehran demonstrate the look of the Islamic Republic by depicting young women cloaked in black chādor and maghna'e wearing no makeup, and young men with beards, short hair, slacks, and round-collared shirts with no place for a tie, which is seen as Western. But what the observer sees on the streets of Tehran is vastly different from these images and indicates the gains achieved by this embodied social movement.

Even without the images of women in chādors that are found in stores, outside universities, and in bathrooms throughout the city, the Iranian young people know what they *should* wear, and perhaps this knowledge of what it means to "act Islamic" and behave according to Islamic ideology is evidence of how Islamification has permeated their lives, and even the lives of secular youth. As Varzi notes, "because of lived experience within this strong public social sphere, the citizens of Iran know how to act Islamic and how they should represent themselves and their world."[14] In other words, they know how to act and dress Islamic (according to Islamic laws and dress codes), with or without images to guide them, which shows that by virtue of wanting to rebel against Islamic moral rules, they have mastered them and perhaps to an extent internalized them. When asked how they know what proper Islamic dress is, whether

Figure 3.1. What they *should* wear. The maghna'e is a full-head covering showing only the round part of the face, from forehead to chin. © 2006 by Nader Davoodi. Used by permission.

it was ever taught to them, their response is always *"Midunim,"* we just know. They have chosen not to adhere to these rules and to make a statement by dressing differently.

It is also important to remember that there are definitive cycles of enforcement and leniency in regard to Islamic dress, and these cycles are also somehow just known by many young people. "For example, we know that in the beginning of summer there is always a crackdown where the morality police want to flex their muscles and say 'we know it's summer but you aren't going to get away with wearing next to nothing,'" explained Neda, a twenty-two-year-old graphic designer who resides in the center of town. "So we know. We just know that for a few weeks we have to play their game, dress more modestly, and cover our hair a little more; but after those two weeks we can go out in tight coats and lots of makeup again. It's like a little game between us and them. First they assert their power, then we push back. This way everyone is feeling like they have some say," she explained. I, on the other hand, could never manage, throughout my many months in the country, to just *know* how to dress or behave during different times of the year or in different spaces. Many young people also know in what parts of town they can get away with different styles, and others know that certain religious holidays are accompanied by a crackdown so they avoid the streets altogether. "Like, we just don't go out when it's near the anniversary of *vafāt-e-Khomeini* [the death of Ayatollah Khomeini]," explained Sherry, a twenty-three-year-old school teacher. "We know when are the right times of year, and what we should wear and when," she added. But how do you just know the rules? How does one know to wear one outfit to the bank and another outfit to the grocery store and another outfit depending on the time of year, I always wondered. "We just *know*," explained Nina, a friend and key informant. "Just like you know what to wear to school and what to wear to the theater in New York, we just know how to dress here. We were raised with that understanding, and we are just pushing the envelope to see what we can get away with!" she said.

Iranian Fashionistas

There is a subtle difference between looking like a bache maruf (cool youth or famous kid) and looking javād (unfashionable) or *omol* (conservative).

For men, being a "cool youth" involves wearing hair gel, a spiked haircut or fauxhawk (a variation on the typical mohawk) or long hair, along with designer jeans, large jewelry or other accessories, and designer sunglasses that are worn at all times of day or night. For women, looking cool or chic involves hip and form-fitting māntos, bright headscarves, makeup aplenty, and designer handbags, shoes, and sunglasses. Young men might be accused of being *javādi* if they have a more conservative, short haircut that does not require the use of hair gel, if their jeans are too tight or do not look designer, or if their shirts expose too much of their chest or shoulders. Young women are seen as omol if they don't wear makeup and if they are seen wearing a loose, long mānto and maghna'e or chādor.

Figure 3.2. What they *do* wear: Hipsters in Tehran.
© 2008 by Bamdad. Used by permission.

Although some young women in the southern and middle parts of Tehran wear chãdors or maghna'e or both, with no makeup or other adornments, most young women have broken from this uniform. Women all over Tehran now wear brightly colored headscarves that resemble shawls in a Greta Garbo or Isadora Duncan style that falls back to reveal hair touched with highlights or dyed an array of colors. They cover their bodies with black, tan, or sometimes pink or red form-fitting coats that are often quite tight and leave most bodily curves exposed. Some of the new mãntos have three-quarter-length sleeves that expose the forearm up to the elbows; others are so short that the woman's hips and thighs are barely covered. "Sometimes our mãntos are more revealing than your tank tops or bikinis, right? They are more exciting in a certain

Figure 3.3. A stylish man. © Bamdad 2008. Used by permission.

Figure 3.4. A stylish woman talking on her cell phone.
© 2007 by Nader Davoodi. Used by permission.

way," Sima, a twenty-four-year-old fashion student, once remarked as she squeezed into a gold lame mānto and buckled a silver belt over the coat, which was so tight, I remember wondering if she could breathe. She had also intentionally worn a midriff-baring tank top underneath the mānto so that when she sat down at the coffee shop her navel showed through the open buttons of her coat. When I pointed this out to her, she smiled triumphantly. In recent years, many Iranians who used to spend a lot of money on clothes they wore only in private spaces (such as in the home, at private parties, or in gender-segregated beauty salons) now also spend their money on fashionable māntos and headscarves to be worn on a variety of occasions. These māntos and hejāb (sometimes referred to collectively as *rupush*) have become fashion themselves rather than garments that cover fashion.

Many young women in both the northern and southern parts of the city wear lots of makeup, including blue, green, purple, and gold eye shadow; mascara-layered or fake eyelashes; up to four coats of foundation and blush; and bright red or pink lipstick. Their eyelids are lined with thick layers of blue or black eyeliner that is dramatically drawn out to their temples, giving the effect of stage makeup, or as one of my male informants once noted, "it makes them look like drag queens." Somehow, in the heat of summer and under layers of manto and headscarves, their makeup remains flawless, and there is very little need for them to dab at their foreheads or upper lips to manage the perspiration. These young women see their makeup as a form of art as well as resistance. They are quite proud of their skill in creating a certain look and frequently offered to teach me their skills. "I see my makeup as my art," explained Sheida, a twenty-five-year-old lawyer from the easternmost part of Tehran. "I think I'm an incredible artist, and I like my art to be seen and appreciated each day on the streets. It's my way of being visible," she noted.

It used to be that the further south one traveled in Tehran, the more conservative would be the clothing styles one saw. This is still true to a certain extent, and a portion of the young women in the southern parts of town wear maghna'e with an accompanying dark, loose mãnto, especially outside mosques and universities.[15] However, young women of the lower classes are increasingly seeking to imitate middle and upper-class style. They play with their appearance in order to play with their class and other identities. Setareh, a key informant and former professor of anthropology at Tehran University, took me to the southern portions of town and introduced me to some of the lower-class young women she had met while conducting research on life in the slums of Tehran. When we met Maryam, a nineteen-year-old university student, she was rushing out of her house in an area known as *Shahrak-e-Pardis*, or Paradise Village, a set of housing projects just outside the city. Maryam was hurriedly painting her nails orange and fishing a pair of strappy sandals out of her bag. "So sorry you have to see me like this," she apologized as her bag fell open to reveal makeup, nail polish, perfume, and a red and silver glittered headscarf that she tied over her black maghna'e. "It's just that, well, you know, Setareh *jun*,[16] in front of my father and in the house we wear the baggy mãntos and these old ratty black maghna'es. But when we go out, well, we can't go out like that. That look makes us depressed." We helped her collect her belongings and offered her a ride to her destination, which turned out to be a coffee shop in the center of town, where she was meeting her friends for a night out on the town. After we dropped her off, Setareh explained to me that this was a common occurrence among the lower-class women she studied. "They don't have access to satellite TV or the Internet, but they do watch the other women on the street and they do see newscasters on regular (non-satellite) television. From all these images they piece together an idea of what they think it means to look modern, you know?" said Setareh. "Even if it isn't correct, right? I mean it's funny, almost, tying a colored headscarf *over* your black one! But they just don't know any better, and they are trying to imitate the kids who are trying to imitate MTV. It's all getting very confusing." She noted that these young women often go to the nicer parts of town and stroll around, waiting for men in nice cars to pick them up. Setareh maintained that these lower-class young women created a fantasy world for themselves when they left the house, and this was their costume. Setareh and several of her colleagues emphasized that changing one's outerwear style was an easy way to play with one's identity, and more important, to play with the comportment of Islamic ideology.

Another phenomenon related to how style and fashion spread from uptown to downtown was pointed out to me by my informants: many young people from the lower-income parts of town work with and for families and young people in the wealthier neighborhoods. I spent much of my time in 2005 and 2007 interviewing hairdressers, makeup artists, massage therapists, athletic coaches, nannies, cooks, housecleaners, and home assistants who lived in or came from lower-class areas and worked for upper and upper middle-class Tehranis. Many of the young people I interviewed who were from upper-class families had servants their own age who had started to imitate their styles and comportment. I also often met young people from lower-class parts of town who worked uptown all day and they told me they learned from their uptown clients and customers how to be in fashion. So, by 2007, young men and women in the lower-class parts of town looked almost exactly the same as young men and women in the wealthiest neighborhoods in Tehran. "Everyone has fake Gucci purses and shoes, even the poorest women," commented Nassim, a twenty-three-year-old housewife from one of the wealthiest parts of town. "There is no point in these labels any more, 'cause everyone has them," she added, referring to her Louis Vuitton purse. Another young woman, a computer analyst from northern Tehran, noted that "the women from pāyin shahr [downtown] look just like the women from bālā shahr [uptown], but when you get really close to them, I mean like one or two centimeters away, and you smell their perfume, you can tell it's cheap. Or you look at their lip liner and you can tell it's not *hesābi* [of good quality], that it's cheap, that they didn't pay a lot for it, like I did for my Chanel makeup. But other than that, they look just like us!"

During the summer of 2007, I spent time at several shelters and drop-in centers for women in the southern part of town. When I walked into these shelters, which were overcrowded and understaffed, I noted that the women standing in line to receive a hot meal or feminine hygienic care looked just like the women I had seen in the northern part of town. These women, who told me they couldn't afford tampons, pads, toilet paper, underwear, or food for their children, opened their purses to reveal multiple tubes of lipstick, several eye shadows, and lip liners and eye liners aplenty. "When we manage to make some money, we spend it on looking good, looking like the uptown women," one young woman told me when she saw my surprise at all the makeup in her purse. "I know, you are probably wondering why we wouldn't just buy *navār-e-behdāshti* (feminine products for menstruation) with our money, but we feel better with this makeup; it makes us feel like the other young women and helps us get the attention we need to feel better about ourselves," she explained. Although looking at a person and assessing the color and style of their headscarf or mānto did not necessarily reveal personal characteristics or political viewpoints, looking good and fashionable seemed to be a priority for many of the women with whom I interacted, regardless of their socioeconomic status.

Most of the young men in the lower-class parts of town also seek to emulate middle-class young male fashion. Although some young men in the southern portions of Tehran wear traditional baggy pants, long-sleeved shirts with vests, and small caps that resemble the fez found in Morocco and Turkey, lower-class young men who dress conservatively are almost as rare as young women in chādor (except, of course, for the young men who are members of the morality police). Many of the young men in Tehran's downtown district try to emulate the uptown or North Tehrani boys, who wear tight pants with matching tight T-shirts, long hair with blond or bronze highlights covered in layers of hair gel, clean-shaven faces, large eye-catching jewelry, and large sunglasses, which they wear at all hours of the day or night. Because many of them know that women are very label conscious, some of the men wear shirts, pants, or jewelry with large designer logos clearly displayed. The young men of the working and lower classes are increasingly blending into the Northern Tehrani style. Hasan, a twenty-year-old man I interviewed at a runaway shelter, did not have enough money to buy food. His sandals were falling apart and hidden under dirty jeans that were obviously hand-me-downs. He didn't have enough money for food or shoes, yet his hair was highlighted, although he later explained that instead of hair color he used hydrogen peroxide, which was less expensive and could be procured from a drug store near the shelter. I asked him why he had spent his money on highlights instead of food. He smiled as he leaned into the door frame where he had been standing, "I know where my priorities are, that's why. I have to look good for the ladies. You interested?"

Looking Good and Being Good-Looking

It is important to note that the conventional wisdom of "don't judge a book by its cover" should be applied to many young Tehranis and their styles of dress. There are many reasons that young people dress the way they do, and two people who dress similarly do not necessarily have the same priorities, political views, or reasons for comporting themselves in the same way. When I met young women who wore a lot of makeup, bright headscarves, and tight mantos but did not like to go out to parties and spent most of their free time studying, and then met young women who wore maghna'e or châdor but loved to go to parties, engaged in multiple-partner sex, and used drugs recreationally, it reminded me that looks don't necessarily indicate persona. Just because a young man wears a lot of hair gel and spikes his hair a certain way, or just because a young woman wears a brightly colored headscarf and tight manto does not mean they are trying to make a political statement. Nor does it mean that they are shallow and overly focused on fashion. For some people, outwear is an art; for others, it is a way to play with their identity; and for many, it is a response to peer pressure, a hobby, or a way of attracting the attention of members of the opposite sex.

Just as in most other countries throughout the world, in Iran people have different reasons for their stylistic choices, and I don't want to make the mistake of saying that every young woman who wears lipstick or every young man who uses hair gel engages in sexually and socially un-Islamic behaviors (such as socializing with the opposite sex, engaging in premarital sex, drinking, and dancing) or is trying to make a political statement. Nevertheless, style, fashion, and looking a certain way have become an integral part of conversations, attention, and energy for many young people as well as for members of the regime, the families of young people, and researchers seeking to understand and analyze the meaning and significance of changes in Tehrani youth culture.

On the streets of Tehran, both uptown and downtown, if one listens to the conversations of young people and observes their daily patterns, the focus on outer appearance for both men and women is striking. Some young women, especially middle- and upper-middle-class secular Tehranis, spend vast amounts of time at beauty salons and gyms and in dressing rooms, sometimes staying for up to two hours to make up their faces before going around the corner to the market. The time, energy, money, and attention that women devote to hair removal and that both women and men devote to plastic surgery often exceed the time and money spent on other causes. Even young people without money find ways to emulate those who have money in less expensive ways, such as substituting hydrogen peroxide or tomato paste for hair color and using homemade body sugaring (sugar melted into a waxlike substance that removes hair) instead of waxing for hair removal. In 2004 Tehran was named the nose-job capital of the world by popular news agencies such as BBC and CBS, and it is no surprise. As you walk the busy Tehran streets, you can see men and women proudly walking around with white tape and bandages over their noses. In contrast to the United States, where people often hide during their recovery period, in Iran, several informants told me, even those young adults who do not have surgery (for whatever reason, including that some of them have nice noses naturally) purchase white tape and gauze from the pharmacy and pretend they have received the surgery, because it has become a status symbol and, for some, a symbol of modernity. "I got my nose done by one of the best surgeons in town," said Vida, a twenty-five-year-old nurse. "It's gorgeous, isn't it? I think that's why a lot of people who come from America like me, because I just *look* more modern than some of these traditional women." Although many people outside of Iran enjoy the apparent paradox presented by Iranian young people's focus on appearances, most people do not ask why this phenomenon is taking place. Many chuckle at the fact that nose jobs are so popular in Iran or talk about the increase in makeup use, but they fail to recognize that makeup, style, and behavior are essential parts of a social movement, and that the success of young people in consuming makeup, fashion goods, and hair products should be seen as a sign of a changing Iran.

The dedication and skill of some of these young women in grooming and appearing polished is also evident. I routinely spent the better part of one day a week talking to the women who could afford to patronize a particular beauty salon. Many came early in the morning and spent the rest of the day at the salon. They took their rest and relaxation there, ordering lunch while catching up with the other women and chatting away on their cell phones. Beauty salons in Iran are gender-segregated,

Figure 3.5. The look of the sexual revolution: A woman applying makeup and smoking a cigarette in a public park. One would not have seen this in Tehran twenty years ago. © 2006 by Nader Davoodi. Used by permission.

and there women discuss topics ranging from sex and contraception to politics and economics as they wait for their highlights to set. "Can you believe this election?" commented a woman who worked at the salon I frequented as she yanked my hair straight.[17] "I mean, things were getting so much better here; we were making progress. Now what will happen? What can we do about it?" She turned toward one of her co-workers. Her comments sparked a heated in-depth conversation about the various candidates and the importance of participating in the electoral process. Many of the women working at the salon, as well as the clients, had not voted during the first round of elections in the summer of 2005 but had rushed to the polls for the runoff between current president Ahmadinejad and former president Hashemi Rafsanjani. Their preferred candidate had not even made it to the secondary rounds, and they now lamented their lack of participation. Comments about one another's eyebrows, hair color, and nails were constantly thrown into the conversation.

The women often articulated that in the absence of an option to express dissent or unhappiness with the regime overtly, they were concentrating their efforts on looking good as a way to speak back to the regime and embody that which the regime seeks to eliminate. Appearance therefore took on a different significance for them, and although people often get lost or caught up in the effort to look a certain way, that effort is still a significant part of the current young adult social movement. For many, getting away with looking un-Islamic by wearing makeup, tighter mǎntos, and bright headscarves is a marker of success and means they do have the power to change the system, and this power gives some of them a sense of agency and citizenship. "I remember fifteen years ago they were beating up women and taking everyone who wore nail polish to jail," remarked a thirty-year-old beautician who lives in the southern part of town but works uptown. "Now look at us; we can do what we want. I can wear orange toe polish, and that's that. If any member of the morality police tries to touch me, I will scream at him, and everyone will support me. I can wear my nail polish, and lipstick too! That means something. That means we are getting to them, that we *do* have power, that they are more afraid of us now than we were of them ten years ago!" she said triumphantly.

Speaking Through Their Clothes

The Tehrani young adults who are creating a new sexual culture use their clothes and styles as codes to communicate with one another and to express identity. Leila, the twenty-year-old urban planning student from Azad University, often told me that "young people in Iran are undergoing an identity crisis; we know we are changing, but we are not sure who we are or how to tell the world who we are. Some, like me and my friends, express this identity in our style. We wear colorful headscarves and tight māntos. It is our way of expressing how we are changing." Although these changes and silent statements may not be acknowledged by members of the Iranian diaspora or by consumers of Western media, the Iranian Islamist regime does see the changes and is struggling to respond to some of the calls made by the youth.

Any violation of Islamic dress code used to be grounds for punishment, but things have changed. For example, during the first decade and a half after Islamification, young women wearing tight coats or open-toed shoes were harassed, physically threatened, and often jailed for not adhering to Islamic dress codes. Women who wore lipstick might have had their lips slashed with razors by men and women who sought to promote Islamic ideology, and women who wore nail polish were punished with lashings. Today young women wear makeup, form-fitting Islamic clothing, and nail polish and toe polish without punishment and with limited harassment, if any. These changes reflect changes in the state apparatus, which has been forced to permit young adults' new styles.

Many of my informants were quick to point out that changes in various styles have ultimately led to changes in responses by the morality police. "Now young people don't have big problems anymore. We can put on style the way we want to, and our parents don't even care," explained Morteza when I interviewed him at a shopping mall in Shahrak-e-Gharb. Morteza is a twenty-year-old university student whose eyebrow, nose, and lip are pierced. He wore a fauxhawk, baggy jeans, and a tight white T-shirt over which hung three large silver chains. "It's not just our government that is changing, it's our culture, our parents," he emphasized. Another young man who was strolling the halls of the shopping mall with Morteza also commented on the notion that parents changing is an important indicator of cultural change beyond government change.

"Yeah, you know, five years ago, if I'd walked around with this nose ring, my hair all done up, and these fashionable clothes, my mother and father would have *mizadan dar-e-kunam* [given me a kick in the pants] and kicked me out of the house. I still live with them, they see how I walk around, and they don't say anything. That means something," he told me as other young hipsters walked past us at the mall. These changes were part of what my informants called the social revolution. Leila emphasized that, for her group of friends, having changed the responses of the morality police to the point where young people now had some control over and choice in what they wore was an important milestone in their social revolution. It was also of no small significance that many of their parents seemed to accept their new styles, and the youth saw all of this as an indicator of changes in culture, not just in government.

Iranian youth also often explained to me that they use style as a form of intentional communication, to signal their identities to one another. One of my informants, Nazanin, a twenty-three-year-old photographer, told me,

You know, we can tell the different types of young people just by looking at them. What they are wearing and how they are wearing it gives it all away. The ones who are against the regime might wear tight outfits and looser headscarves, or the boys might grow their hair long and shave their faces. The ones who are over the top, wearing too much makeup and too many colors and too much jewelry, these are the ones who have just rebelled against everything Eastern and Islamic and want to be Western. Others who are more subtle are just sending a message to the regime: we don't like what you are doing. This I say to the morality police by wearing my light shade of nail polish. I'm against the regime, but I'm not necessarily in favor of being a painted doll either.

Nazanin says she is making a statement by wearing light makeup and somewhat tighter clothing, but she feels that those young women who wear too much makeup and clothes that are too form-fitting are communicating values that are overly Western. Although she does not agree with the values promoted by the Islamic Republic, she feels that her style makes a subtle statement. She says she identifies other people who are "of the same mind-set" as herself by seeking out women who have a style similar to her own. "I just know that they will be like me and like sports and like to discuss literature," she tells me. "I just know by how they look." Although, as mentioned earlier, looks are not always an indicator of personality, many young people have told me they can get a sense of a person's stance on a lot of social issues by paying close attention to subtleties in their style of clothing and appearance.

Ali, a twenty-four-year-old salesman, agreed with Nazanin's comments, but he added that it is especially true when it comes to seeking out women. "You know, I can just tell by looking at a girl what kind of girl she is. I can tell if she is going to be one of those women who is high-maintenance, I can also tell if she is going to be, how do you say, like, liberal or conservative. And believe me, I have no time for conservative women. But one look and you can tell, that's sad but true. I guess it's the same way with us guys too, but obviously I notice the women more," he told me while checking out a new female customer who had walked into his store. The young woman was wearing a tight, white mānto and a turquoise headscarf that revealed her bleached blond bangs in the front and her ponytail in the back. She was also wearing capri pants with Converse All Star sneakers, and her acrylic nails were decorated with flower-patterned rhinestones. Ali smiled at her and then looked at me. "See, that's the kind of girl I want to date, and I just know that she is going to give me her phone number before leaving," he said. He described how he and his friends would look for certain signs when choosing women to date or marry. He said they would never marry a woman who wore a chādor or maghna'e, but they didn't want to marry a girl who was too made-up either. Ali indicated that the more fancy the women were, the more available, he felt, they were for dating and ultimately perhaps for marriage, or perhaps just for sex.

Women also assess men's appearance when choosing partners. Many of the women I spoke with emphasized that they sought out men who wore designer labels and tight clothes, and had long hair coated in hair gel. "I like the boys who wear *shalvarak* [capri pants] or designer jeans, with tight T-shirts, really tight," said Nilufar, a twenty-year-old university student. "I also look at their watches and shoes to see if they are designer; that's a pretty good indication to me if this is going to be my type of guy or not," she added while showing me her Guess watch. Her two friends nodded in agreement and pointed out three or four "good candidates" in the coffee shop in which we were sitting. "See those guys over there, the ones in the corner? Those are the guys who are going to be like us, you can just tell," said her friend, pointing to four young men in tight T-shirts and jeans, slicked-back wavy hair, wearing Gucci, Prada, and Dior sunglasses atop their heads, and large gold chains with matching bracelets. I looked over at them, and one of them winked at me and turned up the collar on his Diesel denim jacket.

Urban Iranian young adults use their style not only to express their identities but also to signal one other. These codes and the identities they project in public spaces help these young adults to define themselves to other like-minded young people. Roya, an eighteen-year-old high school student in Mashad, often talks about codes and passwords used on the street. She describes her favorite after-school activity of strolling down the streets in her newly purchased tight manto, which her parents (and the morality police) disapprove of:

Yes, I like to go to Boulevard Sajjad two, three, four, OK, actually six times a week to strut around with my friends. Of course my mom doesn't know; I tell her I'm going to a friend's house, which I do, but I only go there to change into my more translucent headscarf and apply more makeup. You see, a transparent or chiffon headscarf is a code; it means that you are open to being talked to by the opposite sex. Another thing we do is walk past each other, and if we see a guy wearing a T-shirt or nice sunglasses and a necklace, well, we know where we stand with him.

As mentioned here, what these young adults wear sometimes becomes a symbol of who they are and a way to play with their identity. Some of the young women I interviewed described that when they wanted to be invisible or discreet, or when they wanted to be certain of not being stopped by the morality police or nosy neighbors, they would wear a chãdor. When they wanted to enter the professional arena or had work or errands to take care of at government-run centers, they would wear a loose mãnto and a maghna'e. On days when they wanted to be noticed and wanted to meet other young people who were "like-minded," they would wear tighter mãntos and colorful headscarves. Finally, when they wanted to meet potential partners, they would add heavy makeup and open-toed shoes. Other young women added that when they were fed up with the regime and wanted to do laj bāzi, they would wear shorter pants and "sexy" māntos (with ankles and wrists revealed) and extra coats of makeup. In a culture where heterosexual interactions are subtle and full of subtext, and where seduction is communicated without words, style and body language are heavily relied on for heterosexual mating. In these many ways, style is used to communicate politics, identities, and seduction, all without a single word.

Revolutionary Fashion

When asked about why they adopt certain styles, many young Iranians note that they do it explicitly to defy Islamic authorities; many of them see style as a form of warfare. "They tell us to wear uniforms, they want to force us to wear what *they* want us to wear," began Azita, a nineteen-year-old student at Azad University, while smacking her lips together to be sure her lipstick was evenly distributed. "But I think you have to live your life, you have to wear what helps you express yourself, you have to speak to the outside world in some way. If I want to wear this, then so be it, nobody can tell me what to do." For Azita, wearing heavy layers of makeup and tight clothing is her way of expressing her frustration and her refusal to comply with the regime's mandatory Islamic dress code. When members of the morality police were stationed outside her university with damp towelettes and forced women to take off their makeup before entering, Azita and her friends (like Asana in Chapter 2) responded by adding a few extra coats of makeup before they left the house in order to preserve the base layers after they had mockingly gone through the motions of taking off some of their makeup. "They can't make us back down; they make a rule, we will find a way to break it," she stated defiantly. As Varzi notes, "Islamic moral law was not effective with a majority of the Iranian young people because they did not take the laws seriously. With so many rules and contradictory advice on which rules to follow, it was impossible not to break rules constantly. Teenagers were often applauded (by their parents and peers) for breaking rules as a show of strength and revolt. Eventually they begin to see themselves as above the law, not part of it."[18]

Sepehr, a twenty-two-year-old man who grew up in Mashad but has spent the last few years at Tehran University, agrees with Azita. "What we wear is a symbol of our freedom," he told me, referring to his own T-shirt and tight white capri pants. "Without our looks, well, we might as well just go and die; it's a way to entertain ourselves, to make ourselves feel better, and to show that they [the regime] can't touch us." He indicated that his looks and style were something he could personally do to express his distaste for the regime. He felt that this bodily subversion helped him feel like he was doing something to change his environment.

Homa, who was wearing blood-red lipstick, large gold earrings and bangles, and a tight pink manto the first time I met her, vividly described her frustration with the morality police and how she wanted to use her body and clothes to make a political statement. This is how she expressed her sentiments:

I hate them. Last week one of them stopped me while I was in a taxi and told me to wipe off my lipstick. I was on my way to a party, but I did it. But some days I just want to run naked into the streets and see who comes up to me. Come and get me, you bastards! I dare you! [She screams.] See how I wear tight clothes and red lipstick? I know I shouldn't, but I just want the komite to come up to me so I can run my mouth at them. I hate them!

Homa was emphatic about rebelling against authorities and her parents with her style of dress. Although she lamented the time she had to spend getting ready in the mornings, she said she got private satisfaction in knowing she was doing something she was not supposed to. She, like many young women, said that this was their way of showing they still had ultimate control over their bodies and appearances, that they were above Islamic law.

Kimia, a twenty-year-old architecture student at Tehran University, echoed Homa's sentiments. "For me, defiance is like fashion, you know? It's fashion to live on the edge. So I wear clothes that show how I like to live on the edge. I do it to show solidarity with my friends. I mean what can they do, arrest all of us?" For Kimia, fashion and defiance were part of the same realm of experiences, and a place to manifest refusal.

As noted earlier, many of my informants talked about their style as a form of laj or laj bāzi. Asana (introduced in Chapter 2), twenty-one, and

Sonbol, twenty, also described their styles as laj bāzi. "Yes, women and boys wear whatever they want right now," began Asana while Sonbol nodded in agreement.

They do it for the laj. People aren't happy about the government, but they don't know what to do. They, well we, dress the way it makes us feel good to. The komite just want to scare us; they do everything in their power to show their control. It's not that they are morally offended by lack of hejāb. It's that it shows diminishing control. This seems to be a power struggle. We want to say to them, "You don't control us," and the conservatives want to say, "Yes, we do." The way we dress is the battleground.

Asana and Sonbol felt that this was their way of feeling good about themselves, showing solidarity with their fellow young adults, and making a statement. On their way to our interview, Asana had been stopped and harassed about her translucent turquoise headscarf. *"Hejābet ra rāyat kon!"* (loosely translated "guard your headscarf"), the officer had grunted. Asana had responded by telling the officer to *"cheshmata ra rāyat kon!"* (that is, "guard your eyes"), a popular response to accusations of bad hejāb because according to Islamic moral guidelines, men's eyes should be averted so that even if women are not "properly" attired, men should be able to shield themselves from their appearance. After that, the officer fined her twelve thousand tomans (the equivalent of US$13) for "un-Islamic behavior and appearance." Asana rolled her eyes as she recounted the story. "You know what I say to that? Success!" she said, smiling.

Consequences

Young men and women alike sometimes expose themselves to risks by putting on style the way they do. This is what makes fashion among these young people more than just consumerism or shallowness. Also, if wearing a Gucci scarf were truly just a symbol of consumerism, it would not have been, at one point, a punishable offense, and the morality police and Islamic ideologues would not have been so insistent on proper dress and comportment. The implications of putting on style are huge. Men and women have come together to rebel in the same ways, and they face the same punishment. Women, to this day, sometimes receive fines for wearing nail polish. Men whose hair is too long or whose haircut is "too fancy" are often arrested and their heads are shaved. Women whose hejãb has fallen too far back (although it is not always clear how far back is too far, and it often depends on the time of year) are sometimes arrested, jailed, fined, and whipped. Although it is true that the komite cannot arrest all young people who violate laws by manifesting un-Islamic appearances, many people, especially the leaders of changes in fashion outside Islamic dress codes, have suffered in these last few years while attempting to carve out a space for dressing creatively. It was the summer of 2001 when the women in Tehran first decided to take to the streets in open-toed shoes without socks. Some of my female informants, who said they were among the first several hundred women to do this, were taken to jail and whipped. Similarly, they often pay dearly for each additional millimeter they push back their headscarves, and for each extra centimeter of skin they expose through rolled-up pants and shirt sleeves.

Arefeh, a young woman from Tehran University, was limping the first time I met her in 2004, although it wasn't her limp that caught my eye but the gorgeous blues, greens, and oranges of her headscarf and mãnto. It was only after staring at her for a few moments that I realized she looked injured. When I asked her what was wrong, she smiled and said, "I am an ex-convict." This left me puzzled. She went on to describe her time in prison. "I have just spent four days in prison because I went out in the streets wearing a bandana instead of a proper headscarf," she said, laughing. "I am so proud of myself though; that bandana was a lot easier to manage than this shawl, and a lot cooler too. So what? So we are going to get arrested, but if we get the rules changed so we can wear those, it's worth it," she remarked, opening another few buttons of her turquoise mãnto so that the better part of her neck and collarbone were exposed. As I looked down at her green capri pants, I noticed markings from a whip surrounding her ankles. Arefeh caught my eye. "Yeah, they whipped my legs this time. Told me that would teach me to show my ankles in public. Yeah, a lot of good it did," she said, smiling, as she pointed to her still-exposed calves and open-toed shoes.

During the first few summers I spent in Tehran (2000–2002), I watched the komite load dozens of defiant young women into their cars and haul them to jail. The morality police would wait at popular hangouts with rulers to measure the length of young adults' pants (both men and women). For each centimeter the pants were raised above the ground, the young people were fined 5 tomans (US$6) per leg. If the pants were found to be more than five centimeters off the ground, the wearer was arrested and often, like Arefeh, faced the whip.

Many of my informants, as well as members of the diaspora who travel to Iran during the summer, have called the summer of 2002 the "summer of the cockroaches"[19] because during that summer, komite members would wait outside of well-known beauty salons with bags and buckets of cockroaches. They would catch the women wearing nail polish or toe polish, dip their hands into these buckets, and set cockroaches and spiders loose on their toes. This action was considered lenient punishment for minor offenders relative to the punishment of women wearing open-toed shoes, makeup, and clothing that strayed from the Islamic dress code, who were arrested, taken to jail, and often whipped. Although this enforcement was carried out on only a few hundred young women, it was intended to scare other potential offenders, but this was not the effect. One afternoon as I was conducting my usual participant observation at one of the beauty salons in the northern part of town, a group of ladies were discussing their latest run-in with the cockroaches. "I don't know if I should do orange polish anymore," began one woman, taking her seat at the pedicure station in the salon. "Why not?" asked her friend. "It looks so fantastic on you!" The other woman sighed as she pulled a pair of socks and tennis shoes out of her bag. "Well, then," she sighed, "I guess I'll have to wear these as I leave the salon. Just last week when I came here to get this lovely pink color," she said picking up a bottle of fuchsia nail polish, "as I was leaving, two goons were waiting outside with those bugs and they let 'em loose on me!" She made a face, and then her friend did too, but no one seemed shocked but me. "Yeah, it happened to me two days ago," shouted another woman above the roar of the blow-dryer on the other side of the salon. The hairdresser switched off the blow-dryer immediately. "Look, it happens," she said. "That's just part of the risk we take, and it's the price we pay for looking beautiful." All of the women smiled. *"Bokosh-o-khoshgelam kon"* said one woman,[20] and the others repeated the phrase in unison. I looked down at my light pink fingernails. Negda, one of the managers of the beauty salon, who had become a friend of mine, saw the worry in my eye. "Don't worry, honey, it doesn't really scare us; we still wear our nail polish." She smiled and added, "They probably won't get you for that color, and even if they do, well, it will be something to write about in your book, right?" Luckily they didn't get me that day.

BUT ALL OF THIS HAS CHANGED, and young people are no longer punished in the ways they used to be for wearing "bad Islamic dress." This change is due to changes in the state, as well as to the courage of many young people who have constantly pushed the limits. Many young people like Arefeh and Asana are not afraid of the authorities and welcome their harassment. They see it as a part of daily life. Some also see it as a way to communicate with other like-minded young adults, and as a way to make a statement to the society that dissatisfies them. Soheila, a twenty-two-year-old travel agent with fake red eyelashes and red snake-skin sandals to match, told me during the summer of 2007 that she is no longer afraid of being arrested.

You know, maybe the first time I wore a tight coat, the first few times I was caught and arrested, yeah, it was scary. But then you say to yourself, this is the life I'm choosing for myself, and you know that by going out looking like—well, like me, like the way you do—you might get arrested. So every time you go outside you are ready to be arrested, but not scared. Definitely not scared anymore.

For many of these young people, the risk and the attention it draws from political authorities is part of why they do it. They like the defiance and the danger. Standing up to authority is also a vital component of their choices of fashion. "The louder the better" say many of my female informants, referring to the colors of their mãntos and headscarves. Many note that the gains they make outweigh the risks they take. Yassi, a twenty-two-year-old computer technician, found this defiance and risk exhilarating. One afternoon while we were strolling down the street, she told me, "See, all of this backlash is part of the same thing. See, look at me; I'm wearing short, tight red pants with a see-through scarf. No way we would have been able to get away with all of this or with having boyfriends a few years ago. But we risked it, enjoyed the moments of risk, and we succeeded!" She smiled and adjusted her headscarf to match the sunglasses in her hair. "Now we can have our boyfriends, look good, and feel good about what we are doing. It was so worth it."

Although style and appearance are not the extent of this revolution, as my informants repeatedly told me, style and pushing the limits of appearance are major aspects of the demand for social change that some informants call the sexual and social revolution. Their outerwear and public comportment are also the most public forms of their resistance, a conversation of sorts with the state and the regime on a daily basis.

Young adults in all classes have found creative ways of keeping up with changes in appearance and style. Because much of what I have described as outward rebellion is tied to style of dress among middle- and upper-middle-class young adults, one must ask how less-privileged young Tehranis are able to rebel if they cannot always afford stylish clothing or to pay for private areas of congregation for sexual encounters. Although I did not interview many young people from the lower classes, through my interaction with health care and service providers and scholars who work with members of the lower classes, as well as through much observation, I was able to see how even these young people have embodied the social and sexual revolution.

So, although much of the public aspect of the social revolution depends on consumption, as this chapter has discussed, young people of the lower classes participate through creative means of procuring material goods that are considered in fashion. Young women who are not able to afford expensive headscarves that are in fashion (such as Louis Vuitton, Chanel, or Gucci) purchase fabrics that are similar to the fabrics used by designers and make headscarves that they then wear in the style that is in fashion. Similarly, young men who cannot afford expensive hair highlights use inexpensive hydrogen peroxide to achieve the same golden blond highlights in their hair. And whereas young women from the middle and upper classes spend endless hours in beauty salons getting manicures and pedicures, and wear only makeup from Western designers, young women of the lower socioeconomic classes purchase bottles of nail polish and share them among a group of friends. Instead of paying for expensive manicures, they provide these services to each other free of charge. Instead of wearing MAC cosmetics, they use *sormeh* (bits of charcoal) for their eye makeup and inexpensive pharmacy brands of lipstick (which are often shared by siblings and friends).

As Varzi notes, "baseball caps do not attest to a 'Westernized identity' any more than a hejāb points to an Islamic one; rather such forms of Western clothing show a certain degree of rebellion."[21] It is possible, however, that these baseball caps, Gucci headscarves, and Prada handbags could be both forms of Western clothing *and* signs of rebellion. Rather than concluding that young people are trying to imitate the West or just trying to stay in style and succumbing to peer pressure, it must be acknowledged that their appearance and comportment have made a clear statement to the regime, which has indicated its assent by allowing changes in appearance to take place. Young Tehranis have created a new style of dress that defies strict Islamic dress codes, and they are continuing to push the limits of what they can wear and how stylish they can be. This new style of dress attempts to incorporate global fashion trends and has become a way for young people to play with their identities, to communicate with their peers, to demonstrate their disapproval of the regime, and to assert some amount of agency over their lives. These young adults are politically engaged and believe that changes in the regime and political sphere will be achieved by attacking the moral fabric that has been woven by the current regime. These attacks come in the form of, among other things, changes in outward appearance. Although this struggle to attain freedom in their appearance has had consequences and many have been punished in the process, young Tehranis have made many gains in changing strict moral dress codes, which has translated to gains in social freedom. Taking the process a step further, the changes that these young adults have succeeded in pushing for have perhaps also destabilized the regime, whose source of power is its policing style and morality. Gone are the days of public lashings for "bad Islamic dress," gone are the buckets of cockroaches. Now young women and men wear revealing fashions that are explicitly un-Islamic and get away with it. This outcome could be a commentary on the successes of the youth movement, and a symbol of the ways in which the state is trying to adapt.

4 Meeting, Mating, . . . and Cheating in the Islamic Republic

In Iran, we don't say, "OK, we are gay or we are, what? Lesbian?
No, that's so American of you to even *ask* such a question. We are
not homosexual, we are not heterosexual. We are just sexual. Get it?

    Mahnaz, female, twenty-five

It's not a big deal, men and women interacting, you know? It's a
very normal thing, men and women interacting like this, eating
pizza, drinking milkshakes, having our fun. See, it's totally fine,
right? But they have put it in our heads that what we are doing
is wrong, but it isn't, you know? It's fine, but they have made us
believe that what we are doing, even getting together for ice cream,
is wrong. *They* are the ones who are wrong.

    Reza, male, twenty-five

EVEN THOUGH DATING is against Islamic tradition in
Iran, and against some Persian family rules that suggest arranged marriages, young Tehranis have created their own rules
and rituals for heterosexual dating.[1] Although there used to be a distinct dichotomy between *dokhtar-e-kharāb* (a "bad girl," or woman who
sleeps around) and *dokhtar-e-khub* (a woman who is "good" and "proper"
and who "saves" herself for her husband) there has now emerged a third
category among some of my informants, and among some of their parents as well. Today young men and women say it is somewhat socially
acceptable, or even *sālem* ("normal" or "healthy") for a young woman to

have had one or two boyfriends before marriage. Sexual experience with these partners is further legitimated if the young woman is "in love." The third category, "normal" women, is beginning to emerge among Tehrani young adults and their parents. This development has changed the discussion on sexuality and created a conversation on dating. "Youth culture and dating have changed in Iran because people have changed, families have changed," said Tannaz, a twenty-four-year-old computer science major at Tehran University. "It's now okay to be in a *ravabet-e-sālem* (healthy relationship). Having a few partners before marriage is normal. It's OK; even my parents are OK with it," she said. Indeed, many parents with whom I spoke indicated they had no problem with their children, especially their daughters, having one or two partners before marriage.

After discussion with many informants, it seems to me that these attitudes have changed as a result of three main influences: (1) exposure to an online youth culture that shares ideas from around the world about dating and socializing with the opposite sex; (2) an increase in women's participation in the public sphere due to more women being educated and attaining positions in the workforce, combined with increasing numbers of women spending time at local shops, cafes, and parks; and (3) changes in sexual behavior that are causing a shift in attitudes and ideas. So, as more and more young people learn about male-female socializing around the world and are exposed to members of the opposite sex at school, at work, and in local recreation spots such as parks and squares, dating and interaction with the opposite sex becomes somewhat normalized. As dating and socializing between men and woman have normalized, more young people have been engaging in relationships, including sexual relationships, with members of the opposite sex. The increase in the young adult population also means that, besides people dating more, there are more people dating; and the more people date, the more socially acceptable dating becomes. As dating has become more socially acceptable, attitudes toward sex and virginity have also gradually shifted.

Although dating has become more popular in Tehran, negotiating the dating scene has delicate rules and procedures, and some of the young people use signals or codes to indicate their interest in dating. The process of dating and the procedures of courting and conduct, once interest is expressed, are still being refined among this group of young adults. Because of forced gender segregation by the regime, which used to harass young, unmarried couples, it is a challenge for some young people to find the physical space in which to date. Regardless, many of them do date, and they have developed their own styles of doing so and are creating a new approach to dating that does not exist in Iranian communities in the diaspora, and that did not exist in Iran in previous decades.

The mechanics of meeting potential dating partners are somewhat complicated in an environment in which interaction between men and women is heavily monitored. Some young adults meet their partners in cars, some at parties or in school, but many meet them through friends and in social circles. Often the first interactions between a young man and woman take place in a group setting, as nine of my informants explained to me, and move to being one-on-one when the relationship becomes sexual. Saara, a twenty-year-old student at Azad University, explained this when referring to her own dating experiences. "Well, for me, it's only been in the last year that I have started formally dating people I've met on the outside, like in the formal way of getting a number or giving a number," she began. "That's not usually our way; we don't always go out and give our numbers to date formally. More often than not, what happens is that there are boys I know or who are *ashna* [known] and then you keep seeing them in outings with your friends or cousins or whoever, and then from there it grows into a relationship. Getting a number and formally going on dates, no, that's not really how it goes here," she explained.

Nina, twenty-three, also noted that she tended to begin her relationships in group settings. She indicated she felt more comfortable meeting young men that way. "I mean, we don't really go on dates," she said, referring to the lack of one-on-one contact at the beginning of a courting relationship. Nina often dated her brother's friends, or people who worked in her brother's company, and would join them on group outings. "I don't even know what I would do on a date, like with just the two of us in the beginning? Sitting there staring at each other, not knowing what to say? The way we start dating is that while we are in a group we flirt with each other, show our interest, and then we go from there to other things. Then, before you know it, you are in a relationship—hopefully a healthy one" she added. She also indicated that dating members of her brother's social circle had a safety factor in that, because they were known, at least by her brother, and thus were less likely to be *shaytoon* (rascals), she could be comfortable with them. She also noted that not having one-on-one dates was safer because it kept the couples less visible to the watchful eyes of the morality police or nosy family members. "Plus, that way [being a friend of her brother's], at least the guy knows who I am, where I come from, that I come from a good, hard-working family. It feels better. Maybe this way he will respect me more." Many of the young adults described this phenomenon of being *motmain* (sure) of their partner, or the importance of dating someone who was ashna or *adam hesābi* (a good, solid, and respectable person). For the women, being sure of a boyfriend means trusting him not to gossip about the relationship or to ruin the woman's reputation at the termination of the relationship. For the young men, being sure of a girlfriend means trusting her not to be sexually involved with other men, and being sure that she does not have any sexually transmitted diseases.

Much of the challenge of dating, according to the women, begins after the initial set of first dates. Paranaz, a twenty-one-year-old university student introduced in Chapter 2, expressed a negative view of dating in Iran that was echoed by four of my other informants. She and other young Tehrani women blame a lot of their dating complications and woes on the regime. "I hate the way we have to date here," she explained as she climbed into my cousin's car. We were now three women sitting in the front seat of a very small Peugeot. Although we were sitting quite close to one another, Paranaz was not deterred from raising her voice for dramatic effect. "They don't let us do normal things, so I don't really get to know my boyfriend here. No wonder people don't figure out that they hate their husbands until after marriage; we have artificial dating here," she screeched. I had to move over a bit to keep my hearing intact. "See, we don't get to spend a lot of living, ordinary time with our boyfriends, because of the Islamic Republic," she continued, now at a more normal volume. "The Islamic Republic has created an artificial dating bubble." I looked at her, a bit confused. "See, whenever we get together with our boyfriends, it's to go out or to go have sex and then go home. We don't get to sleep with them, like, I mean sleep over; we don't get to see what they are like on a daily basis," she explained, turning down the music (for which I was thankful because music often impeded my recording of interviews conducted in the car, and often resulted in my informants shouting answers at me). "And they don't get to see what we are really like either. Like me, I'm horrible in the mornings. First of all, when I wake up my hair is everywhere, my face looks bad, and I am a real *jadugar* [witch]," she said, screwing up her face into a scowl for added effect. "I throw things at whoever wakes me up, and I'm not nice until about 11 A.M. But my boyfriend doesn't know this about me. He sees me only once I've collected myself, made myself look all nice. And then, if we get married, he'll be in for a shock, and it's the Islamic Republic's fault. It's their fault we have so many problems."

Paranaz was not the only young woman to blame the Islamic Republic for her relationship problems. Some of the divorced women I interviewed blamed the regime for their divorces as well, echoing Paranaz's sentiments. The problem, they said, was that they did not truly get to know or understand each other while dating because of all the social restrictions placed on them by family members and the regime. All of my informants concurred that the artificial dating bubble created by the Islamic Republic harmed their relationships with both dating and sexual partners.

Sonya, a twenty-three-year-old lab technician at a hospital in the northern part of Tehran, explained to me how her approach to a young man differs depending on whether she is interested in him as a sexual partner or as a dating partner. According to her, and to ten of my other female informants, men who were exclusively sexual partners were preferably people of a different class and from outside the woman's social group, and dating partners were members of the woman's social circle and considered potential marriage candidates. According to Sonya and the other women, there are three reasons it is better to sleep with men who are from different backgrounds: (1) because there is less chance of someone the woman knows finding out; (2) because men in the woman's own class, who are considered ideal marital candidates because of their finances, do not want to marry the women they sleep with; and (3) because the women can maintain some kind of power over the men. "It really depends," Sonya said one afternoon as we drove around the city looking at various young men and rating their desirability. "If you want a guy to go home with and just have sex, yeah, those are the guys you meet in cars or in the squares. But when it comes time for dating, it's totally different. Plus, you tend to date guys in your social group, so you have to be careful, make sure they don't think you're *that* type of girl," she explained pointing to a heavily made-up young woman standing on the street corner puffing on a cigarette. (Many of my female informants commented that smoking on the street was seen as a sign of being a dokhtar-e-kharāb, that is, bad girl, and thus they avoided it.) "You don't want the guys in your friend group to think you're a *jendeh* [slut]," she said. "Our environment has a lot to do with this dating stuff. Reputations, gossip—it's too much pressure. Sometimes guys will, out of their frustration, mind you, go and sleep with, like, four or five women at a time from the southern part of town. He'll go and have his fun because he knows he can't marry any of them. He'll lie to them, tell them he loves them, and they won't get anywhere. He'll spend a month with her and then her and then her—you get my drift?" she asked me. I nodded. It became clear that both women and men distinguished between partners suitable for sex and those suitable for dating. I also observed this phenomenon when I spent time in the lower-income parts of town. Every now and then I saw a nice car with three or more quite-done-up women in it enter one of the poorer neighborhoods while the women kept their eyes peeled for men to take home. Similarly, on more than one occasion when I was at a gathering of male informants, a group of women arrived late in the evening. When I asked the hosts of these parties, "Who are these women?" they responded that they were "women from pāyin shahr whom we have brought to entertain us."

Sanaz, Laleh, and Alaleh described the steps leading up to their commitment to a sexual relationship with the men they were dating as being delicate and particularly complicated. They explained it to me as a game. "You know me," Sanaz giggled, "I like to play with them. I say to them, no, I can't touch you there or you can't touch me here. But if you really like me, you will wait, you know? Be patient; that's how you get them to respect you," she explained, emphasizing the importance of gaining respect from one's partner. Respect is of the utmost importance for many of the young women who are seeking to uphold their reputa-

tions, but only with regard to their partners who were of the same socioeconomic class as them. The theme of respect in a relationship was
also evident in Nina's statements. "Then you play games, make them
work for it; that's how you have to do it. Even though I was dying to
be with him, really *be* with him [meaning to have sex]," she said, referring to her latest boyfriend, "I had to play hard to get. So even though
at certain times I would want to be with my boyfriend, I would pretend
like I had to go home; I had something to do, I would say. Make 'em
work, that's what you have to do. That's how you end up in a serious
relationship," she emphasized. Women's skill of playing hard to get is
highly praised, particularly by other women. It was important, however,
only with the middle-class men they were dating. They usually were not
as concerned about impressing or playing hard to get with the lower-
class men with whom they engaged in only sexual (as opposed to dating) relationships.

"I think women talk to men with their bodies," said Khodi, a twenty-
three-year-old military officer in training. "That's how they do it. We
aren't really good at communicating with them with words, so that's
how we read things: we read their bodies," he explained. For more than
ten of the young men I spoke with, reading women and understanding
their desires was a mystery. Although young adults around the world
may complain about the same issues, in gender-segregated societies
these delicate negotiations between young men and women are particularly challenging because many young men (especially those who
don't have female siblings) do not interact much with women their age
until entering university, and even then they continue to shy away from
female classmates.

"They play games, these women," added Khodi's friend Hossein, also
a twenty-three-year-old military officer in training. "It's like you never
really know what they want, and how to deal with them, I don't really
even know how to talk to women because I don't even have a sister. It's
all like blind dating, and it's very confusing." Heterosexual interaction at
a young age is difficult in any situation, but in Tehran it is compounded
by the fact that young women and men have been separated from a young
age and told not to intermix. Thus, for some of them, interacting with
members of the opposite sex and figuring out what they want or mean

becomes an arduous task. Some upper-middle-class young people have opportunities while growing up to meet members of the opposite sex at parties hosted by their parents or relatives. For young people from religious or lower-class families, who do not have these same gatherings, or for young people who move to Tehran from the provinces, interaction with members of the opposite sex who are in their age group is limited, and thus as they get older it becomes a challenge. Young men and women at universities describe much of their communication as forced or awkward, and even parents and members of the Ministry of Health and Ministry of Education recognize communication problems among their youth.

"Women and men have a different way of life here; everything is hidden, underground," began Reraj, the twenty-three-year-old medical student I often encountered at coffee shops in the northern part of town. "They have their own lives, but it's like they have two different lives when it comes to dating," he said, sipping on a cappuccino. "Women don't meet a guy and go to the movies or dinner or something. No, they just get together and go to someone's house and have lots of sex, you know? Just like, go right to each other's homes. That's the way our lives have become here in Iran," he added. Reraj, as well as four other young men I interviewed, felt that because of the environment created by the regime, he couldn't date young women in what he considered a healthy way. He said that being in Iran limited their interactions and often made him feel bad about how he treated many of the young women. He noted that relationships often became sexual very quickly because they lacked public spaces in which to date.[2] Reraj claimed that because young men and women cannot just date casually and go through the motions of courting such as dinner and public outings (although in recent years this has become increasingly common), they are confined to expressing their romantic emotions in private spaces that easily lend themselves to sexual encounters.

Two students from Tehran University, Mahmood, twenty-one, and Hooman, twenty, felt that the Iranian women they came across and dated were often playing games with them. These games frustrated both men but also made them even more curious about the young women and more determined to figure them out. "Women have the upper hand here. It's tough. They have the power, they hold the reins," Mahmood told me angrily. I remember being taken aback by this statement, but when I shared what he had said with my female informants, they all agreed that in relationships they had the upper hand, but in marriage it was their male counterparts who enjoyed more power. "In Iran that's just the way it is. They [the women] have all the power, and it's annoying," Mahmood described. "But it's also confusing because then when you try to take control you say, 'Hey, do you wanna dance?' or something like that, they look at you and say no! But they sit there waiting for you to ask them, constantly throwing seductive glances at you, and then it's like they take pleasure in saying no. I don't get it!" he exclaimed.

While Mahmood was confused about the power dynamic the young women were trying to enact, Hooman was angry at the games the young women played to maintain their power and, as he said, "trick" the young men into giving the women what they wanted.

With an Iranian girl, if you want to sleep with her, you have to get involved with her emotions. An Iranian girl, if you want to sleep with her, she will first ask, "*doosam dari?*" [Are you in love with me?] But, well, that's if you are lucky. Some aren't satisfied and will ask, "Are you going to marry me?" you know? For the women here it goes, first engagement, then sex, *then* love. Haven't you heard the joke about the porn movie? [*Pauses and waits for me to shake my head to indicate that I haven't.*] So why do Iranian girls watch porn movies all the way to the end? [*I shrug my shoulders.*] Give up? To see if the girl gets married in the end! [*Laughs.*] You women want to make sure that before you have sex, the choices are set, no going back. By the time you have sex you have already made your choice; the door behind you is closed and you are not going back.

Hooman seemed quite frustrated by the women he described and asked if I understood where he was coming from. I told him I could see his point.

You see? *Barikala!* [Well done!] But even though this progression of things is not natural, you know? It's not. For a man, he likes to make his choice based on the sexual encounter, not after the sexual encounter, and then you are trapped. This becomes a game: I won't give it up, I won't give you what you want until you give me what I want. Give me the ring so I have you trapped; at that point you can't go anywhere.

He felt deeply resentful that the women he had dated were always trying to trap him, and he indicated that he had become quite good at evading young women's pressures now that he had gained more experience.

An older guy knows how to deal with these women and how to spin it better than a young guy. He knows better how not to get trapped. Like a twenty-four-year-old guy, for example, he will start in with a girl and won't say right away, "I want to have sex with you." No, he will be more subtle than that. He will first try to take the relationship forward. He will try to evoke the illusion of an engagement, make her think that this is the situation they are in, without making any promises, to make her more comfortable. Then he'll go in for the sex.

Hossein agreed with Hooman and Mahmood that Iranian women play a lot of games, but in his view these games are also based on economics. "Women are tricksters," began Hossein at a party one evening. He pointed to several women across the room. "Yeah, them, they are devils. Iranian women these days look for, well, it's not about, it's less about looks and them liking your type; it's more about what car you drive, what clothes you wear, and where you live," he said. He pushed up his shirt sleeve and pointed to the Gucci label on his watch, and motioned to the Diesel label on his jeans. "They look at that stuff, that's how they size you up, these women; within five minutes they have you figured out." He finished his vodka martini. I then asked him if he ever looked at women and tried to size them up on the basis of what he perceived as their economic situation or style. "It's mostly the other way around," he told me, "because men are just looking for sex; women are looking for a husband."

Young people in Iran frequently have serious partners and are comfortable dating regardless of the efforts of the regime. As mentioned earlier, they see the creation of a dating scene as a vital part of the social and sexual revolution. Because many parents are now more accepting of their children's dating habits, and because young people have created the third category of "normal" for young women, many young people have felt increasingly comfortable dating, being seen in public on their dates, and talking about their partners in front of friends and family. This is a definite shift in practice from even a decade ago, when most young people (but especially women) hid their relationships from family members and even friends. Some of my informants' families, I observed, allowed them to bring their partners to family gatherings and acknowledged them as partners instead of denying these relationships. This growing acceptability of having boyfriends and girlfriends is evidence of a cultural shift—in both theory and practice—that has taken place against the backdrop of the present regime. In fact, five of my informants pointed to their increased dating as a symbol of the gains they had achieved in relation to the state as well as to their parents. Despite the challenges put forth by the Islamists, by traditional moral codes mandating that young women keep their reputations intact, and by the difficulty of cross-gender communication, some of my informants reiterated that dating in Iran isn't difficult at all, and that they are involved in relationships more often than not.

Several of the young people I spoke with talked about their parents' acceptance of their boyfriends or girlfriends. "Yeah, my parents are cool with me having a boyfriend," said Azita while showing me a picture of her most recent boyfriend, who stood with his arm around her father. "They invite him to our parties, and it's really fun," she told me in the summer of 2004. When I saw her the following year, she had broken up with that boyfriend and was now bringing home another one. Many of the young men I spoke with also brought women home to meet their parents, and their girlfriends often became part of the family. Bahram, twenty-two, and Narges, twenty-one, had no plans to get married, yet they were intricately involved in each other's lives. Narges was very close to Bahram's mother and family. "They are almost like my own family," she told me when I saw her at Bahram's uncle's house. She referred to her boyfriend's uncle as *dai jun*, a term of endearment for an uncle, and saw Bahram's brother as her own. This opening up of parents and family members to the idea of long-term dating was described by my informants as symbolic of ways in which the culture is changing as a result of young adult behavior, and it is seen as a landmark or milestone in gains achieved by the sexual and social revolution.

Like a Virgin

According to interpretations of hadiths (Islamic scriptures) and sharia by Islamists, premarital sex is *haram*, this is, a sin against Islamic values and culture. Some scholars have noted that premarital sex and extramarital sex are threatening to the entire Muslim *umma* because they can cause a state of fitna, or chaos, that can undermine productivity, community, and the state.[3] It is for this reason that among members of the Islamic regime and religiously devout Muslim families, virginity is highly valued, and any deviation from it is grounds for punishment. Some of the parents with whom I spoke (especially those from the most religious and sonnati, that is, traditional, families) indicated they would disown their children if they found they were engaging in premarital intercourse. Many believed it was a sign of disrespect and dishonor for their children to engage in such activities. This attitude was made even more clear to me when during the summer of 2004 I received news of the public execution of a seventeen-year-old girl who had been turned in to the authorities by her grandfather, who *suspected* her of engaging in premarital sex. Public execution is not a common occurrence, which is why even though it took place in the northern part of Iran, the news spread nationwide. The girl was hung in a public square while her grandfather and other members of her family watched. "She had spoiled herself and ruined us," he was rumored to have said through tears when looking at his granddaughter's corpse.

Even though being convicted of premarital sex is grounds for severe punishment by authorities and family members, many of the young women I spoke with were comfortable with the idea of having sex before marriage. When I asked them how they came to consider premarital sex acceptable, they noted that although their parents might be upset if they discovered their daughter having premarital sex, in all likelihood it would not lead to harsh punishment. Furthermore, they pointed to evidence that the parents of many of their peers had turned a blind eye to their children engaging in premarital sex and adopted a "don't ask, don't tell" policy.

Although young women do need to worry to some extent about harsh punishment from parents or authorities, they seem more concerned with how they will be perceived by potential partners if they are no longer virgins. Although some of my female informants indicated that they are increasingly comfortable with the idea of not being virgins at marriage, several of the young men said that although it was not a necessity, they preferred to marry a virgin. This paradox puts many of the young women in a difficult position, especially in light of the increasing social pressures on dating and because the age of marriage is slowly rising (unofficial estimates put the average age today for men at thirty and for women at 26).[4] On the one hand, these women want to be active members of their peer group, to date and participate in the changing sexual culture. On the other hand, there is a lot at stake for them. If they lose their virginity, they are no longer considered good candidates for marriage, they could become estranged from their parents and family, and they could remain single. For some of the young women, losing their virginity also means losing face with their parents, but not engaging in sexual behavior means losing face with their female friends. These concerns have led to the formation of a group of women who I call the "everything but" women, drawing on a name given in the United States in the 1980s to women who were willing to engage in all forms of sexual behavior except vaginal penetration. Some of the young women I interviewed did choose to receive hymen reconstructions (a surgical procedure in which the hymen is sewn closed; it is illegal but occurs widely in Tehran) while some remained "technically" virgins. Hymen restoration is one of the oldest and most widespread medical practices in Iran. There are even old, prerevolutionary jokes about the need for women to get zippers installed because they were demanding multiple rounds of these procedures. Regardless of which road they take, virginity issues are a major concern for young women and men alike (and have been for many years, although, as I have said, this is beginning to change), and premarital sex was the topic of much discussion among my informants.

"What's important is that women keep their integrity—not necessarily their virginity, but their *shakhsiyat* [personhood]," said Hooman. "They have a lot more at stake than we do," he concluded. Many young men realize that the young women are in difficult situations, and they are unsure of their own stance on virginity. Some of them had been raised to think they were supposed to marry virgins, but spending time with their peers had changed these ideas to a certain extent. "To me, I don't mind if my wife isn't a virgin," added Hooman. "As long as she hasn't slept with all of my friends, it's OK." This seemed to be a good compromise for Hooman, and for many of the other young men as well. His cousin, Ali, echoed Hooman's sentiments. "Of the women I've been with, most of them—in fact, none of them have been virgins, and it's OK." When I asked him how important it was for him to marry a virgin, he responded that it was not a requirement at all. "I don't mind if my wife isn't a virgin. I don't think you can even find any real virgins in Tehran anymore!" he joked. "No, but seriously, as long as she hasn't been with everyone I know, it's OK," he added quickly.

Sharare, a twenty-five-year-old English teacher, also indicated that she believes most of the young women in urban areas are no longer virgins. She said that those who claim they are have either received hymen reconstruction or have engaged in nonvaginal forms of sexual relations, which to her meant they were no longer virgins. "I'm telling you, here in this oh so religious country, 99 percent of the women are having sexual relations before marriage," she began. "And it's really intense because we are still in a country where virginity is an important thing, a main issue. So the kids might be rebelling against this tradition or something, but virginity is still held in high esteem, so people are going to have to get operations until everyone accepts what's going on." When I asked her about these operations, she responded, "Hymen reconstructions. But even this is problematic, and I'll tell you why. Me and my sister both have experience with this. The places you go to get it done, if you aren't rich, which we aren't, are these strange health houses or nurse houses. And there it's not even a doctor that performs it but a nurse, a regular nurse who has maybe worked with doctors but is still a nurse. It's not healthy, really. And you know it has resulted in people doing these things in secret more," she explained. As she painted a picture of the health houses, I was taken aback because the only women I knew who had undergone the procedure had gone to a gynecologist. Many members of the large population of young women who couldn't afford to see a doctor were not comfortable talking to me about their experiences with unwanted pregnancies and would change the topic. "It's not easy, this virginity thing," Sharare added, reading the concern on my face. "That's why women have gotten creative, you see? So a big thing here is doing it from behind, how do you say it?" I explained the term *anal sex* in English. "Right, 'anal sex.' They do a lot of that, and at young ages. For them it's a way to keep their virginity intact, but I think they are just making fools of themselves ," she added.

Some of the women I spoke with were still grappling with questions about their own virginity. It seemed that although the tone of discussion about sexuality and dating had changed, many young women are still concerned about the social and reputational implications of premarital sex. This could be because the double standard for men and women has not been eliminated, and because although many parents now accept that their daughters may have boyfriends, they still have not completely accepted premarital sex. Many young women believe that premarital sex is acceptable but wonder if it will ruin their chances of marriage (this was not a concern for women who indicated a desire to remain single).

Nina, one of my key informants, who was introduced in Chapter 2, often became sad and frustrated when we talked about premarital sex. She went back and forth on the issue, and told me it was never really resolved in her mind. "You never know who to believe in this country," she would complain. "I don't know, are we supposed to be virgins like they say?" she asked, referring to the members of the regime, the morality police, and her teachers. "But since when did anything *they* say make sense? Since when did any of their rules have our happiness in mind?" she lamented one day as we walked through the park. "But at the same time we kinda have to be virgins if we don't want to let our parents down and we want to get married. But on the other hand, the psychologists tell us it's good to have had a few experiences before marriage! What am I supposed to do?" Nina always looked sad when discussing this subject, and it tormented her greatly. "Like my boyfriend," she began again. "We haven't had sex, because I'm not sure I'm going to marry him; but he confuses me, and my guy friends confuse me more." I often tried to console her on this issue, but it didn't always help. "I don't know, because the guys say on the one hand they want a girl who is untouched by others, but on the other hand they want a girl who is sexually experienced, so what am I supposed to do?" she persisted. I tried to explain to her that the double standard—or the virgin/whore dichotomy—she was referring to was an issue in many parts of the world. She took no consolation in this and kept insisting that women in Iran had more at stake. My friend Mahnaz, a twenty-five-year-old aspiring dance teacher, echoed Nina's sentiments as we were discussing virginity one afternoon after our weekly dance class. "I just don't understand: are women supposed to be virgins and not have a lot of sex, or are we supposed to be readily available to our men?" she asked. Two of the other women in the class added their thoughts as well. "One must maintain their virginity, well, technical virginity anyways, in order to keep people from gossiping," said Souri, a twenty-four-year-old computer technician. "You don't know how it is here in Iran, Pardis," she told me. "People talk, and you don't want them talking about you like that. If you aren't a virgin they think you're a slut, and that ruins your chances at marriage. Be careful, my friend," she cautioned, referring to ways in which talk of virginity was still bound up with ideals about marriage.

Asana nodded at Souri's statements. "Remember what I told you?" she reminded me. "Souri agrees with me." I remembered the conversation Asana and her friend Saara and I had had about virginity. Both of them were "everything but" women, and I recalled my frustration at their frustration. "In terms of sex, well, you know in the Islamic Republic there is very little we can or are supposed to do here," Asana had begun that afternoon as we finished off a king-sized pack of peanut M&M's my mother had sent to me from the United States. "Back when I was young it was even worse, but still, that didn't deter us. In fact, well, you know that I was definitely *chaytoon* [mischievous]. But even with all the obstacles and all the stuff they were filling our heads with, I managed to have sexual relations with three guys during my teenage years. But I was careful. I only let them go halfway in, or between my thighs. I'm still technically a virgin," she had told me a few months earlier. That same afternoon, Saara had jumped into the discussion, pointing out that not being a virgin decreased chances of marriage. "Oh sure, you can have sex with him, if you want," she explained, both to Asana and myself, referring to Asana's dilemma about whether to sleep with her most recent boyfriend. "But in the end he's not gonna propose to you, and you are not going to be the one he is going to marry. It's bad because we can't be open with our boyfriends, especially if they are ones we want to marry. We just have to keep reassuring them that yes, you are my first, you are the first boyfriend I've had. It's not ideal, but he won't marry you if he doesn't think he's your first." She seemed angry and confused. "But he will have anal sex with you and all that. But as long as you are a virgin. I don't get it either, myself," she added, shaking her head. Five other young women who were also students at Azad University echoed Asana and Saara's sentiments and frustrations during various conversations and interviews.

Nazanin, the young photographer introduced in Chapter 3, shared Saara's aggravation. She had been engaged to a man she loved, but because she wasn't sure the marriage would happen, she had decided not to have "full penetrative" intercourse with him. "Let me tell you, Pardis, it's still really important in Iran to be a virgin," she explained. "Very important. Like that guy I told you about, my fiancé; that's why I didn't have full intercourse with him, because I wasn't sure we would marry. And here, if you want to get married and you aren't a virgin, then it becomes a real problem. That's why I had to be careful," she explained. Nazanin was one of the first of my informants to talk so candidly about virginity. I was delighted and asked her to continue. "It's very important to be a virgin, and those who aren't, well, they go and get surgery before marriage. A lot of people in our culture are really sensitive about this issue. And it's tough here, because you have a lot of young people, and they aren't doing that much else, you know? And some, well, not all can get married easily all the time, because getting married isn't so easy any more, because boys don't have enough money to support a wife, so the women go and do what they can do and then go for the surgery later." Nazanin was referring to the potential marriage crisis in Iran due to the rise in the average age of marriage, and to young men delaying marriage because, as they report, they cannot afford it.

Nazanin did not marry her fiancé at that time, but she did marry later. When her current husband asked if she had ever been with another man, although she considered that she had "been with" her former fiancé, she lied and told her current husband he was her first partner in every way. Eleven of the young women I spoke with were nervous about these lies and asked if I knew of a way they could check to make sure their hymens were intact. Other than referring them to some of the nicer gynecologists I knew, I didn't have much advice for them.

Naghmeh, a twenty-five-year-old beautician, told me she too had lied to her husband. Like many of her friends, she believed this lie was necessary for the overall health and well-being of the relationship. "Does he know you weren't a virgin before marriage?" I had asked her when she revealed to me that she had undergone the hymen reconstruction. "No, we just don't talk about it. Like a lot of my friends, we have adopted a 'don't ask, don't tell' policy. But he knows I'm a good girl," she said, smiling, meaning that she was faithful to her husband. Many women felt that as long as they were faithful to their husbands, their past was not a real issue, and honesty about previous partners was unnecessary. When I asked her husband one evening if his wife had been a virgin at marriage, he responded, "*maaloome*" (of course).

Many of the young men I spoke with indicated they knew they were being lied to when women told them stories of their virginity. Several young men swore they could tell when the girl had undergone a hymen reconstruction and was not a "natural virgin." Many of the young men indicated they understood that the women were under significantly more pressure than the men to remain virgins, and that they had a lot more at stake, but they resented being lied to. As blogger Gypsy once told me, "Women are supposed to be virgins, but of course they aren't. But it's because they are supposed to be that they aren't. I know that. But it's funny, you know? Whenever I go with a girl, she says to me, 'You know, I am a virgin, but because I am really flexible and stretch a lot, I won't bleed when we first have sex.' How funny is that? I'm always like, yeah, right!" he said laughing. When I asked him if women often told him this story, he chuckled again and responded:

Yeah, and they think we buy it too! I mean it's like at my school 90 percent of the women are "flexible" and don't have intact hymens because they stretch or fall or something. But me and my friends, we looked it up once and in a book we found it said that in one thousand women only one might be in that special case where the hymen accidentally broke some other way. But why is it that all the women we meet have that special case? Do they think we are dumb? But we play the game, 'cause it isn't that big of a deal for us.

Although Gypsy and his friends said they knew that a lot of women fabricated stories about their virginity, they emphasized that it wasn't that the women weren't virgins that bothered them, it was the lying, which later caused further distrust. It seems that in recent years men have accepted that women may have had one or two partners before marriage (and this is increasingly accepted as fewer and fewer girls remained virgins), but they cannot accept being lied to. "It's like, if you start your relationship with lies like that, where are you going to go from there?" asked Amir M., a twenty-five-year-old property salesman. "I used to have women tell me, oh, it's because I ride horses that my hymen is broken. But the truth is, my fiancée has been riding horses her whole life, and all that resulted in was her hymen being tighter and bigger, almost like a muscle. It was so hard for us to break that thing, it killed us to get rid of her virginity," he said, gritting his teeth for effect. When I interviewed his fiancée a few weeks later, she told me her first sexual intercourse experience with Amir M. had been very painful. When I asked her if she thought her hymen was tighter because she rode horses and if that was the reason it had been so painful the first time, she shook her head. "It's because I was foolish and waited so long. I didn't want to have sex before marriage, so I waited until my boyfriend and I were engaged before letting him have sex with me, and now I kinda regret it, 'cause I wish I had had other experiences before him."

Amir M. emphasized repeatedly and proudly that he was his fiancée's first partner. Although many of the men I interviewed indicated they didn't care whether their wife was a virgin or not, some of the men said that nonvirgins made fine girlfriends but when it came time for marriage, they preferred an "untouched" girl. "I know it's kind of backward to think this way, but I guess I do prefer that I be my wife's first sexual partner," Amir Ali admitted to me. "I don't know, maybe because I'm also kind of inexperienced, but I just think that is right, to save yourself for marriage." He often noted that he, like his sister Nina, was torn in his view of premarital sex, but he was now engaged to a virgin and was delighted that he would be her first partner. Another young man, who chose to remain anonymous, once told me a rather chilling story about the importance of virginity to him. He said he had had many girlfriends in his youth, and then one day he met a woman who "captured his heart," as he said, and he immediately fell in love with her. Soon after they got engaged and did the official marriage ceremony (the *aghd*, whereby the couple is legally married under Islamic law) but prior to the wedding day, they decided to have sex. She had told him she was a virgin and swore on the Koran, knowing how important it was to him that she be a virgin. When they had sex that evening, several days before the big wedding, she did not bleed. The young man said he was devastated and outraged, and he accused the young girl of lying to him. "I told her she was a prostitute and that she had been lying to me all along," he began. "I even told her I didn't want to marry her. She begged me, of course, said she wasn't lying, swore she was a virgin, but I wasn't having any of that." As the young man was telling me this story his eyes filled with tears. "I was so angry with her, I told her the wedding was off and that I wanted our aghd to be annulled. I, I, well, I know I was being stupid and irrational, but I was upset." He took a deep breath before continuing. "Two days later she set herself on fire and burned herself to death. In her suicide note she told me she loved me and that I had been the only one who, who—." He stopped midsentence to sob. As he wiped away his tears, I told him he didn't need to continue, but he did anyway. "She said I was the only man she'd ever been with and that she took our love to the grave. Later I found out that women don't always bleed when they lose their virginity." At this point he stopped and looked at me. He took a deep breath and a gulp of tea. "I was so stupid. Now I've lost the only girl I've ever loved. Now I don't even care if she really was or was not a virgin. I loved her, that's all that mattered."

Attitudes toward virginity are changing to accommodate the changes in sexual and social relations being enacted by the youth. As increasing numbers of young people across religious and class lines have entered into relationships, the idea of premarital sex has become more acceptable. Additionally, as young people have become part of a globalizing youth culture through exposure to the Internet, to satellite television, and to Iranians in the diaspora, attitudes toward mandatory virginity before marriage have continued to soften. Many young men and women indicated to me that virginity is no longer a major issue among young people, but some parents and "traditional" young people still value virginity for women. However, as parents become more accepting of their sons' and daughters' dating habits, and as more traditional youth find themselves in relationships, this attitude will continue to shift gradually. It may not ever be completely acceptable not to be a virgin, but in the last seven years I have witnessed a softening of views on this issue as a result of the young adult sexual revolution. Some women feel they must still uphold traditional norms that mandate their virginity; however, many young men are becoming comfortable with the idea of marrying nonvirgins. It remains to be seen how this conversation will evolve.

Till Death Do Us Part?

The theme of marriage and sexual relations inside and outside of marriage was a recurring one in my conversations with young Iranians, particularly among my female informants. Of the women I interviewed, thirteen were married, four were engaged, and several saw themselves on the route toward marriage with their current boyfriends. It seemed that for many of these women, marriage was seen as a goal or necessity and a way to achieve social status. In fact, during my time in Iran, older women with whom I interacted impressed upon me repeatedly the need for me to marry soon because I was fast approaching thirty, and past thirty my prospects for marriage would decrease significantly, I was told. Cultural pressures to marry, and to marry well, are significant, and important factors in considering women's desire to find and attention to finding a husband. Some of the young women I spoke with, particularly those who were not yet married, viewed marriage as a ticket to freedom, as gaining them reprieve from their families, and as a free and safe space in which to have sex. However, much of this discussion was tied to the issue of appropriate marital partners. Many of the women and some of the men emphasized the importance of finding a partner of the same background. Sex both inside and before marriage was discussed frequently by the married women I interviewed. Questions about conjugal debt, extramarital sex, and the importance of emotional fidelity were among the subjects these women brought up when discussing their marriages.

Regardless of whether they were married or single, the issue of marriage and of sex within marriage was an important one for virtually all of the women with whom I spoke. Although they enjoyed their experiments in both heterosexuality and homosexuality prior to marriage, and in some cases after marriage,[5] they still took the task of getting married, and of marrying well, very seriously. All skills had to be honed, and one had always to be prepared physically (by being coiffed at all times) and mentally for the prospect of a good catch. Marriage was among some single women's favorite topics, and their ultimate goal. Women repeatedly reminded me that marrying well and wanting to have a family were not at odds with their involvement in the sexual revolution, or opposed to movements toward more rights for women. "We are feminists, yes, but that is not at odds with wanting to be a good wife and have a good family," Asana would often remind me. It was clear that marriage was a goal for many of these women, but this goal did not conflict with their political or social activism, nor was it a reason to shy away from participation in the sexual revolution. "We can be many things at once," said Mojdeh, the twenty-five-year-old factory manager, repeatedly. "A participant in the sexual revolution, a feminist, a wife, and an activist all at once," she emphasized.

I can speak from personal experience that attitudes privileging traditional marriage and the family are alive and well in Iranian families, and among Iranian women in Tehran. One afternoon while I was hanging out at one of the usual beauty salons in Tehran where I spent time observing and talking, one of the ladies asked me to come to the back room. She smiled and asked if I wanted my legs waxed. I hadn't realized they needed waxing, but in an effort to appease her I permitted her to do so. Suddenly she started laughing. "What is so funny? Why are you laughing?" I asked. She pointed to the hair on my legs. "Without waxing all of that, how can you hope to catch a husband, huh?" she asked. I looked at her, utterly confused on so many levels by what she had just said. "You must marry soon," she told me. "Your time is running out. If you wax all of this you will feel more sexy, so you will be more sexy. That's how you'll catch your man," she explained. I was dumbfounded. I decided I didn't want any waxing at all, pulled on my pants, and walked back to the front room. "I didn't mean to upset you," she said, following me out to where ladies were seated from wall to wall. "It's just that, well, we all think you should be married by now. Maybe if you were married you wouldn't just sit here and stare at us all day," she announced loudly so that she caught the attention of several of the other customers. One of them started to scrutinize me. "I know why she's not married," she announced to the woman who had been shouting at me. "Look at that nose!" she said, pointing at my profile. I didn't know what to do with this. When I got home I called my friend Laleh. She too had frequently given me the "Why aren't you married?" speech, so I thought she would be pleased to hear about this. To my delightful surprise, she was empathetic. "You know they don't mean any harm, darling," she began, trying to calm me down. "It's just that they are concerned for you. They think they are helping you by telling you all of this. They really do." I was so frustrated. I couldn't understand how insulting me was supposed to indicate compassion and sensitivity. "It's just that they can't imagine you are happy without a man in this society, because it's just so hard here to get by without one. Not just in terms of money, but status and society too," she told me. "Also, some of those women might be threatened by you. They can't understand why you, who seemingly have it all, aren't married. This confuses them, scares them, and makes them question themselves," she said. I took a deep breath. "When I first met you, I felt the same way," she continued. "But then I got to know you and realized that in your world you can be complete all on your own. And to tell you the truth, I envy that," she added warmly.

During my last visit to Tehran in 2007, however, I met fifteen young women who told me they never wanted to get married. Also, friends and family members stopped harassing me about when I was "finally" going to get married, and I was even told "good for you" when I told shopkeepers, beauticians, and other acquaintances that I wasn't married. Although I am not able to judge how much of a shift in society-wide attitudes this indicates, the fact that some people were not seeing marriage as necessary was an indicator of some cultural change, which three of my informants attributed to the sexual revolution.

Although for some women marriage had become less of a priority, for others it was still a necessity. Nassim, who had just gotten married, wanted to talk about nothing other than the fact that she had just attained her goal of marriage. She too was confused by me and could not understand why I didn't share her excitement. "I'm so thankful, thank God, I'm married now," she told me the afternoon I interviewed her. "I was getting a bit older, but thank God I did it, and married well; look at him," she said gesturing toward her husband, who was now doing cannonballs into the pool. "I'm so lucky," she said, looking longingly out across the courtyard. She looked at me as though expecting some kind of enthusiasm on my end or a pat on the back, which never came.

"If you ask me, that is a big risk. You asked about risk before. The biggest risk in life, the worst thing that could happen to you, is if you don't get married," she began, tossing back her bottle-blonde hair. "I always say that marriage is the biggest and most important decision you make in your life. It's the best thing ever. Thank God I'm married now. You want to see my ring?" she asked, flashing a smile.

Setareh, my anthropologist colleague from Tehran University, often commented on this idea of marriage as a goal for young women and lamented that Iranian society had placed such a high value on marriage. "All women want to do is spend their time looking good to try to catch a husband; that is their main goal," she explained. "If they are already married, then their life's goal becomes to serve their husband better. I mean, not everyone, but a lot of women," she would often tell me. Setareh agreed with the observation that young people are seemingly engaged in a different kind of social movement, and that their obsession with fashion and how they look has deeper undertones in some cases. She also recognized the cultural shift that is under way and enabling many young people to have partners and engage in social and sexual activities before marriage. This is a social phenomenon that did not exist when she was their age, a mere ten years ago. She would add, however, that the obsession with marriage frustrated her. She believed that women should, and sometimes do, look good for themselves, and that they should focus on their own lives more than being preoccupied with marriage. Several of my other informants expressed similar sentiments.

Many of the young women I spoke with who were not yet married saw marriage as both a "way out" and a "way in." Marriage is seen as a way out of their families, away from their oppressive parents and brothers, a legitimate escape from the home. It was at the same time seen as a way into a certain status as an adult, an indicator of maturity, as well as a way into certain social groups or classes and a way to be seen as mature and respected by older women. My married informants agreed that being married has helped them attain new levels of freedom and social status, but they noted that this had come at a cost—a secret they were hesitant to share with their unmarried female friends. There is a perceivable discrepancy in this attitude toward marriage in that married women are often unhappy yet marriage remains desirable for young women. Although they are unhappy, married women often have access to parts of the social sphere that they did not have before marriage. For the unmarried women, marriage is still a goal and represents an ideal that holds the promise of perhaps bettering their lives, because it brings them freedom, although at the price of unhappiness with their partner and feelings of conjugal debt.

"You know what I've been thinking a lot, Pardis?" asked Saara one afternoon as we sat lazily in my living room eating yet another bag of M&M's I had brought from the United States. "Tell me," I responded. She answered, "I think to myself, what if I just go with a guy that I don't like that much, marry him, and then get a divorce, you know?" I didn't quite understand what she meant and was busily writing notes to myself when Asana chimed in. "Well, I used to think I should wait and marry for love, but my family is driving me crazy!" she said, taking a fistful of candy. "At least if I get married, and then perhaps divorced, I will be in control of my own affairs, not them. I will have control of my own life, and after I'm married I can go and do whatever I want," she said. Saara smiled and decided to add her perspective. "Plus," she began, "that way we can legitimately get rid of this virginity and do what we want once we are married women," she said, alluding to the fact that many of her married friends were having extramarital affairs. Asana nodded and then continued sharing her own thoughts about her family. "In a way, I really want to divorce my dad, and this seems to be the only way of doing that," she said, realizing this almost as she was saying it. "And if I have my own income [Asana was planning to be a school teacher], I'll do just fine, be married, send my husband to work abroad, away from me, and live on my own, 'cause that's somewhat more acceptable," Asana finished determinedly.

This was not the last time Asana made comments about wanting to get married to get away from her father. The following summer when I saw her, she was seriously dating a young man she described as less than perfect, but she added that he would do the job fine because she could no longer handle the strict rules her father imposed on her. "I just want to get married to get out of my father's house," she reiterated. "I don't care if my husband is less than ideal; it's worth it." For Asana, Saara, and several other women with whom I spoke, marriage represented a legitimate way for them to leave their parents' homes. It also earned them a certain level of maturity in their parents' eyes. Many commented that their relationship with their parents improved drastically after marriage, because they felt more respect coming from their mothers and fathers.

Several of the young women I spoke with noted that being married was a status symbol that earned respect not just from parents and family members but also from friends, and even from professors and teachers. "At our school, people who have boyfriends or aren't married like me have to be a lot more careful," explained twenty-one-year-old Shahrzad. "Professors are more lenient with the married women, and they, the married ones, are such troublemakers! Oooh! Watch out! They go more with different boyfriends than us, and they get away with it!" she exclaimed. Shahrzad noted that as a single woman she had to be much more careful than married women did about her appearance and her actions, especially at school, because they could easily be misconstrued by her teachers and peers, who would tell on her "at the drop of a hat." She looked forward to the day she would be married so that she could relax and not worry about harassment from teachers and relatives about when she was finally going to get married. Shahrzad's sister, Sanam, took this idea of marriage as freedom one step further, noting that "married women can get away with taking risks more than we single women can." When I asked her what she meant, she responded:

Like a married woman can go out and try to pick men up at two o'clock in the morning and no one will say anything. She is a *zan-e-shohardar* (woman with a husband); she can do anything, get away with anything. If they stop her, she can say, I was out buying something for my husband. Or the husband himself will come to her defense to keep his pride intact. But us, we can't even go for ice cream at two o'clock in the afternoon with our girlfriends without getting harassment from them. It's just not fair.

More than a dozen other young women agreed with Sanam's assessment that marriage is a shield against punishment from parents and the morality police. I myself witnessed this protection mechanism when I would tell members of the morality police that I was married and watch their reaction to me change. Instead of continuing to harass me, they would tell me to call my husband or go be with him, or they would threaten to call him themselves and tell on me. (Of course he was a fabrication.) When I would play the game of begging them not to tell my husband, they would tell me to learn to be a good wife and then send me home. Before I began pretending that I was married, however, I would be harassed for up to half an hour by the komite before they would let me go. On another occasion I lied about being married to see if it would help me purchase some books at a crowded bookstore. At first I kept trying to get the salesman's attention, asking if he had a certain book. He ignored me. When I went up to him and told him I was buying the book for my husband, his tone changed completely. He said he was so impressed that I was coming to buy books for my husband, and he became incredibly helpful, assisting me in choosing several books and then giving me a free bookmark at the end. Although it is possible that these are coincidences, they did help me to see the point of view of many of my informants.

While Sanam pointed to her married friends and talked of the freedoms they had earned from their parents, Nassim noted that her husband provided protection for her at parties when they were threatened by the komite. She indicated that the morality police believed a married woman at a party was not a threat if her husband was there to "watch over her" and "police her." "Marriage is so much more than sex and companionship," she began. "Marriage is also protection, and it earns you a lot of respect in a lot of people's eyes." Here Nassim was alluding to the notion of marriage bringing respect that so many of my informants mentioned: in Iran a single woman is a threat, but a woman with a male owner (her husband) is much less threatening and thus more acceptable. "Plus, if the komite catch us at a party, it's all good if you are married; they aren't going to bother you. You are better off than if you are single; you aren't so much of a threat," she explained. She then stopped a moment to light her cigarette before adding, "Especially if you are there with your husband, there is very little the komite can do to you if your man is there to protect you. Plus, they will leave you alone and go after the singles; that's just the way it is." Although I was not able to corroborate her statement, because it seemed that everyone at parties was being arrested, I understood her point about the status of married women.

A factor that contributes to making marriage a way into certain social circles and earns a lot of young women respect is the suitability of their marital partner. Finding what they call a "good" husband is almost as important as marriage itself. Parents emphasize that marrying well is vital for the family's image and for the child's image, and it can be a worthwhile investment.[6] For this reason, they suggest certain young men for their daughters to date (and young women for their sons to date) in the hope that they will enjoy each other's company and choose to marry. Although the official practice of arranged marriage has dwindled significantly in urban Tehran in the last decade, parents are still not shy about indicating the importance of their role in finding suitable partners for their children. Many of the young people I spoke with had accepted these notions and were seeking partners that would fit the suitability criteria outlined by their parents.

"Well, I wanted to get married right," Naghmeh told me. "So I knew I had to choose a man, and a good one, you know? My mother had taught me right. So I did. I chose a good one, and got married. I'm very lucky," she added, opening her pocketbook to fish out a few pictures of her husband and children. Although her marriage was not arranged, she had relied heavily on the opinions of her parents as to whether this man was a suitable partner.

Many of the young men I spoke with were aware that young women looked at them with this unspoken suitability list in mind. "We know," began Mahmood. "We aren't stupid. We know they are looking for certain material things. They want guys of a certain class. It's hard, but *na khodagah* [without knowing], you go with people in your range, that's what you do." Mahmood's friend Hooman echoed his sentiments:

The same way that guys look at women's bodies and their sexiness, women are interested in a guy's power, in his economic situation, his potential, his status. That's what is important for a girl. That's why sometimes you see beautiful women with ugly men—probably because the guy is either rich or powerful, and almost certainly comes from a good family. Especially Iranian women, these are things they look at and look for. Because in Iran our culture tells them this.

Hooman's friend Hossein also noted that the economic situation after the revolution was partly to blame for young women's overemphasis on finding wealthy husbands. "Since it's kinda like Iran has become a poor country, now the women look to, like it's not about, well, it's less about *ghiyafe va tip* [looks and your type] and more about what car you drive, what clothes you wear, where you live. That's what makes you a good marriage candidate, if you're a guy," Hossein explained. After speaking with these guys, I began paying close attention to young women's eyes as they interacted with men they were meeting for the first time. Because many of my male informants had told me repeatedly that women look at men's watches, necklaces, and the keys in their hands to discern the make of the car they drove, I watched to see if this was true. Sure enough, when I spent time at coffee shops, restaurants, and parks where young people met each other, the young women's eyes would dart to the men's wrists and hands. They also looked at men's clothes, sunglasses, and pocketbooks to determine their suitability for interaction and perhaps marriage.

Although many of the men found it frustrating that women judged them on the basis of their socioeconomic status, one young man revealed that he too looked for these things when choosing a wife. "If you want to get a wife, or if you want to start a family, your wife has to be a woman whose parents are known, who you know, whose parents are on the same level, if not higher than yours." He emphasized the last part of this sentence. "This is very important, so of course I look for a *dokhtar-e-pooldar* [rich girl]. It's like that over here. Yeah, you have to go through this," he admitted, both to himself and to me.

Having *gereftan* (gotten), as they would say, a good marital partner ensures respect and admiration from peers. I remember one afternoon when a group of my female informants was discussing one of their girlfriends who was absent. She had just married, or "gotten," one of the superstars of Iran's soccer team, and everyone was admiring her skills in conquering him. "Mona played her cards exactly right with the soccer star," began Laleh. "Yeah, he's a tough one to land, and she did it with grace and style," added Danielle, a twenty-five-year-old homemaker and mother of two. "But how did she do it? I'm so impressed," said Shakila, one of the younger, unmarried members of the group. "Simple: she played well. She slept with everyone in this town except him, wouldn't sleep with him till he proposed, lied about being a virgin, and played hard to get," Laleh answered. "I'm green with envy, but if she played her game well, then I guess I just have to admire her," Danielle added. These women gave a tremendous amount of credit to their friend and the strategies she used to win a highly desirable husband. Although they were jealous of her, they found themselves respecting her for her skills.

As discussed in Chapter 2, in Iran, sighe, or temporary marriage (also called *mut'a*), is a form of contract, generally private and verbal, between a man and a woman. The man in the relationship may be married or unmarried, but the woman is single. She may be divorced, widowed, or a virgin (although for the first temporary marriage some clerics say that a virgin needs the consent of her father to enter into such a contract). The contract binds the two in a marriage-like relationship for a period ranging from one hour to ninety-nine years. The woman receives some kind of bride price and financial support from the male for the duration of the contract. Under certain legal and financial conditions, an Iranian man is permitted to marry four women permanently and simultaneously. Temporary marriages, although they can become permanent, are allowed without regard to the number of legally recognized wives a man may have already wed. A man can also make several temporary contracts at once (with up to ninety-nine temporary wives), but a woman is not permitted to marry simultaneously more than one man, either temporarily or permanently. At the end of the mutually agreed-upon period, no divorce ceremony is required for the couple to part. After dissolution, the woman must uphold a period of abstinence (forty-five days) to ensure the identity of the father of any children conceived during the sighe period. Theoretically, children born from these marriages are equal to those of *nikah* (permanent) marriages, the objective of which is procreation as opposed to the objective of temporary marriage, which is sexual enjoyment.

Temporary marriage is a highly debated practice in Iran, and different groups give different connotations to and have different perceptions of it. Many women in temporary marriages are young divorced women from lower-class backgrounds or occasionally middle-class women. Women who are or have been in temporary marriages reduce their chances of permanent marriage for several reasons: the objective of exchanging money for pleasure seems immoral to some people, so sighe may be perceived as similar to prostitution, which is inherently illicit; and the issue of virginity as ideal comes into play. Sighe was among various forms of marriage in pre-Islamic Arabia and is still accepted as a norm among many lower-class communities, but although the Islamist regime has attempted to revive the practice in present-day Iran, it is a marginal and stigmatized institution that is considered immoral, illicit, and out-of-date, particularly by middle- and upper-class women. Many citizens believe that temporary marriage defies and undermines the true meaning of the institution of marriage. The exchange of money (the bride price) offends many of Iran's modern urban middle-class women who have adopted the idea of "love" marriages.[7] Such payment is seen as degrading not only to the woman involved but to the relationship itself. A majority of the opposition argues that temporary marriage, whether religiously sanctioned or not, is merely a veiled form of promiscuity and a shameful cloak for illicit relationships. The idea that temporary marriage is a step toward modernization also strikes discord in Iran due to opposing views on modernization and on modernization as a form of Westernization.

The institution of sighe may have been always accepted and rarely questioned for lower-class women as a liberating way to express their sexuality, choose their partners, or get to know their selected husband before marriage. For educated, urban upper- and upper-middle-class women, sighe may be seen as a threat to family life, a creeping in of immoral values, and a male prerogative. A topic of heated debate among the entire population, temporary marriage is technically a religious and legally accepted practice, and touted as a social "solution" in modern-day Iran.

Throughout my time in Iran I was surprised that more young adults did not engage in sighe or temporary marriage. The primary reasons told to me for *not* engaging in sighe were that even though it permitted young people to date more easily, travel on trains and buses, and so on were that (1) sighe has in recent years become associated with legalized prostitution and thus is seen as a "bad" thing to do, and (2) women who have never been married are required to obtain their father's permission for their first sighe (in fact, some say he must testify that his daughter is a virgin, whether the marriage is temporary or permanent). Therefore, even though sighe was used in the years immediately after the revolution as a cover for dating so that members of the opposite sex could socialize with each other more easily, today it is generally frowned upon, as it was by most of the young people with whom I spoke, as well as by their parents. Also, many of my informants added that because the social environment had shifted to the extent that they are now more able to get away with traveling and socializing with their partners (a testament to how things are indeed changing), sighe is no longer as necessary as it was in previous years, and thus was not worth ruining their reputations for.

THE TWO ISSUES DISCUSSED MOST among my married female informants were conjugal debt and the utilizing of sex to negotiate with their husbands or to procure material items, and fidelity—or more often infidelity. Of the thirteen married women I interviewed, all but one repeatedly talked about this notion of conjugal debt, and seven out of thirteen of them admitted to carrying on some form of extramarital affair.[8] Most of them indicated that they were unhappily married and no longer enjoyed their husband's company; however, none of them indicated that they were ready or willing to file for a divorce.

It seemed that many of these women, although they utilized sex to achieve what they wanted from their husbands, were sexually unsatisfied by them and engaged in sexual relations with them reluctantly and mostly as a negotiating tool. "Yes, it's true, my husband makes me want to vomit," said Laleh, making a wrenching gagging sound and pretending to stick her finger in her throat. "But I am a woman who wants to be comfortable. I want to *bokhor-o-bekhab* [sleep well and eat well],[9] so I give him sex and he supports me." She smiled. Another woman indicated that when she gave her husband sexual favors, their relationship was better and calmer, and she was able to live with him more peacefully. "I want to do good things for my husband, honestly," said Katayoun, a twenty-five-year-old homemaker. "It's hard though, but when I'm good to Jafar in bed, you should see him the next day; he is a different person. From the moment he wakes up he is totally different, and nice to me and buys me things. The relationship becomes tolerable."

Many of the women alluded to using sex as currency, though reluctantly, in order to win material items or sometimes more freedom from their husbands. "Because I know that Thursday night I want to go out with my girlfriends," recounted Danielle, "I'm going to give myself to my husband tonight so he'll let me go, and maybe if I'm really good he'll give me money to buy a new handbag!" She giggled hopefully. Mahnaz agreed with Danielle but noted that she often had to work harder than she wanted to in order to win this freedom. "I hate my husband, like I mean he absolutely disgusts me," she said, shuddering as she spoke. "But I'm ready to do whatever he wants, and sometimes I have to get wild, so that I can go out with my friends or, more often, with my boyfriend. But it's hard work, I'm telling you," she added. This notion of transactional sex within marriage is not new, nor unique to Iran, but having the women discuss it so candidly would not have been commonplace two decades ago.

Having a boyfriend or lover, or having the desire for one, was a common theme among the married women I interviewed. Only two of them identified themselves as "happy" in their marriages. In fact, during my time in Tehran I did not meet many happily married women at all. Many of these women were unhappy because they were not sexually attracted to their husbands and thus were sexually unfulfilled. "It's like a closed factory between me and my husband," Danielle told me one day, scooping up her six-month-old daughter. "It's a wonder this one was ever born. I think that's the last time we had sex," she added, kissing her baby and then handing her to me. "But I can't, I just can't have sex with my husband. It doesn't work and we can't talk about it." When I asked her why, she responded that she wasn't attracted to him, and added that he wasn't good in bed. "I didn't know that he wasn't good in bed because, believe it or not, he was the first man I slept with," she said. I was surprised at this because Danielle seemed to have very progressive views on sexuality; the thought that she would remain a virgin until marriage was interesting to me. She must have read the surprise on my face because she responded, "Yes, the first *man* I slept with. I had been with women before him, but I was very young when I married. Just barely seventeen." When I asked her what she did to overcome the sexual barrier between her and her husband, she smiled and put a hand over her daughter's ears. "Well, he was the first, but then I caught up real fast. Now I have a few lovers! Thank God for them!"

Laleh also often boasted of her lovers and would venture to bring them to parties or dinner at her home when her husband was away. She repeatedly told me how much she hated her husband and how she preferred her female friends for intimacy and her male lovers for "good, raw sex." When one of her lovers started boring her, she decided to take on a new one. She took me on a date with a prospective man so I could watch the way affairs unfold in Iran. As we sat down to lunch that day, I got the distinct feeling of being a third wheel. "Nonsense," Laleh told me. "You are like my sister. Plus, this will be good for your book." As we walked into the restaurant, she told me she was nervous and excited. I noticed she was grinning from ear to ear and had added an extra layer of makeup to the usual three or four she usually had on. When we arrived, she spotted him sitting in a dark corner. We sat down. The conversation was limited and awkward; the two of them seemed to prefer simply exchanging coy glances. During appetizers, they asked each other about their respective marital statuses and family situations. When he left to go to the bathroom between courses, she assured me that, given his background and accessories, he was wealthy. She emphasized that he wore an Omega watch that was so new he must have purchased it from outside of Iran, which meant he had the means to travel. During the main course, they discussed geography. It turned out that his family (he had a wife and children) lived outside Tehran but he came into town for business during the week. He owned an apartment building in the city, among other things (he indicated he was a real estate mogul, which delighted Laleh) and used it as a place to bring "guests" while he was in town. By dessert they were flirting openly, and it seemed certain their affair would start shortly. "That was wonderful," Laleh said as we drove home after the meal. "So satisfying! I think he's going to be great in bed," she giggled.

Mahnaz also often talked about her extramarital affairs. She referred to her boyfriend as the real love of her life and the man who "should have been the father of my children." She told me in 2004 that she was in love with her current boyfriend and had been for two years. When I visited her in the summer of 2005, she had just broken up with this man, who was also married, because it was adversely affecting her marriage. "I would go to sleep thinking about him and wake up thinking only of him. Every day, every night, all my thoughts were with him. It was terrible, but also wonderful. I loved him so much," she said longingly. "He was so hot, so good to me in bed. Without him I would never be able to have orgasms with another person," she added, fanning herself. She took a deep breath before continuing. "Now I'm done with those kinds of affairs. Now I want someone who can satisfy me physically, but I don't want to fall in love with him. Love is hard and it messes up your family, I don't want that. I can't understand it, but why don't I feel it for my husband? I don't know. I love you more than my husband, that's for sure," she said throwing her arms around me and resting her head on my shoulder.

Mojdeh too described her intense feelings for a lover she had taken and how it had disrupted her life with her husband and daughters. She told me the whole story of her affair, blaming her husband for its beginning but blaming herself for the problems it had caused in her current family situation. "For many years I was unhappy with my husband. He made me feel sexually inferior and ugly," she began, taking a sip of coffee and leaning back in her chair. "Then, when our daughter was born sick, it was a heavy toll on our relationship. We started fighting and things were really bad. He told me I had gotten crazy and that I needed to seek help. He told me to go to a psychologist." She paused and smiled at me. "So I did. I went to a psychologist and started telling him about our problems. Well, the first few sessions I didn't really realize but he had started hitting on me, telling me I was beautiful and telling me he couldn't imagine how anyone wouldn't want to have sex with me—because, by the way, my husband didn't want to have sex with me for many years," she explained. She stopped again and thought for a moment before continuing:

Well, a few sessions later he approached me and sat close to me. He unbuttoned the top few buttons of his shirt. He was so hot. "Don't you want to touch me?" he asked me. And well, that's how it started. We started sleeping together and then fell in love. He became my love, my life, my everything. But it ruined me because I could no longer be a good wife or mother when all I thought about was him. I still love him, but now I need help, I need to find another therapist. I don't know what to do. I think I may have gone too deep.

It was very hard for Mojdeh to talk about her lover, and she did so only in private with me. Though some of her friends talked openly of their affairs, Mojdeh was very quiet about hers, and she did feel extreme remorse now but believes it was her husband's fault for driving her to this point in the first place.

Some of the women felt remorseful about their infidelities while others didn't. Most indicated dissatisfaction with their husbands, but not a single one of them ever said they wanted a divorce. For some it was because they felt financially bound to their husbands due to their lack of education and the employment situation for women in Iran. Others didn't want to face the social consequences of divorce, and still others felt that although they didn't love their husbands, being married was better than being divorced or single (because they received financial and social support from being married), and thus worth the headaches they had to put up with. Having female friends and a social and intimate outlet other than their husbands was a necessary lifeline for all of the married women I interviewed. Virtually all of them indicated that their friendships with their female friends were some of the most important parts of their lives, and they relied on interactions with other women to help them navigate their lives in an environment of distrust. Many women noted that they couldn't trust their parents, teachers, coworkers, or even their husbands. They emphasized repeatedly that their female friends were the only people who "understood" them and with whom they felt completely at ease.

"Cyber Cheating"

In a country where socializing between men and women is heavily regulated, Internet meeting and mating takes on new significance. Out of the young adults I interviewed, more than one-third indicated that they had at one time or another engaged in some sort of heterosexual relationship through the Internet.

For some of these young adults, the interaction took the form of a courtship in which the young man and woman met on a Web site such as Orkut and exchanged e-mails for a time before arranging a face-to-face encounter. At least five of the young people I interviewed noted that they had met their current boyfriend, girlfriend, husband, or wife through an online site. They recalled exchanging photographs and po-etry and engaging in instant messaging or "chatting" before meeting their partner for the first time. Many said that this form of encounter felt "safer" and allowed them to get to know their potential partners before taking the risk of being seen on a date with them. "Going on a date *is* risky in Iran. I know it's hard for you to conceptualize that, but for us it's a reality," said Gohar, a twenty-year-old university student. "By meeting the person online first and getting to know him that way, we can be sure that taking the risk of a first date will actually be worth it," she added. Several other young women expressed the same feeling about online dating.

Other young people described their use of the Internet to engage in safe cybersex. According to them, cybersex is safer than sex because it is easier not to get caught, because engaging in anonymous sexual exchange online does not involve being in the presence of a member of the opposite sex. "My parents don't let me go out that much," explained Roji, a 19 year old beautician. "But I still like to be a part of what my friends are doing, so I just do it online," she said, referring to her friends' engagement in sexual activities. "I love to chat online, and I love to have romantic encounters with boys on the Internet. Half of them probably send me wrong pictures, but I don't care. I just imagine what they look like while we are exchanging hot sentiments," she added. Young men said that cybersex was a socially safe way to learn about sex without the embarrassment of being in the physical presence of a woman. For some young people, socializing with members of the opposite sex is still a new experience, and many young men do not know how to interact with young women or how to court them. Thus the potential awkwardness of the first encounter is a source of extreme anxiety for many young men. "I love chatting online and having sexual relations with a cyber-girlfriend because I'm not as shy or awkward," described Shahram. "It's hard for me with women. I get shy and I don't know what to do with them, so this way I can work on my sexual style, my sexual courtship, before the real thing. Plus, this way my reputation stays intact. No one knows about my cybergirlfriend—not my parents or my friends—so no one can give me a hard time about it," he added quickly.

Still others (especially married women) with whom I spoke noted that the Internet provides a "safer" way of cheating on their husbands. Some women described cybersex as an outlet for their sexual frustrations.

Others said it was a way to pass the long hours of the days and weeks when their husbands were away. And many claimed that "cybercheating," as they called it, was not "real" cheating, because the anonymity of the Internet made it so that their husbands would never find out and that their cyberpartners would never find them or blackmail them.

In a society where gossip is rampant and reputations and respect are important, many people rely on the anonymity and privacy of the Internet, arguably the only sphere in which they can enjoy any privacy to facilitate what the regime and society view as "immoral" encounters. Because the regime seeks to legislate on people's bodies, on their sexualities, and on intimacy, and because they have the right to enter private homes at any time and arrest all "moral offenders," young people have delved deeply into the safer space of the Internet as a venue for seeking out intimacy.

Let's Talk About Sex

P: What is the meaning of sex to you?

H: When you go inside someone, and it takes place between two people. It's a, like a fling, but a very good fling. It's like that in the beginning, but later on it becomes more serious. That's what sex is. Yeah.

The punishment for premarital sex ranges from one hundred lashings to death by stoning, depending on the severity of the sexual crime and the nature of the interaction (homosexual encounters and adultery are punishable by death, although this is rarely enforced). As has been discussed, Iranian traditions also uphold the importance of virginity, specifically for women. It is for these reasons that I was surprised to find that a majority of my informants were having sex before marriage. The number of partners before marriage ranged from two to twelve for women and three to sixty-five for men. Women who were concerned with maintaining virginity elected to use oral and anal sex in addition to "outercourse" (heavy rubbing over clothing) and *laye payi* ("between thighs," whereby the man inserts his penis between the tightly squeezed thighs of his partner instead of going inside the vagina). Many of my informants described their sexual experiences as taking place in public venues (such as cars, parks, or abandoned warehouses) while others told stories about sexual encounters in private homes when parents and other family members were away.

Some of the young adults described their *first* sexual experiences quite vividly, and noted that they met these first sexual partners mostly in public areas such as in cars or on the street. Although some people expressed feelings of guilt that accompanied these first (usually premarital) sexual encounters, many (men and women alike) took pride in the loss of their virginity and emphasized that the pleasure they experienced far outweighed any personal guilt. One of my informants, Seppand, age twenty-two, decided to tell me, as we were driving around in his car, the whole story of how he lost his virginity one afternoon.

My first sexual intercourse was my first year of college. We, me and my friend, picked up two women in a car, his car. Hot women, really, and cool. So the women got in and then asked us to stop the car. There were actually three of us guys and the two women. Then the one girl said I should come in the backseat with her and pushed the other into the front seat. Once I was in the back seat, we started getting sexually involved while driving around. Then my other guy friend wanted to get into it too, so he did. Then the other guy and girl got into it. Lots of penises being pulled out. Then they gave us their numbers and we hung out a bit more, but not much.

Seppand was exhilarated just telling the story. He was glad to have finally gotten rid of his virginity at what he considered the late age of nineteen. He also didn't seem ashamed that it took place in a car or in front of his friends. When I asked him if he had worried that he may have gotten caught in the car, he responded, "Come on! Who do you think we are? We know what we are doing, we know the right roads to take. Plus, that's how it's done here: women get in your car with you. We can't exactly invite them home, you know."

Another young woman, Nanaz, twenty-three, described her first sexual experience, which was quite similar to that of seven other young women I spoke with. Nanaz said that her first sexual partner was a man she had met at several parties but did not know very well. "I mean, I kind of knew who he was, a lot of my friends knew who he was, but I didn't know him well." she began. "But one night, at a party thrown by one of my friends, he started flirting with me. He was so cute, and I was really excited about the attention." Her voice rose with enthusiasm. "So, we were talking and flirting and drinking, right? Then we started kissing on the dance floor, until someone suggested we go somewhere more private. This seemed logical, so we went outside the party to where his car was parked, a Patrol [a type of sports utility vehicle], so it was roomy, and from there I just couldn't stop. We kissed, then did other stuff. And, well, yeah, we had sex. It was amazing. Didn't hurt, felt great. I'm really glad," she explained, smiling. "I don't regret it at all," she added quickly.

Many young people, men and women alike, described sexual adventures in cars. It seems that a lot of sexual and social activity is centered around driving and cars due to the paucity of public spaces where young people can gather freely. As mentioned in Chapter 2, many described their cars as an unregulated private bubble floating through heavily regulated public spaces. In their cars young people feel free and in control of their lives. They can play their music, talk politics, and flirt with members of the opposite sex, all while driving past the morality police and clerics. The car also gives young people a distinct sense of power and escape. They said they felt they could always "outdrive" the morality police and escape harassment as long as they were in a car. Additionally, the car is a status symbol for many young people, and young men in particular described the car as an essential accessory for dating because many of their encounters take place in their cars. During the time I spent in Iran, I conducted more than a quarter of my interviews in cars, and spent almost a quarter of my days riding around in cars with friends, family members, or informants. As mentioned, the car is a popular mating spot because it allows semi-private use of public space. Young adults pick each other up in cars, and pass phone numbers, notes, and sometimes beverages and drugs between each others' cars. Sometimes just a look exchanged between a young man in a car and a woman on the street is enough of a signal, and although it is not sanctioned by the morality police (and young people face arrest and serious punishment for doing it), the young woman might get into the car and drive around with the young man, sometimes to an abandoned spot. After this, the young man might drop her off in the same square in which he found her, or he might take her to her next destination.

After this phenomenon was explained to me, I was no longer shocked when notes and phone numbers were passed to me by young men in cars or on motorbikes who passed by. I remember that within ten minutes of my arrival in Iran in 2004, as my cousin and I were driving home from the airport, a young man in a car next to us passed me his phone number. He kept trying to talk to me, but in my confusion and jetlag I could hardly respond. Over the next few weeks this was a common occurrence. Upon my return from Iran I recounted this story to a female friend; she had a similar story to tell.

I remember when I arrived at the airport, my cousin picked me up in her new car. As we were driving—now, it was the middle of the night, mind you—down the highway at full speed, I saw a guy in a car next to us trying to catch my attention. First he had his music turned all the way up and was swerving around our car, I guess trying to show his car tricks. Then he started yelling out his window at us. "Ladies!" he said. "Come on, you wanna come home with me?" I started laughing and looked at my cousin, who seemed totally unruffled by all of this. "Ladies!" he yelled again. "I have a DVD player in my car!" he said smiling. I guess that was supposed to have done it for us. He has a DVD player in his car; I guess I was supposed to swoon.

"Well, that's how we meet guys here," said Roji. "We get dressed up and go to the main squares and streets. Sometimes we drive around in a friend's car trying to meet guys; sometimes we just walk the streets and either wait for a guy to drive up in his car, which gives us a good idea of what he is like, by the mark of his car, or sometimes we meet other guys who are walking down the street." Roji's friend Bita further explained the basic ins and outs of heterosexual meeting on the street. "If you meet a guy on the street, the guy might throw something down in front of you, like keys or his book or whatever. If you bend down to pick it up and give it back to him, it means you are interested in sex. That's how it works." Although I never witnessed such a scene, when I asked Asana if this was true, she told me it was but it happened mostly between younger people (specifically youngsters between the ages of fourteen and eighteen). When I asked her and Saara if they had ever witnessed this taking place, Saara shook her head, but Asana said it had happened to her once in her neighborhood, Shahrak-e Gharb.

Yes, once I had a guy throw something in front of me, when I was fifteen years old. I was out in the street, I think I was walking to my friend's house, when I saw three guys walking toward me. One of them took out his keys and threw them in front of me. I stopped, looked at the keys, then looked at him. I knew this was a code. I had heard from my friends that boys did this, but this boy wasn't very *khoshtip* [good-looking]. So I looked at the keys again, looked the boy in the eye, and then walked past him and his friends. As I walked away I heard his friends tell him he had made a fool of himself. It made me feel good.

Throwing something in front of a woman seems to be one of the many unspoken sexual codes to express sexual interest. Another code I was made aware of by Shahrzad and later by Laleh and Alaleh was flashing car headlights while driving during the day. I had often seen men flash their brights as we drove past them, but I never knew what it meant. When I asked Shahrzad, she explained that men flashed their lights when they wanted the women in the car to pull over so they could flirt with them. Many of my informants reiterated that in this environment, so much of sexuality and sexual interaction is unspoken. Ten young people with whom I had informal conversations (often while riding in a taxi) told stories about meeting people in shared taxis and becoming sexually involved with them either inside the taxi or at another arranged spot. On three separate occasions, five men told me stories about showing their interest in a female passenger by placing their feet over the woman's feet. If the woman did not move her foot, she was expressing interest as well. This response was the signal either to engage in some flirting or sexual interaction, or to arrange a time and place to do so.

Many of the public taxi and private *āzhāns* drivers I interviewed recounted stories about sexual behavior that occurred inside their vehicles, sometimes involving the drivers themselves. "Yeah, kids come in here, come into the backseat and start talking to each other in hushed voices," began one āzhāns driver. "Some of them know me, they know I don't care and that I have a comfortable backseat. So when they call the service, they request me. I guess I'm becoming famous among the kids." He smiled. When I asked him what the young adults did in the backseat aside from talking, he became a bit flustered but nevertheless answered my question. "Well, *khawharam* [my sister], it isn't proper, and excuse me for saying this, but what *don't* they do? They tell me to take back roads at night, and then they kiss and moan and such, such things, well . . . yes, such things." He shifted in his seat and attempted to dab the sweat from his forehead. Another taxi driver spoke of his own sexual escapades in his own taxi. "You wouldn't believe how interesting it is being a taxi driver, Khānum [Madam]," he told me. "The things I go through, the things I do, even I'm ashamed of them, but still, I like it and I can't resist." When I asked him if he felt comfortable disclosing these things, he sighed and looked at me in the rearview mirror. After a few minutes he adjusted the mirror and began to speak. "You seem like a nice enough lady, and trustworthy too. Well, I'm going to tell you a story, a good one; you won't believe it but it's true." I settled myself into the seat and pulled out my notebook. He didn't seem to mind in the slightest my taking notes and began to speak a bit more slowly so I could catch every word. "Well, one day a woman on the street flagged down my cab when there was no one else in it. So I stopped, and instead of her getting into the backseat, where passengers usually sit, like yourself, she got into the front seat with me. She was hot and sweating and fanning herself; she made a comment about the weather and looked over at me. Then I saw she was staring at me, and I couldn't help but want to look at her," he said, glancing back at me for effect. "She was wearing a chādor and maghna'e, like she must have just come from work, or maybe she was one of those women from the payin shahr [downtown]. Anyway, after a few minutes she pushed aside her chādor and pulled up her long black skirt. She took my hand, slid it between her legs—as I'm driving, mind you—and put it inside her," he stopped and wiped a few beads of sweat from his forehead before continuing. "It was hot in there, and moist. The whole car ride I played with her. Then when we arrived at her destination. She got out of the car with a smile, but without paying," he said, explaining that women often perform sexual favors so they won't have to pay for cab rides. He then held his hand to his nose. "It happened months ago, but I swear I can still smell her and feel her on my fingers." He sighed.

Yet another āzhāns driver, who looked young enough to be part of the age group I was studying although he wouldn't reveal his age, talked of his own success in sexual relations. "Being an āzhāns driver is great 'cause you get to drive women around, freely," he explained. "Like, if they stop you and say, 'Who is this girl?' you say, a passenger and you show your driver's license." He showed me his license. I nodded in agreement, remembering a female friend of mine from abroad who had spent a summer in Tehran dating an āzhāns driver. She had said the same thing and noted that she felt at ease dating him for this very reason. "It's great 'cause I can drive my girlfriends around for hours and we just talk and make out, and it's really fun. We can go wherever we want! The sky is the limit with this car! It's my ticket to freedom!" he exclaimed.

It is possible that these colorful stories and accounts are embellished. It is also possible that much of what they say is not true, particularly because I had no way of verifying their information, and I had only small amounts of contact with them. Although some of the accounts may be exaggerated, the narratives speak to an ideal or a fantasy of sexuality and sexual practices that can be enlightening and descriptive of the sexual culture.

Pleasure, both for themselves and for their partners, was a theme often alluded to by many of my informants, especially the young women. Perhaps this was because they were more comfortable discussing pleasure with me than the young men were. In any case, the young women often reiterated that giving and receiving pleasure was one of the most important aspects of sexual relations, if not the very definition of sex. "Sex to me is when two people get together and please each other," answered Nilufar, who was introduced in Chapter 3, when I asked her to define sex. Most of the women who discussed the importance of pleasure in sexual relationships reiterated the importance of making sure that both parties enjoy the experience. "I want to make my partner feel good, I take pride in it, but I also make sure that I feel good too," said Nahid, a twenty-year-old journalist in training. "My pleasure is important to me. If I'm not feeling good, it's not a good partner for me and I get out," she noted. Alaleh echoed Nahid's sentiments: "The problem with my ex-husband was that he didn't please me," she explained. "That was the root of all the problems with our marriage. I couldn't please him sexually and he couldn't please me, though we both tried. I'm a hot girl, I have sexual needs. Thank God for my hand," she said, kissing and then wiggling her fingers. "Without these," she said, "I don't know what I would do!"

All of the married women I interviewed indicated they turned to masturbation to pleasure themselves. Although masturbation is said to be "un-Islamic," and the schools teach young people that it is a terrible thing to do, many of the young women I spoke with said they often masturbate, with and without vibrators and other toys or props. They told me they purchased their sex toys from black market vendors. I did not see any of these vendors myself, but three of my informants showed me sex toys they had purchased from them.

Masturbation was alluded to in some of my in-depth interviews, but it was most openly talked about in the dance class I attended three days a week. There the women would practice their *varzesh ha-e-sexy* (exercises for sex) and discuss various sexual and self-pleasuring adventures. It was also a forum for the younger women in the class to talk to the older women and gain insight and advice from their experiences. The questions they posed to their older counterparts and to me included, *Is masturbating normal? How and where can I get a vibrator? What is the real deal with oral sex? Is it dirty and bad? I like giving blowjobs; is that bad? Why does male ejaculation taste so bad? Is it true that you must be able to make yourself orgasm before you can have an orgasm with a man?*

"Ladies, I have heard they are selling vibrators in Bāzār-e-Tajrish; let's go and buy some!" Laleh announced after dance class one evening. The women all screamed and giggled in delight. They told me they had procured vibrators from other countries through their friends or on the black market outside the bāzār, because a lot of the Web sites they could be ordered from were blocked by the Islamic Republic's filtering system, which had created something of an intranet that was Islamically approved. Some women said they used household appliances instead of proper vibrators, as well as cucumbers, eggplants, deodorant bottles, or other household items; others said they turned to a combination of cybersex and masturbation. They would go into chat rooms where they could meet both women and men, and they would masturbate while talking online. Finally, some of the young women said they often masturbated while on the phone with a friend or potential lover. They said that sexy conversations coupled with a little masturbation helped them achieve the pleasure they were seeking.

These discussions of masturbation and the importance of pleasure in women's sex lives painted a picture of Tehrani women as strong and in control of their own bodies and sex lives and as having the ability to make definitive and clear decisions for themselves, even if some of those decisions do not comply with traditional conventions of morality. Women in Iran are increasingly asserting their agency in the workforce, in the public sphere, and in the bedroom. It is important to recognize these developments against the backdrop of a repressive regime and an international media that seek to portray Iranian women as passive and without agency.

Pleasure, desire, mobility in cars, and desire for both heterosexual and homosexual encounters have combined to popularize group sex as a phenomenon among this population. A popular location for group sexual encounters is the northern region of Iran, close to the Caspian Sea. This area is popularly referred to as "the North," or Shomal, and is reachable in a few hours by car. Many young people spend evenings there with their partner or partners, and groups of young men or young women go there to find potential partners. "You know lots of people go to Shomal, to the jungles of the north, and do their things there," explained Reraj. "They go there, deep in the jungle, and have lots of sex, with lots of people; it's really something to see. I love it," he said averting his eyes from my gaze. When I asked him about going to their homes, he responded, "They go to their homes too, but for the big group sex scenes, it's all in the jungle. I looked at him skeptically. I'm serious," he said. "People go there all the time. And the sex parties there are really *mofasal* [elaborate]. Sometimes guys host parties there and have a set of women come, and then a little later another set of women joins them. It's not a visible place; you have to park your car and then walk a bit into the jungle, and then a lot of us stay in villas or campgrounds nearby."

Gypsy echoed Reraj's statements about the prevalence of group sex in Shomal. "Have I ever had group sex? Well, yes, with a few women at a time, but who hasn't done that? But I've watched really elaborate orgies too," he told me. "Let me guess," I said, "Shomal?" "Yes," he responded. "One time there was this girl and she was trying to get me to participate in an orgy. She wasn't my girlfriend or anything, she wasn't anyone's girlfriend, come to think of it. She was just plain horny. Anyways, she got to talking to me and wanted me to come to this big group orgy in Shomal. So I went, but didn't do it, just watched. It was cool," he said, smiling.

I also was privy to a few of these group sex parties both in and just outside of Tehran. One of the ones I attended wasn't all the way up north but instead took place in the summer home of the daughter of a wealthy cleric. Her parents were out of town for a week; apparently they had gone to make their religious pilgrimage to Mecca. This young woman decided to host an orgy at their garden estate just half an hour outside of Tehran. I did not know I was to be attending a sex party that evening. I was just told to come to this "hot party" being thrown by this young woman who was known for her parties. "It will be good for you and your research," my friend Sanaz had told me the night before. I was hesitant given that the hostess was the daughter of a cleric. "Even better," Sanaz had said. "They've got our backs this way; there is no way the party is getting busted up. I'll pick you up at ten," she said, hanging up the phone. The next night I was ready when she came to pick me up. We piled into the car of an old friend of mine, Kian, a regular at some of these party scenes. The car ride to the garden was full of excitement as everyone talked about how great the party was going to be. When we pulled into our destination, however, I did not hear the usual party sounds. It seemed quite silent, given that there were supposed be thirty or more young people there already.

We parked the car at the edge of the garden and walked through the dark to get to the center of the party. The ground beneath my feet was uneven and I grabbed Kian's wrist to steady my steps. He reached into his pocket to fish out his lighter to give us some light. We walked for about ten minutes before I began to hear techno music coming from one of the structures several yards from where the main house looked to be. "Where are we going? Where is the party?" I asked nervously. No one responded. We continued walking toward the music, and as we got closer I realized it was a small-scale bathhouse, or *hamam*, that the family had constructed. on the property. Sanaz took off her mānto and rusari (headscarf) and urged me to do the same. I did and then placed it next to hers under a nearby tree. The bathhouse was dimly lit but techno music blared from one corner. Steam enveloped the room, so I could not see much as I first stepped inside. I reached for Kian's wrist again and didn't find it. He was gone, and I wouldn't be seeing him until the next day. As my eyes adjusted to the light and steam, I noticed that there were forty or so young people present, all naked or in undergarments, kissing, touching, dancing, and some having oral, anal, and vaginal sex. I hadn't realized that I was coming to a group sex party, but there I was. I tried to walk to a corner to remain inconspicuous (although I was quite conspicuous as probably the only person in the room who was fully clothed). I tried to count the number of bodies and to ascertain who was doing what and with whom, but it was difficult because of the steam. I saw groups of three, four, and five people, men and women, engaging in sexual acts with both genders. After ten minutes I began feeling faint; the heat was getting to me, and the blaring lull of the techno beat was giving me a headache. I looked out across the room trying to find Sanaz and Kian. Sanaz was kissing and being kissed by three men, and Kian was nowhere to be found. (Later he told me he'd been taking Ecstasy at that point, in a back room where drugs were being distributed to interested parties.) I began feeling uncomfortable and weary. I was not accustomed to this kind of scene, but I was glad to have observed a group sex occasion to corroborate stories from my informants. After another fifteen minutes, I left the bathhouse and wandered over to the main house, hoping to find at least a few people who weren't engaging in group sex. When I entered the house, it was quiet. The lights were on but it seemed to be empty. I walked into the kitchen, found a glass, and filled it with water from the sink. As I took a big gulp and began to steady myself, someone walked into the kitchen. "Can I help you?" he asked. Judging by his tattered clothes and broken plastic sandals, I assumed he was a *kargar* (worker) in the house. I apologized and told him I was a friend of the hostess and just looking for water. "They are out in the bathhouse," he told me. I told him I had just come from there and wanted to find a telephone to call an āzhāns to go home. I wondered if this older, kind man knew what was happening out in the bathhouse, and if he did, what was his reaction? I wondered if he ever told the hostess's parents about their daughter's parties, or what his impression of the whole situation was. I was about to ask when he handed me the phone, ordered me to tell the cab driver where I was going, and shuffled off down the dark hallway. The āzhāns came and took me home.

SOME PEOPLE MIGHT CHARACTERIZE the behaviors I have described here as hedonism. Some might say these young people are doing this as a last resort. Others would say they are succumbing to peer pressure to behave a certain way. The youth themselves, however, characterize these behaviors as part of a larger project of social change—a project in which women are asserting their agency, both sexually and socially, and young people are carving out a social and sexual space and creating a social movement with the goal of changing the sociopolitical climate as well as ideas about and attitudes toward sex. The aftereffects of these changes in sexual and social behavior and ideas remain to be seen.

5   Caught!

The Imam Khomeini revolution is the revolution of values.
Sign posted outside many major hotels in Tehran

The Islamic Revolution is not about fun; in fact there is no fun to be had in the Islamic Republic.
Ayatollah Khomeini

Men and women [in Iran] have no need for reproductive health care services until they are engaged as no one engages in sexual relations prior to that moment.
Minister of Health, Tehran 2004

July 2000
Her face flushed, Yasaman, nineteen, looks around the crowded Tehran apartment that at the moment resembles a cross between an American fraternity party and a curtained bordello. She takes a sip of her Russian vodka martini. "The difference between you youth in the West and us here in Iran is really very simple: when you want to have fun you go out, and when you want to pray and be spiritual you stay in. In Iran, when we want to pray and be spiritual we go out, and when we want to have fun we stay in." Persian pop music blares from large speakers, and everywhere there are pairs of young flirting and drinking Tehranis. Yasaman glances over at her best friend, who is tucked away neatly under a boy on a nearby couch. The dimly lit room is filled with other young couples occupied in the same activity. As Yasaman sits down,

her purple miniskirt is pushed up so high that she catches the attention
of a boy across the way. She shrugs and nonchalantly lights a cigarette
after handing one to me.

Soon Yasaman will leave her friend's house party. Like the other
women in attendance, most of whom she goes to school with, she will
carefully don a navy blue hejāb to cover her hair, and wrap a long,
flowing coat over her skirt and sweater. On the street, accompanied
by a male friend, she will keep her eyes lowered, carefully blending
into the streams of veiled women moving along Tehran's crowded city
streets. Like thousands of urban teens in Tehran, Yasaman's public and
private worlds could not be more different, but she wonders how long
her dual life can exist before she loses herself.

In Mashad, a city far east of the capital, a group of women and men
gather. Everyone piles into the car of a young man named Siamak, who
turns up the latest single from 'Nsync that he has bootlegged from
the United States. He starts driving as everyone talks and laughs and
explains to me that our destination is one of the hottest spots in Mashad
for people to meet each other. As Siamak rounds a corner, he spots
some members of the komite and shouts for everyone—or at least the
women—to duck as he drives past them. He turns the music down and
we dive beneath the seats so that only the boys remain seen. The women
giggle and scream and take another puff of the miniature hookah that
holds remnants of opium, hash, and marijuana.

The duality of public/private in Iran has changed, and young people are using the social and sexual revolution to make their public and
private worlds more alike. Frustrated by having to project one persona
on the street and another behind closed doors, they are trying to make
their public worlds more open so they can be the same person at home,
at school, in the mall, and at work. More and more of the behaviors and
conversations that previously took place underground are now taking
place aboveground. This social and sexual revolution of young Tehranis
has been created against the backdrop of the Islamist regime.[1]

By not adhering to Islamic laws on dress, comportment, modesty,
and male-female fraternization, young people are rejecting the notion
of being Islamic subjects. Policymakers in Iran are increasingly trying

to find ways of inspiring belief in Islamic ideology, especially among the youth. As Varzi notes, "at play in Iran's understanding of its own world is the notion of a public secret. Everyone in Iran knows that religion does not exist on the level or in the form that it appears to exist on the surface. Even Islamic policymakers know this, which is why it is crucial that the surface remain untouched and unquestioned, and the secret never voiced."[2] However, in the last decade or so, the secret is beginning to be voiced, and is becoming less of a secret. As young people live out their resistance and seek to change their social lives, the smooth surface covering the secret is being broken. The state appears to have adapted to its youth by no longer punishing them in the way they once did, and the behaviors of the young people indicate that their sexual and social revolution has been a success and their resistance is threatening the entire social and moral order of the Islamic Republic.

As has been mentioned in the preceding chapters, many of the young people I spoke with called their own actions laj or laj bāzi, which can be loosely translated "playful rebellion." "I think we do certain social behaviors as political statements. I think it's our form of laj," said Gypsy, former political activist turned blogger. Gypsy had been politically involved while living in Tehran, until early 2005, and had been one of the more outspoken bloggers in his group. When I interviewed him in 2004, he said he joined the party and social scene as another way of getting back at the regime. "It's the komite, you know? They kept pushing us down, and they were the ones who made social issues political, and, well, the youth responded with their laj. Now it's real laj bāzi, and it's great! The more we party, the more we laj, the more progress we make. It's only the last four or five years that this has happened. People were having lots of boyfriends and girlfriends, and the more they had, the more the authorities got lax, so it seemed like it was working."

Many people credit the regime for defining the battleground and creating what they call an enghelāb-e-farhangi, or sociocultural revolution. The young people I spoke with said they had decided to go to extreme opposites on all the values embraced by the Islamification of the 1980s and, by association, by the regime. "The regime complains about the youth and our cultural revolution," began Asghar, a young jewelry salesman residing in the northern part of Tehran, as we were drinking tea in his shop one afternoon. "But it's their own fault that the young people have become like this. They breed this version of Islam. They tell us *this* is our culture, Islam. It has been beaten into us, and we don't like it, so we young people, we reject everything that has to do with religion or their version of culture. We want to move to be more Western. They hate the West; by default we love it!" he said, finishing his tea. A young woman who called herself Suzi (the Anglicized version of the Persian name *Sousan*) echoed Asghar's sentiments. "I don't like that they lie to us," she said, pulling out three strands of peroxide-blond hair from underneath her headscarf.

The Islam they preach is actually turning us against Islam. I used to be into *namāz* (praying) and fasting. Then, when I entered into the dormitory, my viewpoint totally changed. The kids didn't understand why I did what I did. They said I just believed what I read and what I was told point-blank, without any dispute. They told me that Islam was about love, we must pray with love in our hearts, but that's not what this regime has turned it into. This regime focuses on "don't wear nail polish or lipstick when you pray." But why? Instead of teaching us to love God, they harp on stupid things like makeup. So what do I do? I respond to their stupidity by wearing makeup! I resent them. That's why I look like this now: because they don't want me to!

Another young woman also commented on the regime's focus on makeup and expressed her confusion. "What I'm trying to understand is why can't I do namāz while wearing nail polish or makeup? Why do I have to wipe those things off for doing namāz? Why can't I present myself to God the way I want to? The way I present myself to my friends? I have so many questions. The regime is full of contradictions, and then they wonder why we don't want to follow." Her boyfriend, Saasha, a twenty-one-year-old religious studies major, took her sentiments one step further:

They sit for hours and tell us, when you want to enter into the bathroom, enter with the right foot. If you sit on the floor, cross this foot over this one. They even sat around and came up with a law that says, "If an earthquake happens and a man from an upstairs apartment *falls* into a woman from the downstairs apartment and she gets pregnant, the child is not a bastard as it is God's will!" Ay, *Khoda* [God]! We are really out of it, this regime is really out of it. This is what they want to teach us. They want to focus on going to the bathroom, and when and where to have sex. There are more important things, like creating a better bus system, but they have chosen these things to focus on, so this is how we fight back, by focusing our attentions on social, sexual, and cultural relations.

Majid, another religious studies student who had moved to Tehran from Mashad, echoed Saasha's statements. "It's not good, though,'cause now lots of kids make fun of God and the prophets," he said sadly, "and there are some kids who don't even believe in God anymore. It's really *hayf* [unfortunate], you know. Religion is becoming a joke. I have a coworker who is a total atheist, and he laughs at us whenever we talk about God. I'm serious, he just laughs. Now, you tell me, is this a successful theocracy?"

Reza, the twenty-five-year-old filmmaker introduced in Chapter 2, described his frustration at the authorities for turning Iranian men into "sex-starved animals." He thinks the fundamentalists deserve to be betrayed. "They are so sick, you know. They want us not even to think about women, and what does that result in? Incessant planning and scheming about how to get women! See, in London or Paris you go to a pub and women are all around, and no one pays them that much attention. In Tehran, a young woman brushes past you at the *meydoon* and you go crazy![3] Desire fills the two of you and you can't wait to go somewhere secretly and just get it out!" Reza told me he is ashamed of his peers because he thinks their judgment is sometimes clouded with desire.

For many of these young people, just doing what the regime doesn't want them to do brings satisfaction. Frustrated by the social parameters set by the regime, they lash out by doing exactly what they are told not to do. "Anything the regime says is forbidden, we like to see what's up with it that it's forbidden," said my friend Golzaar, a twenty-two-year-old psychologist in training. I was interviewing her at a pool party where the crowd was mixing cocktails in a backyard protected from the outside world by a series of tall trees. She sipped her gin and tonic before continuing. "We are curious, so here, when so many things we are told not to do, we want to see what is up with it, you see? They make us curious about things we ordinarily might not have been curious about." Another young woman who was casually sunning herself while half listening to our conversation came over to put in her two cents. "Yeah," she began, "if they just easily let a boy and girl come and talk and just sit and walk through a park and stuff, just let us hang out and say we are friends, then maybe the kids wouldn't run to do strange things in each other's homes. It's because things are forbidden that we want to do them." Indeed, it seemed that many young people spent large amounts of time engaging in "forbidden" activities such as drinking, dancing, and socializing with members of the opposite sex. Additionally, many young women told me that because they are taught that proper Islamic subjects should not draw attention to themselves and should dress modestly and avoid eye-catching jewelry or accessories, they chose to wear brightly colored designer outerwear, jewelry, and significant amounts of makeup. "We want *to cheshm biyarim khodemon ra* [to make ourselves more eye-catching] so as to call more attention to ourselves, just because they tell us not to," said Golzaar, showing me her turquoise rhinestone-studded rusari. "It feels good to push the limit. We aren't doing this just to look good, but that is a nice added bonus," said her friend, showing me her pin-striped mänto and then trotting around the pool to show off her gold lamé bikini.

The notion of certain social activities (such as pool parties and other mixed social gatherings) being forced into the home often came up among my informants and friends. Some were angry about the results. Reraj once told me, "Women and men have a different way of life here. Everything is hidden, underground. They have their own lives, but it's like two different lives they have for themselves—and we're tired of it! It's too confusing! We want to make it like everywhere else, you are the same person outside as you are inside. My friends, they don't, like, meet a guy and go to the movies or to dinner; they just get together and get down, have lots of sex, you know? Just go right to each other's homes, 'cause it's risky to go on a date here. It's not natural, if you ask me!" Reraj and many of my other informants were angry at the regime for creating a situation in which they had to rebel just to assert themselves. Many of my informants echoed his sentiments about wanting to behave the same way at school as they did at parties; they wanted to be the same person outside the home, in the public sphere, as they were in the private sphere. They knew they had already succeeded in pushing the invisible line of

proper Islamic conduct, but they wanted to make the line disappear altogether. "We know that a lot has changed," remarked Asana. "Like now I
can talk and laugh with boys as we walk into school grounds, and I can
wear more makeup, but we still want more! I want to be able to hold his
hand in public!"

Other young adults lamented the lack of proper recreation activities
and blamed the regime for their boredom. They were angry that they
couldn't do in public what they called "normal activities" (often referring
to men and women going to discos, clubs, and outdoor sports areas together), and they said the result by default was their engaging in sexual
and certain other "risky" social behaviors (such as drug and alcohol use),
sometimes out of a lack of anything better to do. Some, such as twenty-
two-year-old Amireh, felt, as she explained it, stuck in boredom, "I mean,
it's a sticky problem, isn't it? Because on the one hand there's nothing to
do here in Iran. The situation in Iran is that there's nothing you do here
from morning till night, because you went to school but now you can't
get a job. But you know you have all kinds of problems. Only problems
in Iran, that's it. Our life is filled with only difficulties—*inkar naakon,
oonkar nakon, na, nemishe, nemitooni, dorost nist* [can't do this, can't do
that, no, don't, it's not right]—and very few pleasures or *tafreeh* [fun],
so if you don't have a boyfriend or girlfriend, well, that makes things
even worse. It's like you have to have that, but then you're not supposed
to have that. So what are we supposed to do? See, at least when you're
with your boyfriend, at least for that one hour, you are really enjoying yourself." Although boredom seems like a luxury available only to
wealthy young people, Amireh is actually not a member of the middle
or upper class and in fact is struggling to make ends meet because her
father (a servant to an upper-class family) has not been bringing home
enough money for the family. Amireh wants to work, has an education,
but cannot find employment. She indicated that long, empty days are
therefore particularly painful because she would like to work, would like
to contribute to the family, but has no outlet.

Soraya, a twenty-four-year-old art history student, agreed with
Amireh's assessment, and was upset by it. "Well, there's a lot of, let me
tell you, people without anything really to do in the Islamic Republic,
and they start to go crazy. They start to get bored, and then they don't

think about their futures and don't think about what they are doing. This leads them down a path of partying, sex, and drugs. I guess it's natural, but maybe more heightened here, right?" she asked. I told her that youth around the world often turn to partying, drinking, sex, and drugs in order to fill voids in their lives, but I didn't think that young people anywhere in the world face the day-to-day difficulty and harshness of life the way that youth living in the theocratic environment of the Islamic Republic do. Soraya emphasized that because young people are underemployed and often frustrated by restricted social freedoms, they are more likely to turn to tafreeh-e-nasālem (unhealthy forms of recreation) to get through their daily lives. I told her I agreed but something needed to be done about the risks young people face due to this behavior.

"The point is that the Islamic Republic has changed things," said Behrad, a twenty-three-year-old taxi driver, when analyzing his relationship to the regime. "They try to regulate our sexual and social lives, but here in Iran everyone does everything, just in secret, that's all. You could say we live a lie, but we're tired of the lie and ready to expose the secret." His friend Hassan, aged twenty-two and a taxi driver, chimed in to point out the similar public/private contradiction that Yasaman spoke of at her party. "It's like my teacher at school always says." He straightened his shirt, pulled down his glasses, and continued in a tone of voice to match that of his teacher: "During the time of the Shah we used to go out and drink and come home and pray; now we go out and pray and come home and drink." When he'd finished his impression, his friends slapped him on the back, handed him another beer, and drank a sarcastic toast to jomhuri-e-Islami (the Islamic Republic). "But now those days are over; we will soon party in public!" he announced.

Politics and the Power of the People

Young Tehranis do not rely exclusively on social and sexual behaviors to express their political dissent. Some of the more ambitious young people with whom I spoke were interested in attaining positions in the *Majlis* (the Iranian Parliament), and most of my informants followed changes in the political sphere quite closely. Throughout my time in Iran I was continually impressed with the amount of time all of my informants spent reading and watching the news. Although they focused much attention on parties, looking good, and relationships, news items and political issues were also frequent topics of their conversation. Because of the Islamic Republic's free education policies (which had resulted in a literacy rate of 79 percent for the nation in 2003, according to the Central Intelligence Agency Factbook),[4] most of my informants were avid consumers of the news through newspapers, magazines, and especially the Internet; although many were more interested in pop culture, songs, and styles from around the world, they also paid attention to the political environment. Many of these young people spent a lot of time discussing the regime, the political moment, and the possibility of change in the country. I was often impressed that all of them, from across the socioeconomic spectrum, were knowledgeable about global politics and knew about current events both in their country and in the world.[5] "We have to be, because we're at the center of a lot of global changes," Diar, my friend and key informant, would often remind me. I heard variations of this statement from two dozen other informants as well. Many of them told me they spent a large portion of their day watching the news on television, listening to it on the radio, and doing Internet searches to assess the nature of U.S.-Iran relations, keep up-to-date on internal laws and religious edicts, or *fatwas*, and keep abreast of changes in rules about or crackdowns on the social activities of young people. They emphasized that being up-to-date on the news was vital to surviving the sociopolitical environment of daily life.

The extent of young adult involvement in politics became increasingly apparent to me during the elections in the summer of 2005. Most of them did not vote, as a form of boycotting what they believed is a corrupt electoral system in which the Council of Guardians chooses the candidates, and because the president, for whom they would be voting, is not first or second in command in the country.[6] (The first in command in Iran is the Supreme Leader, who is not elected but ordained by the clergy.) Furthermore, many were dismayed by former President Khatami, who, according to many of my informants, had "let the youth down." All of my informants discussed the election and the candidates during the two-month campaign period preceding the elections. Virtually all of them knew a bit about each of the seven candidates, and many were involved in campaigns to persuade other young adults to boycott the election. "We're not going to vote, and it's a deliberate decision," said Tina, a twenty-five-year-old housewife and one of Laleh's weekly dance class students, one day in class. When I asked her the reasoning behind this decision, she told me the same thing that many of my informants had been telling me throughout the month of June. "Because what's the point?!" she snapped. "Why would you vote for someone [the president] who has no power in the country? What, isn't he like sixth in command?" Tina added angrily. "Yeah, it's such a hoax," chimed in Azar, a twenty-year-old university student. "The people who have the real power won't let any of our candidates run for the position anyways. Haven't you realized that there are no real reform candidates? Or at least no one who represents *our* interests," she said as other members of the dance class nodded in agreement.

Although most of my informants had decided not to vote and were formally boycotting the election, a few of them were backing the somewhat moderate candidate Mostafa Moein, who was endorsed by President Khatami. "We have to back him; otherwise we could get a really conservative guy, and then what?" said Reza. He and his friends were among the few young people I knew who were trying to get others to support a particular candidate (such as by distributing posters and hosting chat sessions online to talk about the importance of voting) and who still believed in the powers of the president. Most of my informants were disillusioned and disappointed at the empty promises made by Khatami, in whom they had all put so much faith. "We backed Khatami. All of us. Went out and supported him. But what did he do? Nothing!" commented Mona, the owner of the beauty salon I spent time in once a week. Many of her clients (and many of my informants) agreed with her and felt their votes would not mean anything because the candidates did not represent them or their views, because the candidates they had favored had not received approval by the Council of Guardians even to run for president, and because the president has limited power.

Nevertheless, in the weeks leading up to election day, many young people became involved in the campaign of former president and presidential candidate Hashemi Rafsanjani because he was heavily soliciting the young adult population of urban Iran. His campaign consisted of colorful stickers, CDs of techno music mixed in with his words and promises, and outdoor disco balls at campaign headquarters. Although some of the young adults campaigning for Rafsanjani believed in him and felt he would be the best president and perhaps follow in the footsteps of Khatami, other young people who were promoting Rafsanjani on the streets of Tehran confessed they had no intention of voting for him, or for any other candidate for that matter; they were campaigning just because Rafsanjani had promised them money, a job, or a free ticket out of jail if arrested. Others indicated that campaigning was a fun way to pass the time, and a way to be closer to election politics.

Regardless of their personal views on the election, virtually all of my informants, and many young people on the streets of Tehran, were involved in the campaigning either directly or indirectly. Those who chose to boycott the election sought also to promote the boycott, and those who supported a particular candidate spent extensive amounts of time talking about their candidates and the importance of the election. During those months, and at many times throughout my time in Iran, I was reminded that although much of the young adult sexual and social

Figure 5.1. Young people were quite involved in the 2005 presidential elections. Many supported former president Hashemi Rafsanjani. Here a group of young people take to the streets to support their candidate. © 2007 by Nader Davoodi. Used by permission.

revolution is subversive and silent and inscribed on people's bodies, many young Tehranis are overtly involved in politics, and most of my informants are interested in what is happening in their political environment.

Caught!

When discussing their relationship to the regime, most of the young people I spoke with talked about being arrested, detained, and sometimes whipped by the komite. Almost all of my informants had been caught and detained at least once, many of them several times. Experiences with the komite were a favorite topic among these young adults, and they often traded war stories. Experience with the komite was both the price of rebellion and social revolution, and the marker of success. Being caught gained a person a reputation within the group and was a source of pride. Many of the parents I interviewed also told stories of their children standing up for what they believed in and getting caught. Telling these "caught" stories was also a source of pride for many parents who did not punish their children for committing a crime that landed them in jail but rather applauded them and sought to comfort them once they were retrieved from their holding cells.

For some of the young adults, the potential of being caught was just a part of going out; they had adapted to it and viewed it as worth the risk. Some of the young people, particularly the young women, still felt uneasy about being caught, but most of the young adults I spoke with said they were no longer scared of the morality police, and some even spoke about their run-ins with them with pride.

My informants' tales of these encounters with the morality police were each more colorful than the next, and they told them with pride and animation. One afternoon I was talking to Asal, a nineteen-year old student at Azad University, who told me this story about one of the first times she was caught:

> Asal: I'll tell you the story. It was a few years ago, and we were going
> to a party. So we went and there we are drinking and having fun
> and doing, well, you know what, and then the door opens and in
> come some strange-looking guys. I remember it well. I remember
> what they looked like: strange, I remember. I remember turning to
> my friends and saying, "look at those boys; what strange looks they

have." It was weird, and then all of a sudden, more and more of them came in, and we realized, oh my gosh! They were komite, and I remember well, just as I realized it was them and turned to put away my vodka drink, I turned around and one was standing right there.

P: No!

A: You bet! Well, that was it for me: handcuffs, the whole lot. And I was so scared. I remember cowering in the back of the truck and ducking down to use my cell phone to call my dad and tell him we were being carted off to jail.[7] I was pretty scared, and he was pretty scared too.

P: And then what?

A: Well, ah, you see, then we got taken to jail, and we had to sleep there two nights. They took blood tests to see how much alcohol we had in our blood, and you'd better believe we had our share. Then we couldn't post bail for two nights, no matter how hard our parents tried. These guys are merciless. But us women, we had it easier. We didn't face the whip in the end; they just fined us. But the men, they faced the whip.

P: Yikes!

A: But you know, it wasn't that bad in the end. It was a bit scary, but we talked 'cause we were all together, and so we talked and laughed and it was over.

P: Sounds intense.

A: Well, yes, but now we have learned, it's a *tajrobeh* [experience] for us. Now I'm not as afraid of being carted off.

Asal smiled as she told the story. For her, being caught was all part of the experience of going out, and it gave her more experience in handling the morality police. She also saw it, as she later explained to me, as an indicator of her commitment to the sexual and social revolution. Now she goes out regularly and is prepared to be caught. She says she always has an exit strategy; she keeps her Islamic clothing nearby and stuffs a cucumber and mint in her purse to take away the smell of alcohol on her breath. She often says she doesn't care if she is caught; she almost dares them to catch her, because that means she and her group of friends are succeeding. "It's like war with these guys," she would often say. "The fact that they are getting angrier and wanting to bug us more means we're getting under their skin, means we're doing something right!"

Some of the young adults noted that being caught was just a part of their daily activities, and a part of their activism in the enghelāb-e-far-hangi. "Most young people have nothing to do here, no fun," my friend Shahnaz, a twenty-five-year-old English teacher, once told me. "Their way of being active and involved in this mess is to be caught, even ten times a day." She turned up the banned Persian pop music playing in her car and rolled down the windows, a gesture that indicated her disrespect for the rules of *mojaz* (proper, moral, or Islamic-approved music). "One thing people like to do is drive around in cars blasting their music, and then they get caught for it," she screamed above the music. I quickly became uneasy and shifted in my seat. "Like I said," she continued, turning down the music at my reaction, "I'm telling you, a lot of people are having plenty of sex, and they don't care if they get caught. They don't care! In fact they dare them to catch them."

Through observation and from experiences of almost being caught myself, I began to realize that Shahnaz was right. One night during the summer of 2004 I went to a gathering of about twenty young people at the home of one of my informants, whose parents were out of town. She had decided to host a get-together in celebration of her parents' absence. When I arrived at the party, I saw the usual scene of young people huddled in different corners, drinking, talking, and laughing. An hour after I arrived my phone rang and I wanted to have a conversation someplace quiet and away from the party, so I began to search the apartment for an empty room. As I walked down the hallway I saw a young man guide a girl into a bathroom and then shut the door. The next door was to a closet, and then I finally came to one of the bedrooms. The lights were off, so I stepped inside and turned them on. When the lights came on I realized that a young man and young woman were having sex in the bed. They both looked up at me as I stood there feeling very awkward. I dropped my phone, scrambled to pick it up, turned off the lights, and backed out of the room, apologizing profusely to the couple. At that moment, I decided I wanted to leave the party and go home. I said goodbye to the hostess and left. An hour after I left, the party was raided by the komite, who apparently had the same experience I'd had of walking in on that couple. The morality police arrested the couple on the spot. The next day I heard that most of the partygoers had been released after spending the night in jail and paying a fine. The young couple from the bedroom, however, had not been released. I called my informant who had hosted the party. "What happened to your friends I walked in on having sex?" I asked. "They got arrested with us but taken to a separate cell. I didn't see them, and I know they haven't been released yet," she told me. "Well, what is going to happen to them?" I asked, afraid that they would be whipped and held in jail for a long time. "Most likely they'll just force them to get married, and they'll call their parents and embarrass them in front of them," my informant said. "Well, I guess it could be worse, right?" I asked with relief. "I don't know. They are forcing them to get married, and that's pretty heavy punishment in and of itself!" she replied.

A few days later I heard that the couple had indeed been forced to marry but had been released without any physical punishment. I asked my informant to put me in touch with them so I could ask them a few questions. She gave me the phone number of the young woman, who turned out to be a twenty-two-year-old manicurist from the southern part of town who works in the northern part of town. "Are you OK?" I asked when she finally called me back. "Yeah, it's fine. We're married, but we'll try to get the marriage annulled. I guess my reputation will be ruined, but I have to tell you, it was almost worth it!" she said. "How so?" I asked. "The sex was great, and the excitement and adventure of doing what we know we aren't supposed to be doing, then being caught! Well, and it makes a great story!" she added.

Another evening, twenty-one-year-old visual arts student Arefeh was giving us a ride home when she told her "caught" story. I asked if I could take notes and record. While I was busy doing that, my cousin Lily from the United States, who was fascinated by Arefeh, kept asking her questions. Our enthusiasm and curiosity egged her on, and perhaps made the story even more colorful.

> Arefeh: Yeah, it's true, I have just been released, I'm like a fugitive, or an ex-criminal.
>
> Lily: So, you just got out of jail. What was it like?
>
> A: Uncomfortable, mostly. The food was rotten, I didn't eat a thing for two days, and it was just very, well, how should I say it, not a place I'd like to go back to.
>
> L: How awful.

A: Yeah, I'm telling you, they have started up again. They want to scare us, to make us regret all the progress we have made.

L: What were you in for?

A: Well, I was at a party—well, actually, you could hardly call it a party. It was a gathering of a few people, and I was drinking. I guess they had neighbors with a vendetta, so the party got busted up and we all got sent to jail.

L: Sucks.

A: Yeah, one minute you are sitting on a couch discussing politics with your friend, moving aside your empty martini glass, the next minute you are being handled gruffly and sent away; you just don't understand what is going on!

L: Was it really awful in there?

A: No, not that bad. It's always the first moment they bust in that you are scared, but then you go there, to the detaining cell, and you go with your friends and you talk and tell jokes.

L: So, it's all part of the adventure?

A: Yes, but I tell you what, I wouldn't want to go in there alone. While we were there, there was a sixteen-year-old girl, so made up, so done up, I think she was, well, you know, a dokhtar-e-kharāb (bad girl; also used to denote someone who is a sex worker). Anyways, she came in by herself and it was scary for her, and she seemed not so scared. She was a little runt, but standing there telling orders.

L: I don't understand.

A: Well, we were scared for her, so we thought we should invite her to hang out with us so she wouldn't feel scared and alone. But boy did we regret that. She had one heck of a voice, and one heck of an attitude. She put us all in her pocket![8]

L: Like a tough girl.

A: Like a lower-class girl, but then we were all scared of her!

L: Bizarre. So I take it that the whole experience all together wasn't so great.

A: No, and I mean I just got out of jail, but look at me, I am wearing a short, tight mānto with these sleeves [three-quarter length]. I am crazy. You know that they have been stopping women for the silliest things.

L: I hear that they are just at it again, trying to make us do what they want.

A: The other day, can you imagine, my friend was in an āzhāns, in an āzhāns, on her way home. Alone. In an āzhāns. But they stopped her.

L: What for?

A: They said she had too much makeup on! Can you believe it? She was alone and in a car, and they still wanted to bother her. They just want to get on our cases so that we get scared, but it's not working. Really. It's not. Look at me!

Arefeh seemed very calm and relaxed when telling us about her experiences with the morality police and in jail. When I asked her if the experience had been traumatizing, she told me she was used to it and therefore it no longer scared her. "I used to be scared, when I was younger, and back when they would catch you and potentially whip you," she began. "But these days it's just a different story. They will catch us, round us up, and try to scare us, unless they are flirting with us, but we just end up having fun in the holding cell. They try to scare us by saying, 'We'll call your parents,' but they don't realize that our parents aren't going to punish us. So these days your life is shaped by how open your parents are, and it has less to do with the morality police, and our parents are becoming more and more open each day. We are succeeding in changing the rules!" she added emphatically. Arefeh, and at least six of my other informants, emphasized that because the morality police and the regime had changed so much and become much more lenient, it was now the parents who were the primary obstacle to young people enjoying certain social freedoms. Three of my informants reported that each time they were caught by the morality police, the punishment was that their parents would be called in. It seemed that the state was relying on parents to be the mediators between the state and its changing youth. However, while some parents were harsh disciplinarians, the parents of the majority of my informants apparently were sympathetic and did not punish them but rather paid their way out of jail and took them home to soothe them.

Saman, a twenty-year-old student at Azad University, had a similarly colorful "caught" story, but his arrest resulted in harsher punishment than Arefeh's run-in with the morality police. On the afternoon he decided to tell me stories about his experiences in jail, his cousin pulled out his wallet and showed me a picture of their friend who had been whipped the previous week. His legs looked cut, bruised, and swollen. Apparently he was one of those who had been whipped so badly he had to be taken out of jail by an ambulance. Saman revealed that he himself had been both caught and whipped recently. He turned around, pulled up his shirt, and showed me his back. It was raw with whip marks. He cringed as he carefully slid his shirt back over his open wounds. He sat down on the couch to tell me the story, taking care not to lean back lest his wounds cause him further pain.

P: So, you were caught recently?

S: How did you guess?

P: You're being funny.

S: Yeah, it's true, they got me.

P: And whipped too?

S: Yeah, my back didn't just get like that on its own.

P: And that picture of your friend looked bad too.

S: Yikes! His was really bad. For me, not that much; it was bad, but not that bad. I mean I felt it, it hurt, but it wasn't awful.

P: How and why were you caught?

S: Well, you know they busted up a party that I was at where I had been drinking. But we saw them coming, we did, and then me and my two friends ran away. We each ran in a different direction. Well, I ran to my car right away and jumped in and started driving. I could see that they were chasing me, but I still ran hard and drove fast.

P: Wow! *Na Baba* [no way]! Go on!

S: So I'm in my car, right? And I'm doing all kinds of artiste bāzi, and I'm scared, but then I think I've lost them, so I pull over for a breath. I'm tired and a little drunk, right?

P: Great, not a good combination.

S: Well, my tiredness snapped right out of me when just as I stopped the car the komite came and pulled me out of the car and into their car. Then, well, you know the drill: I went to the jail station and—

P: Let me guess: two nights, right?

S: You got it, plus the lashings on the first night. They weren't horrible, but they still hurt to this day. You want to see them again?

P: Perhaps later, not now.

S: Anyways, getting caught sucks, I'm telling you, but it doesn't make us act any better. If anything, we act up more. Akh! They [the morality police] are such a pain, but me and my friend, I think we're going to a party at my cousin's house tonight. You wanna come?

Neither Arefeh nor Saman seemed traumatized by their recent encounters with the morality police, although there may be deeper mental health consequences from these experiences that they are just repressing. It is also possible that these young people have become numb to the experience of being caught and detained. Arefeh later revealed that she has been caught and detained more than twelve times. It seemed that for many of these young adults, the more times they were caught, the more defiant they became. Instead of making them scared or more compliant, being arrested seemed to have the opposite effect on them; they wanted to act out even more.

One evening I was talking to a group of young men who explored some of these themes. Behzad, a twenty-three-year-old ski instructor, and Shaheen, a twenty-three-year-old scuba diver, both discussed these very issues. "I've gone to a lot of parties, I've been caught a lot of times. I've been lashed, but it's not like I'm afraid of these things," Behzad explained while drinking his vodka and Red Bull. "But when you were younger and not so experienced, were you afraid of getting lashed?" I asked him. "I was never afraid of being lashed," he responded. He took a deep breath and continued:

I was never afraid of the komite. I was lashed twice the first year of my partying. The first time was a little bit scary, it hurt a lot too, but then you get used to it. When you live in this society with these rules, you adapt to things. Some adapt more, some adapt less, and some don't adapt at all and are always scared. But wherever you are, you have to adapt, otherwise you won't enjoy life. This applies to everything.

Shaheen echoed Behzad's sentiments when I asked if he had ever had an encounter with the komite that led to his imprisonment. "Many times," he responded. "How was it?" I asked him. "Well, we're used to it, but if it ever happened to a stranger, they would probably see it as a bit bizarre," he responded. "Were you scared the first time?" I asked. "Yeah, the first time a person is very scared, but you learn that the more you act scared, the more they give you a hard time. A lot of times they just bother you for nothing, like it's a power trip for them," he said. Behzad chimed back in: "Exactly. It's kind of like their own fun," he added. "Yeah, those guys, this is the only power they have, so they just use it to give you a hard time," concluded Shaheen.

Many of the secular middle-class young adults noted that being a part of the middle or upper-middle class actually made them more vulnerable to being caught. Contrary to other countries where privileged kids often escape the law, in Tehran, being wealthy, visibly flashy, or wealthy and idle are grounds enough for harassment. My informants hypothesized that the reason behind this is that many members of the morality police are recruited from lower-class parts of town (although this is now changing due to recruitment from all socioeconomic groups) and thus are *oghdehi* (jealous) of wealthy young adults and seek to avenge their jealousy by giving young people who have more money or education than them a harder time. "Sometimes you have to be careful," began Ali Reza, a twenty-one-year-old university student. "One thing I never tell those guys is that I'm a student. You can never tell them you're a student, especially in politically sensitive times," he explained, referring to the fact that students at Tehran University have been known for political activity, for staging protests, and for being against the government, a crime that in Iran could result in harsh punishment for heresy. "They [the morality police] hate the students; they hate people who have more education than them, which isn't hard, believe me. So I just tell them I'm a swimmer, or a *varzeshkar* [exercise trainer]. That usually works better."

Other young Tehranis complained that they were often stopped for driving nice cars or wearing designer clothes. "We had just gotten our new car, a Peugeot, a 206, really nice," Amir Ali and his sister Nina told me. "And those jerks, those dirty guys, we weren't doing anything and they came over and started harassing us. First they said I was driving badly, then they asked us our relationship to each other, and what right did we have to be alone in a car with each other," Amir Ali angrily exclaimed. Nina chimed in: "We told them we are brother and sister and produced the necessary documents, but they still fined us, and it was a heavy fine too," she said. Amir Ali shook his head. "Those jerks, they deserve what they get," he said. "They deserve to spend their days trying to babysit us!"

The consequences of being caught include, as already described, spending one or more nights in the detention centers that have been set up around Tehran, being lashed or fined, having your parents informed of your activities, and possibly receiving a record of arrest (indicating ex-convict status). Although young people do not always receive a written record of arrest or a black mark on their identification cards, when they do receive these, it makes employment more difficult to attain, which is significant because finding a job is already quite difficult for young people in this age group due to the current economic recession caused by global sanctions on Iran. Some young adults see the black mark as something to be proud of while others are frustrated over the restrictions that having a prison record places on employment access. However, most young people said they were willing to face these consequences in order to achieve their social goals.

I too have my share of caught stories, although, as illustrated earlier, I also had several near misses. On more than one occasion I had just left a party (or decided not to go to one at the last minute) that was then raided.

May 13, 2007

My cousin Shireen kept talking my head off about how young people around town know where the hot spots are and what the hot times are when the komite are gonna come for a search. They mostly know the locations that are likely to get raided and they avoid them. I got tired of thinking about it and decided to go with my other cousins to *hava bekhorim* [get some air].

Five of us decided to go for some fruit juice and to drop my cousin Rita off at school. I was sitting in the front seat and didn't notice anything funny, but at one point my cousin Marjān, from the back seat of the car, quickly told her sister Nelly (who was driving) to turn down the music and told all of us to pull our headscarves forward. "They are right there and they are staring at us," she said in a hushed tone as Nelly turned down the music. I hadn't seen them (the morality police).

Even though I was sitting in the front seat, somehow I couldn't spot them as quickly; clearly these women have eyes that are trained for the komite. I turned my head to see where they were standing. "*Zol nazan* [Don't stare at them]; they will come right over to us," said Nelly. I turned my head back and pulled my headscarf forward. "Of course they are staring at us," said Rita. "Five women in a car, what did you think?" "Well, it's better not to provoke anymore trouble," said Jasmin in between sips of her melon juice. "Don't worry. If they come bother you, if they say *hejābet ra rāyat kon* [pull your headscarf forward], just say OK and pull it forward," Rita explained. "It's true," said Marjān from the back of the car. "We should say "of course, I'm sorry, you are right," but it's a bitter pill to swallow." The light was still red. The morality policeman couldn't stop looking at us. After thirty seconds he began walking toward us with a determined stare on his face. "Oh my gosh, he's coming this way, we're gonna be arrested!" exclaimed Nelly. We all said a prayer for the light to turn green before he reached the car. Thankfully it did, and Nelly expertly accelerated down the street and into a back alley. From the rearview mirror I saw the officer shake his head.

May 18, 2007
So on Saturday we had lunch with informants Moji (who is married with two children) and Laleh at this happening new restaurant near our place called Boulevard. Moji had invited us (my friend Shohreh and myself) to go there and check out the men. I honestly am becoming desensitized to married woman here who cheat on their husbands. Really. Anyways, so we went to Boulevard and, yes, the owner was quite attractive (Laleh had her eye on him) and there were a lot of other attractive men in there, all sort of looking at us out of the corner of their eyes. It's amazing here in Tehran: in the same instant that a woman is talking to you about what to order from the menu, she will be simultaneously tucking her hair back under her hejāb and her eyes will dart from the door (looking for komite), around the room (looking for potential mates), to you (to see where you are looking).

On our way to the restaurant we encountered a member of the morality police while Laleh was parking her car. He looked me,

Shohreh, and Moji up and down to try to see what was wrong with our appearance. Finding nothing, he let us go. That was as close as last night when I was coming home from my friends' house after having a glass of red wine and I watched komite pulling people out of their cars on Valiasr street to stuff them into a bus. I quickly popped a mint into my mouth, pulled my headscarf forward, and slumped down in the backseat of the car. Luckily, my being alone in a cab was no problem for them because we passed the inspection.

Laleh's hand on my leg jerked me back to our lunch setting. "You just sit there, like *mast* [yogurt], doing nothing; come on, get up! Go to the bathroom or something; you need to draw attention to yourself," Laleh said to me as we sat waiting for our food. She puckered her newly tattooed lips and was drawing out her words for effect. I looked at her quizzically. "Well, come on! Don't just sit there. Pretend to spill something on yourself, scream out, do something to catch their eyes. Hurry up," she said nudging me. I didn't know what to do. I didn't want to draw attention to myself, but we were already the center of attention thanks to Laleh's loud, high-pitched laughs and Moji's *ada atvar* [attitude and gestures]. I got up and went to the bathroom shyly. As I looked around the room, I saw that I had caught a lot of people's eyes. I didn't really want the attention, so I slipped into the bathroom and then out. "You are no fun," declared Laleh when I returned. She then pulled out her camera to start taking pictures of us, in the hope that the flash would catch people's eyes. It worked. Shohreh also started taking pictures, and before you knew it, most of the men in the restaurant were looking at us. "Let's try to get some phone numbers," Laleh and Moji said. It's like a form of entertainment here, getting numbers and trying to find guys to sleep with, I told Laleh and Moji. "We don' have any other outlet for our miserable lives," Moji said.

"*Dow shish* [double sixes]," Moji said to Laleh, looking at the gentleman sitting next to us, who was, for the moment, alone. "*Dow hasht* [double eights]," responded Laleh. "Is it really worth it?" asked Moji. I looked at them both, again not following what was happening. "It's a joke that everyone in Tehran knows," Laleh told me. "Moses and Jesus were sitting together in a café in heaven playing backgammon when a beautiful girl walked in. 'I'll roll you for her,' said Jesus to

Moses. 'Fine', said Moses, grabbing the dice and rolling them; he rolled a perfect pair of sixes. 'There, dow shish!' Moses said excitedly. Jesus grabbed the dice, rolled them, and shouted out, 'Dow hasht! I win.' Moses took one look at the woman who walked in and said to Jesus, 'Come on, Jesus, was she really worth a miracle?'" Laleh and Moji laughed as Laleh told the joke. "Now that's what we do when we see a guy: we call out a roll of dice, and only if we really want the guy, like I want that *tikkeh* [piece, or good-looking man], do we say dow hasht." Apparently Laleh was really interested in the guy at the table next to us. She kept casually (or not so casually) looking over at him, smiling, and tossing her hair. Eventually she took off her outer mānto, which was more conservative, revealing a tighter, sexier gold mānto with slits up the sides to show off her legs. Moji changed seats to have a better view of the restaurant and take a look at what was available. After a little while, Shohreh and I got tired of sitting there watching people play these games, so we got up to leave. Moji and Laleh decided to stay a bit to try to get some phone numbers. "Just remember to put your other outer mānto on," I told Laleh, concerned that if she left the restaurant looking the way she did, she would be an immediate target for the morality police. As we walked out, I noticed that one of the young men in the restaurant was staring at me. He smiled at me and made a motion of getting up. I smiled and left the restaurant, but of course our car wasn't there, so we had to wait outside for about fifteen minutes. During that time the young man kept looking at me and eventually got up to come out and give me his card, but I was already leaving at that point.

In the meantime, from outside the restaurant I watched Laleh and Moji finally get some numbers and decide to leave in Laleh's bright green Daewoo (a *machin e tableau*, or "flashy car"). As I waved good-bye to them while getting into my car, I noticed that Laleh was still wearing her "sexy" mānto, and as I looked around I saw several members of the morality police watching her. As Laleh and Moji got into their car and began driving down the street, two komite on a bike rode up and stopped them. I got into my car and left quickly, motioning to Laleh to get out fast, but it was too late; the morality policemen were following her. At that point, they drove out of sight, but I got the whole story from Laleh later. "What happened to you guys?" I asked her the next day at dance class. "*Gereftanemoun* [they caught us]," she said. "Tell me all about it," I said. So she did.

> The one guy came over to my side of the car and Moji jumped out and ran to her car, which was just down the street. I was just giving her a ride to her car! Anyways, so the komite guy came to me and said, "Look, you have to follow me." I was scared but thinking on my feet and grabbed the long black cloak I had at first been wearing in the restaurant to cover the parts of my legs that the mãnto leaves exposed. "Why?" I asked him. "I haven't done anything wrong. Tell me what I've done wrong." I was trying to flirt with him, hoping that would do the trick. It didn't. He wasn't one of those young ones [referring to the fact that in recent years younger men had been appointed to be part of the morality police squad, and these young men often had no desire to arrest other youth and were only playful when pretending to arrest young women], he was an older, angrier policeman. He told me to get out of the car, and I did. He took one look at me and said that I wasn't dressed properly and that I would have to go with him to the station. I didn't want to go, so I played dumb. I kept asking him what was wrong with me, and he kept saying that I had to follow him. Eventually I told him that my husband told me never to follow a man anywhere. I was trying to slip in the fact that I was a married woman with a ten-year-old son so that he wouldn't bother me anymore. "If your husband had any *gheirat* [honor, jealousy], he wouldn't let you out of the house looking like that," he told me angrily. "Now get in the car and follow me." There was a lot of traffic. I told him to go ahead and I'd follow. I followed him down the street and then jumped out of my car and into Moji's car. I jumped into the backseat and lay down. I told Moji to step on it and she drove quickly past them. We escaped, thankfully. Otherwise, they wanted to take me to jail and fine me and create a *parvandeh* [criminal record] for me.

Although I narrowly escaped run-ins with the morality police on these occasions, there were several incidents in which I was "caught."

But luckily I never faced harsh punishment, and I managed to dodge detention and arrest every time.

One evening I was conducting some of my interviews in a parked car (as I often did when my key informants would refer me to friends of theirs). The car was a nice, quiet place to conduct the interviews, away from the watchful eyes of others and the komite, or so we thought. Just as one informant was discussing his opinion of the komite and being caught, one rounded the corner and approached us, yelling from ten feet away, "What are you doing in there?! What is going on in that car. *Poostetoon ra mikanam* [I'll tear your skins off]!!" I panicked and froze. My informant quickly turned on the car. As the komite ran up to us, my informant had already started the car and put it in reverse. He drove backward down the one-way street we were parked in, onto a main street, and sped away, leaving the komite chasing us. He drove quickly, and soon we lost the komite in the back alleys of Tehran. "That's what happens with the komite," he said as I looked over my shoulder. "That was close, though," I replied. "Yeah, but it was fun, wasn't it?" responded my informant. "Admit it, you'd do it again," he laughed as I let out a sigh of relief that we had escaped.

The car seemed to be a dangerous place for me with regard to run-ins with the morality police. In the summer of 2007, when I was on my way to lunch with my friend and informant Sonia, a thirty-year-old housewife and mother of two from Shahrak-e-Gharb, we were caught and harassed by the morality police, who wanted to take us to the *kalantari* (youth holding center). We were driving from our dance class to a popular pizza parlor in Shahrak-e-Gharb when we spotted two members of the morality police on a motorbike driving next to cars and looking inside them to make sure that women were properly dressed. During May and June of that summer there had been an intense crackdown on improper dress in Tehran. Some young adults hypothesized that they were clamping down because they were afraid the youth were getting too out of control. Others said they thought it had to do with the worsening of U.S.-Iran relations. (One informant noted that each time relations with the United States worsened, the regime intensified its crackdown and took out its frustration on seemingly westoxicated, or west-infatuated, youth). Still others said that the regime was trying to distract society by making them focus on Islamic dress codes so they would not harp on the worsening economy or increasing gas prices. A popular joke being circulated on cell phones as a text message read, "Pull your headscarves forward so that you forget the price of gas, the rising unemployment, the worsening economy, and Iran's role on the global stage." These text messages, of which there are hundreds or sometimes thousands per day, are often politicized jokes or political commentaries and have helped the youth in building a virtual community for communication with one another. Regardless of the motivations behind the crackdown, during the six weeks I spent in Tehran in 2007, I watched young women be arrested daily on Jordan and Valiasr Boulevards. As I walked to my house near Jordan Street I saw officers screaming at women, telling them they were under arrest, and on more than one occasion I witnessed members of the komite pulling women out of their cars in the middle of the street and beating them. Bystanders (young and old, men and women) who witnessed such a scene often became infuriated with the komite and would leave their cars and motorbikes and violently attack them while telling them to leave the women alone. I witnessed this happening on two occasions. The fact that laypersons are now attacking the morality police speaks to a shift in opinion and behavior and says that many people (not just youth) are no longer afraid of their own fates and are willing to stand up for the youth.

During this period of heightened attention to Islamic dress codes I tried to lay low and be properly dressed at all times. On one particular afternoon I was wearing a long, loose black mānto and a navy blue rusari. Sonia was wearing a loose beige mānto with a white rusari; however, she was also wearing capri pants, so her ankles were showing. When we saw the komite on their motorbikes we both panicked. "Your pants aren't appropriate," I told her. She looked at me and nodded. "Oh no, what are we going to do?" she asked me. "It's no problem," I told her, "just speed by them quickly so they don't notice." Sonia looked at me as we were approaching the dreaded motorbike and tried to speed up. As she did so, she must have lost her concentration because she somehow slightly swerved, causing us almost to run into the divider, thereby calling attention to ourselves. That was enough; they pulled us over. As Sonia stopped the car, we tried quickly to strategize. "What are we going to do now?" I asked her. "It's no worries, just whatever we do we must *not* get out of the car," she told me. I nodded but looked at her quizzically. "Technically they aren't supposed to touch us; it's against Islamic law 'cause we aren't married or related to them; so if the guy is adam hesābi, he won't pull us out of the car but will instead ask us to follow him somewhere," she explained. "I was told never to follow them, no matter what; who knows where they could take you?" I said, remembering my aunt's advice to avoid following the morality police at all costs. She had warned me that sometimes women are taken first to warehouses where they are raped before being taken to jail. Although I wasn't sure about the accuracy of this statement, I didn't want to take my chances. Sonia and I agreed we would stay in the car and try not to follow them at all costs. The two men parked their motorbike and stormed up to the car. "What kind of driving is that? Are you crazy? Were you trying to get yourselves killed?!" one of them asked angrily. "I'm so sorry," Sonia said. "I didn't see the divider, I didn't mean it. Please, officer, let us pass," she begged. "You think you are so fancy with this Renault car," the other one said to Sonia and then came around to my side of the car and stuck his face through the open window. "You think you are so special with those sunglasses, huh?" he asked me, pointing his finger at my nose. "They are health prescribed, medical glasses," I blurted out nervously, amazed that I had come up with such a lie on the spot. "Get out of the car," commanded the first one. "No, I won't," Sonia answered. I said nothing, pulled my rusari even further down my forehead and slumped in the front seat. "I said, get out of the car!" he shouted. Neither of us moved. "We are both married, our husbands don't like us talking to strange men," Sonia told him. I nodded, quickly trying to invent a husband in my head. "You're married?" the second officer asked. We both nodded. "And your husbands let you go out of the house looking like this? Fancy sunglasses, shalvarak [capri pants]. Where is their gheirat?" he asked. Neither of us said a word. "Call your husbands right now, I want to have a word with them. What kind of man lets his wife go out looking like you prostitutes?" he snapped. "My husband is asleep, he is in Amrika," I said, continuing my lies. "Oh, you're khāreji [foreign] then?" he asked me. "I'm from Iran, but I live over there," I answered. "So you have come here to start *javsazi* [a political scene; a punishable offense]?" he asked. I was silent. I didn't know what the word meant, but Sonia had gotten so upset she took over the conversation. "No, no, sir, she is just visiting. She isn't *seasi* [political]. Please, sir. Just leave us alone. I have two children waiting for me at home and we have to go bring them food; they are hungry," she said. "Two children?" asked the other man. "How old are you two? It's not becoming of you to have children," he said, implying that we looked too young. Sonia nodded. The officer asked us to produce our identification cards. I didn't have mine (which the officer was angry about), but Sonia handed over hers. "Wow, you are thirty years old and really do have two kids," he said incredulously. Sonia nodded. "Well, how old are you? And what is your story?" he asked me. "I'm thirty-five and I have two children also; they are in the United States right now with my husband," I lied. The two officers then spent fifteen minutes lecturing us on the importance of proper Islamic dress and comportment, and why we had to be better role models for our children. The entire time they were talking I was silently praying that they wouldn't arrest us, because I wasn't sure who I would call to get me out of jail (my parents weren't around and I didn't have a man to "answer" for me). At the end of their rant, one of them looked at Sonia's identification card again and then looked the two of us up and down. "We were going to take you down to the station and punish you," he said. "But since you are old, we aren't going to do that. We know you should know better, and we'll hope that your husbands do the punishing for us," he added, then gave Sonia back her card, turned on his heel, and left. We both let out a sigh of relief.

Another of my more terrifying run-ins with the komite also took place in a car, during the summer of 2000, when I was spending time with my friend and key informant Diar. We were driving home one evening and our car was stopped. The komite asked about the nature of our relationship: married, we said. If we hadn't said that we would have immediately been arrested and forced to get married. It was that summer that I learned the ways in which young people had adapted to living under the current regime. They always had a story or lie prepared for the komite; those who were in relationships coordinated false stories of their marriage so that their stories would match if they were arrested and interrogated separately. They knew all the back roads to take to either avoid the komite or escape from them, and they knew when and how they could bribe them, when they could fight back, and when they should run. Diar, thinking quickly on his feet while I was in a panicked freeze, somehow figured out that this was a case that required bribery. The officer asked us how long we'd been married. "Two years," responded Diar. "When is your anniversary?" he asked me. Once again I froze. I didn't know any Persian calendar dates except for my own birthday. "The sixth of Mehr," I responded, the date of my birthday.[9] Diar smiled at the officer and said, "Oh, my friend, it's you. I almost didn't recognize you." He reached into his pocket for his wallet. At that the officer's face softened. "Yes," said the officer, gently. "I just remembered that I forgot to give you *shirnee-e arouseemoon* [the sweets or celebration of our wedding]," Diar said, handing him a wad of money and shaking his hand. That must have done the trick, because the officer smiled, nodded at me, and was on his way. I was terrified, but Diar just laughed and explained that this kind of extortion was part of daily life, especially for young people who drove nice cars and were prone to arrest for being "flashy."

It seemed as though the relationship between members of the komite and many of my informants had undertones of class tension. Setareh, my anthropologist friend from Tehran University, and I often discussed the issue of class and how it was playing out on the streets. "Well, the conservatives and the komite tend to be of lower class," she began. "And the kids they are harassing tend to be of higher class, so they get *oghdehi.*" She then told the story of being on the ski slopes of Shemshack, a popular ski destination just outside of Tehran. She said she had gone there with her friends and had noticed how "over the top" the women there can get with their ski outfits, makeup, and lack of proper hejāb, especially the wealthy ones in their hooded Bogner ski jackets. "As I was sitting down to buckle my boots, I saw a North Tehrani girl sunning herself, as usual," said Setareh. "She was just lying out in the sun; you know, up there they do whatever they want, they do such things that you wouldn't believe. As she was laying there I saw one of the komite guys and you could tell his blood was just boiling. *Why did this girl deserve to act like this and be wealthier and have a better life than him?* he must have been thinking to himself. When some of her buddies came out and they all started joking together, the guy could no longer contain himself. It was too much. He came over and started yelling at them, threatening their arrest. But you know what is funny? It's like young people here are increasingly less scared of the komite, and you find them yelling at them all the time. But yeah, I think the face and personality of these guys has changed too," she sighed and sipped her tea as I continued to fumble with my digital tape recorder. "Like, I'll tell you another story." She began again, after we sat in silence a few minutes, processing our discussion of class relations.

My brother and his friends are really active, like, I mean politically and socially active, although in Iran it's kind of one and the same thing. Anyways, let's not get off track with that discussion. Back to my brother and his friends. They love to pour into the streets and just do crazy things. Well just the other night, after the soccer game, they poured into the streets like a lot of other young people and started dancing. Then one of these guys [komite] came over to yell at them and tell them to stop. My brother and his friend grabbed the guy's hand and brought him into the dance circle. They kept saying to him, "Come on, brother, you don't want to be filled with hate. Let go of your hate. You know that you just want to be young and have fun. Come and dance with us. Just this once, let yourself go." Well, sure enough, the cop started dancing with them! I wish someone had been there to take a picture.

Setareh and I had many conversations about the ways in which the morality police interacted with the youth, and about how this interaction was indicative of the sociopolitical environment. It seemed to both of us that over the course of the preceding seven years (2000–2007, the period during which I conducted my research in Iran) many things had changed. More and more members of the morality police were young men who believed in or were part of the sexual revolution. Therefore, young people in 2007 were not caught as often as they may have been in 2000. Members of the komite did not raid parties at the same rate as before, and while cycles of arrest continue to this day, young people fear the morality police far less now than they ever used to. Perhaps this is due to parental support and the support of most of the Iranian people, who come to the aid of young people who are being publicly harassed by the komite. Perhaps young people have become numb to the experiences of harassment and arrest, and their lack of fear makes it so that the morality police do not derive pleasure out of arresting them. Perhaps komite members themselves have shifted their viewpoints and now side more with the youth than with the regime. It is important to reemphasize that in this social and sexual revolution being enacted and embodied by many young people, there are many levels of debate, discussion, and change.

These "caught" stories demonstrate some aspects of the dance between the youth; members of the morality police, some of whom are sympathetic or unsympathetic youth, some of whom are older and sympathetic or older supporters of the regime; and the state. Being caught is a potential consequence of the resistance and rebellion of many young Tehranis, but it is an aspect of the revolution that the young people accept. Many youth feel that being caught and interacting with members of the morality police are necessary steps to ensuring that their goals of social change are achieved. Today young people feel that they are succeeding by causing a shift in attitudes that has resulted in adults standing up for them more often and morality police harassing them far less often, than they did ten years ago. Increasingly, many Iranians—not just youth who see themselves as part of the sexual revolution, but also older Iranians of varying socioeconomic statures—wish to change the culture, and many members of the state are beginning to share these desires as well. Therefore, although I have focused on one aspect of the tensions between the youth and the morality police, it is important to remember that this is not a simple battle between two opposing sides, but rather a larger project of modernity, with many differing viewpoints.

6   High Risk

August 1, 2004

Yesterday I had an interesting conversation about risk with one of my
cab drivers. Nima, twenty-two and originally from Mashad, echoed
statements that I had been hearing from many of my informants, but
never so succinctly. "AIDS only happens in prisons," he told me while
driving me from my house to a testing center in the Southern part
of town. "If you stay out of trouble, and stay out of jail, you aren't
gonna get it." He seemed convinced that this was the only mode of
transmission for the disease. When I told him it can be passed outside
of prisons, and often during unprotected sex, he was nonchalant. "Well,
I guess you should know your partners, then, right?" he asked me. "But
how well can you really know your partner?" I responded. He sighed
and shrugged his shoulders, "Look lady, if I get AIDS or something,
I'll deal with it then. I have so many more problems that are more real.
I guess if I got it, well, then I got it. Not much you can do, but I'll just
deal with it then." As he said this, I noticed that one of the informants I
was traveling with was calmly staring out the window of the car. "Did
you hear that?" I whispered to her. "He doesn't care if he gets AIDS!"
She looked at me blankly and said, "Look, there are worse things than
just quietly dying of a disease. We have a lot more risks here; death and
disease don't have the same meaning [as they do in America]." It was
then that I began to realize that for young Tehranis, the social risks
of sex far outweighed the viral risks. For many of them, it was more
important to adhere to social norms and rules than to be infected with
a virus such as HIV. It also became clear that safe sex meant "socially

safe" sex. In other words, if young people took the necessary social precautions and maintained their reputations and engaged in socially acceptable behaviors, they seemed to think that they were safe, and the viral issues did not have much significance in their minds.

The sexual revolution enacted by urban Iranian youth has succeeded in creating a shift in the conversation about sexuality and is now succeeding in carving out a space for an important social movement. There are challenges, however, that young adults face in enacting what they call a sexual revolution, as well as ways in which they attempt to minimize the risks associated with their behavior. Although young adults have achieved many gains through their sexual revolution, it is important to focus on some of the consequences of their sexual and social enactments, and to explore the notion of risk as young people see it.

Many of the health risks to which the young adults are exposing themselves are unknown by them. Most Iranian youth reveal that they are uninformed about the consequences of unprotected sex, use of multiple psychoactive drugs, multiple partners, abortion, self-administered

Figure 6.1. Many women have turned to cigarettes and other substances to combat rising rates of depression in Iran's failing economy. © 2006 by Nader Davoodi. Used by permission.

contraceptive pills, and other potential risk behaviors. Because premarital sex is forbidden under the current regime, efforts to disseminate information on family planning, harm reduction, and sex education are minimal and often reserved for couples who are engaged to be married. Young adults who are not yet engaged (or who do not plan to be) currently have limited access to the information they need to make better informed decisions about their behaviors, although this too is changing. In the summer of 2007 I noted that many more young people were becoming educated about HIV and AIDS and contraceptive use before marriage; this increased access to information signals an attitude that was not in place prior to 1997. However, although young people do now have better access to information, many women reminded me that, as unmarried young adults, they did not have access to oral contraceptives such as birth control pills or the morning-after pill, which is occasionally dispensed at pharmacies without requiring a marriage license (although this is illegal because premarital sex is illegal). And if they did have access, they were fearful of purchasing these pills lest their parents or family members discover them. Many of the young women noted that going to a pharmacy to purchase such items (which were often quite expensive) made them vulnerable to being seen in public procuring items that would indicate they were involved in sexual activity. Most informants were deterred by the social risks (and costs) of being caught attempting to purchase contraceptives such as condoms or the morning-after pill, and thus did not feel that these were options available to them. It is important to explore questions of health and risk that have arisen as a result of changes taking place in the sexual and social culture. Additionally, it is crucial to remember that young people's ability to talk with me about some of their most sensitive and delicate sexual and reproductive health issues signals a shift in ideas and attitudes about sex and sexuality. In the summer of 2000, when I first began my research in Iran, it was very difficult to encourage young people to talk to me about their personal sexual health concerns. By 2007, informants would call me to ask questions about safe sex and volunteer their stories with little encouragement. As Dr. Parsan (head of an HIV testing and counseling center in Mashad) told me in May 2007, however, "It's all about the P in KAP!"—knowledge, attitudes, and practices. A KAP study measures sexual behavior and harm reduction strategies. Parsan is elated with the success of his newest HIV education program, which is being promoted in schools and universities throughout Iran. "They have the knowledge, there has been a shift in attitudes, but we are stuck at P, practices. They know about safe sex more today than five years ago, but they aren't practicing it, and we have to understand the extent of this, and why it's not happening."[1]

Tales from the Classroom

From 1951 to 1953, the Shah mandated that the state school curriculum for high school biology students in their second year must include a section on human reproduction, detailing the mechanics of reproduction as well as a description of male and female reproductive anatomy. The Compulsory Education Act of 1953 required children to remain in school until the age of fifteen, and thus this biology and human reproduction curriculum, which was offered to adolescents in middle school (ages twelve to fifteen), was structured to reach all young people passing through the education system. The information presented in this curriculum, which emphasized that both males and females contribute genetic material to the production of a fetus, runs contrary to a central tenet of sharia with regard to reproduction, namely that the child is the product only of male "seed." When Khomeini came to power and reinstated Islamic laws, he suppressed the dissemination of information that stated that males and females both contribute to the child's genetic makeup. He then took this decree one step further and decided to ban all discussion of reproduction and sex prior to marriage, and therefore banned the Shah's former sex education curriculum.[2]

More informal sources of sexual knowledge were available during the 1950s, 1960s, and early 1970s, including the family, television, magazines, and newspaper cartoons, all of which were banned after the revolution in 1979. Prior to the Islamist regime's crackdown immediately following the revolution, a primary source of informal sexuality information was American pornography magazines such as *Playboy* and *Penthouse*. During the time of the Shah, these magazines were bought and sold and displayed openly in private homes. Although in December of 1993 the Iranian Parliament approved a law that mandated capital punishment for producers and distributors of pornographic materials and thus made these magazines illegal, many old copies, or copies purchased on Tehran's black market, still provide information to young people.

After the revolution, the primary formal source of information on any aspect of human sexuality was the mandatory religious curriculum installed in the schools. In these classes, students learned about genitalia and the biological functions of reproductive anatomy through religious leaders' descriptions of the rules of ablution (ritual bathing) and purity and pollution surrounding the body. Religious teachers disseminated information on what to do prior to prayer in order to counter the "polluting" effects of "urination, defecation, expectoration, expulsion of nasal mucus, menstruation, childbirth, ejaculation, and penetration of the vagina (human and animal) to restore spiritual purity."[3] The teachers and mullahs who presented this information stressed that sexual behavior is the most unclean of the body pollution processes.

Currently, formal codified knowledge about sex and sexuality is passed to young people in mosques or during religious instruction. Young women receive puberty education at the onset of menarche in most public schools in Tehran; however, education about contraception and family planning is usually not provided until young adults have entered into a marital contract. (Some young people receive limited information about family planning at certain universities or schools, but most of my informants reported not having been offered these classes.) Today the government requires couples seeking a marriage license to participate in mandatory prenuptial counseling classes (a requirement enacted in 2000 and the first of its kind). To receive an officially certified form documenting readiness for marriage, couples must show proof that they have attended at least one of these one-hour classes, which won Iran the award for family planning from the United Nations Fund for Population Advancement (UNFPA) in 2002. The average age of marriage in Tehran is now between twenty-three and twenty-six,[4] but the average age at first intercourse is roughly fourteen or fifteen, according to my discussions with informants as well as the thirty-five surveys that were filled out as part of my research. There exists, therefore, a gap of about ten years during which young people are sexually active but without access to medical information, resources, or ways to minimize

their risky behavior. This may explain in part the rise of STIs and ig-
norance about contraceptives. Although birth control efforts have been
successful among the married portion of the population, married young
people often do not pass on the information or resources to unmarried
young people.

The sex education curriculum that I was able to observe included
seminars provided at the high school and sometimes university levels,
as well as the mandatory prenuptial counseling course provided for
couples who have legally registered to marry. Counselors, health care
providers, and the teachers who structure and lead these courses differ in
their implementation of the curriculum and in their interactions with the
young people. Many of my young informants claimed that these courses
were uninformative and that their teachers were unapproachable and
unhelpful. Many of the teachers and health care providers I interviewed
complained that the young people were inattentive and rude, and many
of them asked for my help in structuring a sex education program that
would be more appealing to the population.

The current sex education curriculum that was designed and approved
by the Ministry of Education and the Ministry of Health in 2003 for
middle school, high school, and early university students focuses on the
experiences of puberty, menstruation, and changing bodies as well as
on young people's relationships with their friends of the same and opposite sex, with their families, and with community religious leaders. The
first section of the course focuses on the experience of menstruation for
women and nocturnal emissions for men. The details of this experience
are discussed and women are encouraged to recognize that they are "unclean" during this period (so they should not enter mosques or other holy
sites), and men under no circumstances should succumb to the desire to
masturbate even when their hormones are developing. The next section
of this curriculum looks at relationships with friends, family members,
and community religious leaders. Here young adults are encouraged to
break off their relationships with members of the opposite sex. A seminar leader I was observing in 2005, who was brought in to give a sex
education course to middle schoolers, told the students that "when you
are younger, it is OK to be friends with boys and girls and to have different kinds of friends of different ages to play with. As you get older,

however, you must discontinue many of these relationships. Boys should only play with other boys and only those who are their own age. Boys should not play with older boys or younger ones. It is the same for girls," he lectured. When the teacher read this aloud, I could see the faces of the young boys change. "But why can't I be friends with my old friends?" one boy blurted out. "We were friends before; now because I'm changing I'm supposed to change my friends too?" he asked as his classmates nodded in agreement. The teacher barely looked up from the text he was reading. "Yes, my son," he said authoritatively and then moved on to the next section of the course, which was about young people's relationships with their parents. This section told the young adults never to tell a lie to their parents or other authority figures. They were also taught that engaging in acts of sexual mischief would dishonor their families, their religious communities, and God. They were reminded that masturbation was haram (a sin against Islamic values and culture) and that all sexual desires should be repressed until after marriage. After the seminar the leader looked up from his text and asked, "Any questions?" There was silence in the room. After class the teacher shook his head and said to me, "You see, I know that we have a lot of problems here, and that the kids are up to no good, but they refuse to talk about it! I mean, I know the old saying, 'Who among us has not done something just because we should not do it?' I just can't get them to talk to me about what they have done, what they are doing. I don't know what to do." He sighed. A few hours later I saw some of the young people from the class gathered and making fun of their teacher, who was "so conservative," and making jokes about masturbation. This was just one example of the disconnect between teachers and their students that frustrated both parties.

The curriculum for the mandatory prenuptial counseling courses differs significantly from the school sex education curriculum in that it focuses more on married life, family planning, and creating a "happy and healthy home." Both courses are provided to men and women separately. During my time in Iran, I had the opportunity to sit in on several of these courses offered to women. Their content varied from charts and diagrams about the reproductive system to discussion of reproductive health, contraception, conjugal debt, and sexual pleasure. Not surprisingly, the openness and values of the counselors and teachers who lead these sessions vary from person to person, and the instructors sometimes teach the classes on the basis of their own values rather than following a standardized curriculum.

The courses are always provided at a *markaz-e-moshavere*, or counseling center, which often also serves as a one-stop shop for couples wanting to get married. In Iran all couples applying for a marriage license must pass HIV and drug tests and show evidence of having attended these courses. The counseling centers are distributed throughout Tehran.

The first time I sat in on one of these courses was in 2004. The center was located toward the middle of the city, close to Tehran University. Several of my informants had told me to start at this location because they were unhappy with the information they had received there. It took me several tries to find the building because it was not clearly marked and was located on the second floor of what seemed to be a run-down building. I pushed the buzzer and was let in. As I climbed the steep stairs, I noticed how dark, humid, and unwelcoming the center was. Inside, the walls were blank and there were no chairs or benches but rather pillows on the floor. A few young couples were milling about. In one corner of the room there was a tray of tea and cookies, which everyone seemed to be ignoring. I only saw three or four people in the waiting room, and four or five women who appeared to work there were offering tea and ushering guests to either the bathroom, the kitchen, the office, or the classrooms. I asked where the courses were being taught and a woman pointed toward a door down a dark hallway. As I walked down the hallway, I noticed that the atmosphere was quite tense. Two classrooms were provided for the prenuptial course, one for men and one for women. Outside of the women's classroom, approximately twenty-five young women sat in silence, anxiously awaiting the teacher's arrival. After we had filed into the classroom, the teacher began by telling the young women to take out notepads and paper. "You are going to want to write down every word I say because it is important," she said in a high pitched voice. Like many of the other women I observed working at this particular center, she was shrouded in a thick black chãdor, with only her face showing. "Khãnum hah [ladies], the most important thing I am going to teach you in this course is that you must please your husbands, at all costs. This is what will hold your marriage together," she said matter-of-factly. Half of the young women hung on the teacher's every word while the other half rolled their eyes, looked around the room, filed their nails, or snapped bubbles of chewing gum. "Khānum hah," she continued, her shrill voice becoming even louder, "your man comes first. You must always be ready for your husband's sexual needs. If perchance he is watching a football game on television, you should be resting to prepare yourself, or else preparing your bed for the evening. If you should feel overcome by fatigue yourself, make sure always to ask your husband, 'Is there anything else you need from me?' or 'Would you like to have me later?' before retiring." After the course I approached the instructor to ask for an interview. She rudely brushed me off, asked why I was wasting her time if I wasn't getting married, and told me to leave her alone.

During the summer of 2004, I attended two other sessions of this course at the same venue, with different teachers. All three of the women who taught the course focused primarily on the importance of pleasing one's husband and on notions of conjugal debt. One of the teachers alluded to the importance of satisfying the "men who protect us." After these experiences I was surprised that this prenuptial counseling had helped Iran receive the family planning award from UNFPA in 2002. Most of my informants reported that they had learned nothing about family planning from attending these courses, and in fact they had found them quite frustrating. "I mean, how am I supposed to seek out counseling when the counselors see me as less than my husband?" complained Nassim. "I remember the course well because I just took it a few months ago," added her friend Sarbena, age twenty-five. "The part I remember best was the fact that the teacher told me that at twenty-five I was too old to be in this course! She told me there must be something wrong with me that for all these years no one wanted to marry me!" Sarbena spoke to a sentiment common among the seven of my female informants who had taken the course: namely that they disliked being judged by the counselors at the centers. They felt that the judgment passed on them by what they called *Khānum hah-e-omol-e-chādori* (conservative chādor-wearing women) impeded their efforts to access family planning education and resources.

In 2005 I attended several sessions of this course at another venue closer to the northern part of the city, near Tajrish bāzār. This counseling center was quite different from the one I had visited the previous year. It was well marked with a large blue and yellow sign so that it could be spotted from the street. The staff were very friendly; when I entered I was greeted by an information officer, who politely asked what I was looking for. I immediately noticed the many posters on the walls that contained slogans about HIV testing, child rearing, drug use, and harm reduction, all in Persian. Sunlight streamed through the center's windows, and the hallways and waiting rooms were lined with couches filled with young couples and families with young children. The basement was used for treating substance abusers, including providing methadone treatment. The ground floor was for counseling clients on STIs and HIV, and it housed the classrooms for the prenuptial counseling courses. The second floor housed the testing center where couples and individuals could get free HIV, STI, and pregnancy tests. The top floor was for family planning services and pre- and postnatal care. The people who frequented this center were also friendly and were willing to discuss the reasons for their visits. Many reported that they were there for the premarital testing and courses, but several indicated that since their first visit (usually for the prenuptial services) they had returned frequently to receive counseling and family planning services. Three women said they had been coming to the center for five years and were now bringing their infants and toddlers to be seen by the pediatricians on the top floor.

The three female teachers of the prenuptial counseling course at this particular center were extremely friendly and allowed me to sit in on many of their courses as well as to interview them. They had different teaching styles: one treated the course as a lecture, imparting the necessary knowledge to the students and then leaving; the second used a question-and-answer format; and the third used games and exercises to get the information across. They all agreed on seven points or subject areas that were to be discussed during the course: (1) the reason for and *ahamiyat* (purpose) of marriage; (2) the means of disease prevention and contraception; (3) the STI, HIV, and pregnancy testing available to the women, and encouragement to continue routine testing; (4) education about HIV and STIs such as Hepatitis C; (5) marital mental and physical health; 6) relations between husbands and wives; and (7) the timing and spacing of children and options for infertile couples. At the end of the course, the teachers distributed a variety of pamphlets on contraception and disease prevention, as well as a packet of free condoms. Attending these courses was enlightening and impressive. The women who led the courses were open-minded and discussed issues ranging from extramarital affairs and infidelity to the importance of women gaining pleasure out of sexual interaction. One of the teachers even told the women they had the right to refuse sex from their husbands if it was not pleasurable for them. She talked about sexual pleasure as a right, and emphasized that should their husbands achieve orgasm before they did, they were to urge their husbands to continue until they themselves were pleased. These teachers also had a calm and open demeanor. The black chãdors of the ladies in the previous clinic were replaced with white lab coats and loose beige or white headscarves. Two of the teachers wore makeup, and one pushed back her headscarf to reveal burgundy highlights. These teachers were so open and inviting that routinely after the course had ended several young women would line up to ask the teachers their own personal questions. I heard young women telling these teachers about their abortions and their desire for extramarital affairs. Many of them revealed emotional troubles and relationship issues that they were having with their fiancés. The young women seemed to really trust these teachers.

According to the teachers, the students who attended the courses came from a range of socioeconomic levels. They were a mix of women in tight mãntos with heavily made-up faces, women from the university in school uniforms and wearing some makeup, and a few young women in chãdors. Many of the women receiving family planning or testing services were in chãdors and, according to Mrs. Kalhour, the head of the clinic, were from the poorer parts of town. "We are trying to keep our doors open to everyone, to make sure that women from all over Tehran come and use our services," she said. "We are doing our best, but there are thousands of young people we want to help who would never come here. Things in Iran are getting better. The government now funds us to keep the clinic open. Parents bring their daughters and have open discussions with their kids about contraception. We are allowed to promote condoms now. But we still have a long way to go."

Information About Sex

"Yes, we here in Iran, we do know the condom; we know what it looks like, but we don't know what to do with it, see? It's like driving a nice car. Yes, we know what the good cars are, and there are a select few of us who can get our hands on these nice cars, but do we know how to drive these nice cars? No! With sex it's the same: we know there is this thing called a condom, and supposedly we have nice ones, but we just don't know what to do with them. We need education."

   Hooman

Many of the young people I spoke with were grappling with fears and misconceptions about their sexualities and sexualized bodies. Although some experienced confusion about specific sexual practices and acts, most were misinformed about HIV, STIs, and contraception. Many of them had never had an outlet for talking about their concerns and questions and had been carrying heavy burdens on their shoulders for some time. For some, these fears and misconceptions were causing a great deal of strain, and they indicated that one of their biggest problems was not being equipped with the knowledge that could help them overcome their anxieties and feelings of guilt.

"I remember that there was this doctor friend of our family who said it's bad to have sex every day, really bad. He said that too much sex is unhealthy," Katayoun told me one afternoon. She looked very worried and quickly added, "Is this true?" I was not sure how to respond to her question, so I asked if she remembered what specifically the doctor had said was bad about "too much sex." "He just said that it's bad, that there is something wrong with people who want to have sex every day." She stopped and drew in her breath before continuing. "But I like to have sex every day, and I'm so scared that I'm going to get really sick. Can you help me?" she begged. I told her there was nothing unhealthy about her sexual appetite. She seemed so relieved when I told her this, and a few weeks later called to thank me.

Many of my other informants expressed similar pangs of guilt due to their desire to have sex often. "I heard that you can become incapable of having babies if you have sex too often," Asana once told me. "I'm scared too because I love sex, but I also want to have babies someday. Plus, now I'm getting serious with my boyfriend, and I think we are going to get married. I'm scared that I should probably tell him I may not be able to have babies and that I've had a lot of sex before him." She was at the point of tears. "It's not true," I consoled her. I told her that safe sex even in abundance would not result in infertility. Her friend Saara, a midwife in training, was surprised at this news. "I didn't know that," she said. "But I did always think that the amount I want to have sex is bad, and makes me dirty." Many of the young women I spoke with talked about feeling "dirty" or "slutty" because of their frequent desires for sex. For some of them, this feeling had been ingrained in them by family members or, more often, by boyfriends. "My boyfriend was inadequate," said Sormeh. "So he would make me feel bad for wanting sex. For so long I felt like I was sick, like there was something wrong with me 'cause I loved sex. But then I realized it was his problem, not mine. I'm not sick, and my new partners really enjoy my cravings."

The data on HIV and STIs vary depending on the source, but all sources agree that further research is needed in this area, and that given the current sensitivity of the topic in Iran, much of the data currently presented may not be accurate.

Although some data about the HIV epidemic are available, data on STI rates remain virtually nonexistent. According to the World Health Organization (WHO), "there has been a significant increase of total numbers of reported STI cases in the country during the period of 1995 to 1998."[5] The WHO researchers named candidiasis, trichomoniasis, chlamydia, and gonorrhea as the four main infections, accounting for more than 60 percent of total diagnosed cases. In their assessment of STI syndromes, they noted that in 2003 the incidence of young persons (both men and women) reporting urethral discharge was 1.96 per ten thousand, and for those reporting genital ulcers, 8.4 per ten thousand. Other data on STI rates, transmission, and resources for treatment are unavailable, which further highlights the importance of ethnographic research in this area, as well as the need to offer young Tehranis further education about sexual and reproductive health risks and decision making.

The first case of HIV in Iran was reported in 1986; by the end of 2004 there were officially 9,800 HIV-positive cases and 374 cases of AIDS.[6] However, the WHO and the United Nations AIDS (UNAIDS) program placed the estimate of people living with HIV and AIDS in Iran at the end of 2004 at 31,000, with a low estimate of 10,000 and a high estimate of 61,000.[7] This marked discrepancy between actual number of cases and estimated number of cases speaks to the need for further screening and research in this area. WHO and UNAIDS researchers are currently trying to create screening mechanisms for estimate numbers on the basis of in-country research. According to a UNAIDS official in Tehran with whom I spoke, "Based on the reported data, the HIV epidemic in the Islamic Republic of Iran appears to be accelerating at an alarming trend." The WHO and the Iranian Ministry of Health agree that the primary means of transmission of HIV remains injection drug use. In a country with more than two million officially registered drug addicts[8] and more than three hundred thousand identified injection drug users,[9] most HIV centers run by Iranian officials, members of the WHO, and the Center for Disease Management in Iran agree that more than 60 percent of registered cases contracted the disease through shared needles. The UNAIDS officials I spoke with added that there have also been huge outbreaks among injection drug users in prisons. It is acknowledged by UNAIDS officials in Iran that at least 35 percent of people who are HIV-positive contracted the disease sexually. Prior to 1997, the government did not wish to accept Iran's growing HIV problem. During the late 1990s, and in recent years, however, the government (perhaps prompted by reformist president Khatami) changed its stance and began to issue fatwas encouraging HIV research and to fund public media campaigns. In 2003 the government issued a fatwa legalizing needle exchanges, making Iran one of the first countries to do so in the region. In their final report on the HIV/AIDS situation in Iran, the government-sponsored Center for Disease Management wrote that "due to the paucity of research in Iran on high-risk behaviors, little is known about potential points of entry for HIV and about behaviors that may influence the rate at which HIV may spread and take hold within specific subpopulations, their HIV/AIDS awareness has not been studied as well."[10]

In a country where high value is placed on so-called good, moral behavior, admitting to a disease whose mode of transmission is primarily unprotected sex and intravenous drug use is difficult. For many years the regime refused to comment on the incidence of HIV in Iran, and researchers interested in this topic were discouraged from investigating the issue. Since 2003, however, because the government has accepted that HIV rates may be rising, researchers are now permitted to study the epidemic, and there are now a few testing centers throughout Tehran (although very few outside the capital) and several hospitals have opened their doors to HIV and AIDS patients. It is still very difficult to find a testing center, however, and the hospitals and clinics that have been established to serve HIV patients are overcrowded and underfunded. Although some providers and doctors have become more open to working with HIV/AIDS patients, HIV-positive people are still highly stigmatized by the community, and they face difficulties in getting the services they need because most of them have been exiled from their community (that is, asked to leave their families and neighborhoods in Tehran, or the city altogether), and many have lost their jobs.

It is therefore not surprising that my informants had many misconceptions about HIV/AIDS. Most did not know the difference between HIV and AIDS, and many were confused about modes of transmission. These confusions led to anxieties on their part about going to the dentist, the hairdresser, or the swimming pool. During my time in Tehran I researched information being disseminated about HIV. The few times that it was alluded to either on the radio, in magazines, or on billboards, the discussion or the message was centered mainly on drug users and HIV.

Whenever I brought up the topic of HIV in a focus group, it caused intense discussion accompanied by much discomfort. "There is no information out there telling us what we should be doing, why, and how," complained Majid. "There could be all these infected people around us and we don't even know it," he exclaimed, which caused unease among the other members of the focus group. "They could go to the dentist or hairdresser and they might not know they have AIDS, and what if the dentist there uses the same stuff on us that he used on the AIDS guy?" Another member of the group added that she didn't even really know what HIV was, only AIDS, and asked me to explain the difference. When I did, many people in the group were surprised. "There isn't any information here," she repeated. "People don't know what AIDS is—people like me [meaning educated] don't even know what HIV is. It's weird, though, because they think it's out there, that it's not our problem," she added. Another member of the group, a young man, raised his hand and began to speak slowly. "AIDS scares me," he said as some of the others nodded. "But to tell you the truth, [there is something else that] I'm scared of more than the disease." Everyone leaned in closer to listen to him. "There was an article in the paper about this guy who went to the hospital and said he had AIDS. The hospital refused him too. Apparently his family had kicked him out of the house and now he had no place to go." As he told this story I noticed people in the room shifting uncomfortably in their seats. "So, I sometimes think, well, if I have it, I'd rather not know and just die; it might be easier that way than living such a hard life." At this there was uproar, and everyone began talking at once.

Overall, my informants seemed to be split between thinking it wasn't a real threat in Iran, or it was only a problem for drug users, and being very afraid that they might be susceptible to contracting it from the dentist, hairdresser, or swimming pool. One couple I interviewed spanned both views. While twenty-two-year-old computer technician Yassi believed that AIDS was not a real problem, her boyfriend, Hamid, a twenty-three-year-old electrical engineer, felt he was highly susceptible to it. "Yeah, I've seen a few billboards with AIDS stuff on them, but I didn't think it was a real problem here in Iran—more like a thing that happens in Africa," Yassi told me. Her boyfriend quickly grabbed her wrist and shook his head. "No, *azzizam* [term of endearment]. I heard that the dentist and the hairdresser can give it to you and that it's a real problem here in Iran. In the last five years it's become a problem, and some people are starting to talk about it, but it's like, to be honest, Pardis, we have so many other problems that AIDS, well. . . ." He was interrupted by his girlfriend. "AIDS isn't a big problem," she interjected. "No, it is a problem, but we have other problems that seem more pressing, like dealing with the komite."

Many of my informants believed that the primary means of HIV transmission was getting it from the dentist or hairdresser. "What do I know about AIDS?" said Nazanin. "I know it's a bad disease, a very bad one that you have to protect yourself from. And it's not just from sex that you get it. You're likely to get it from the dentist or the hairdresser too." Another young man included swimming pools in his list of how

HIV is transmitted. "It's a bad disease, AIDS, but I can't explain what the disease really is," commented Behrad. "I know that some people have AIDS and some do not. While you can get it from sex, you also get it from the dentist, the hairdresser, or sometimes swimming pools." He said this matter-of-factly, then smiled, puffed out his chest, and added, "That's why I don't swim in public swimming pools."

Others believed rumors that HIV was solely a disease of drug users and ex-prison convicts. "Only drug users have AIDS," said Hatef, an eighteen-year-old coffee shop attendant. "I feel confident that I'm not gonna get it, and I know lots about AIDS." When I asked him about what he knew and whether he was aware that HIV was transmitted sexually, he shook his head. "It comes through blood," he began. "Some people will tell you that it comes from sexual relations, but it's not really from that; it's mostly from heroin users, from them sticking dirty needles into their veins. And also it comes from prisons specifically; that's where it is mostly spread. They don't have needles, and they are forced to share needles, and it is easily spread. Then they come home and spread it to their friends, and when they go back to prison it continues. This is the most normal way AIDS is spread." He wanted to know if I was impressed with his knowledge about HIV and if I understood now why he didn't feel at risk. I was not sure how to respond, and as I sat there quietly trying to figure out what to say to him, he spoke up again. "I don't do drugs with needles, so I'm all good," he said. Again I did not know whether it was appropriate to step out of my role as an anthropologist and become an activist and educator, or whether I should try to process the information he had given me and focus my attention on the interview. This situation came up more than once, and ultimately I decided that at the end of each interview I would spend a few minutes talking to my informants about any gaps in their knowledge that they wanted filled, and often correcting their misinformation. I also began carrying around fact sheets and pamphlets that I had picked up from the various drop-in centers (which unmarried young adults are not comfortable frequenting), as well as information from the various health care providers I had interviewed. This information was often new to my informants, so I would refer them to the nearest drop-in center, hoping they would go there to seek out additional information.

Most of my informants told me that the process of getting tested for HIV or STIs was too high risk, frightening, and difficult for them. Reraj explained to me that none of his friends had ever been tested, nor would they ever want to be. "Why not?" I asked him. "Well, they don't really want to know," he responded. I then repeated my question. "Look, they just don't care," he responded. They either think they don't have it because they feel fine, or they figure what's the point; if they have it they are going to die anyways, right? Why make your last years difficult? Just keep your reputation; getting sick is less serious."

Tara, a twenty-three-year-old computer technician, alluded to Reraj's statements. "Getting tested here isn't really popular. I mean, I'm sure it's expensive, and it's just too scary," she explained. Although I told her there were centers where free testing was available, she reminded me that although the testing was free and voluntary, it was not anonymous. She told me she didn't know anyone who had been tested, and when I asked her why she thought they hadn't, she responded, "Well, it's just too much, and how scary! But I mean, what is the difference? You are still gonna die; might as well die ignorant, right?" I asked her what she found most fearful about HIV. "It's so scary here, the way they tell it; it's the way they give the stories to us that's a problem. They tell us you will die quickly if you have it; you will die for sure, they say. Then they say you will lose your friends and family, no one will want to associate with you. They paint a very bleak picture, so it's like, we'd rather just not know, you know?" she explained, her voice trembling. Like many of my informants, Tara was uneasy in discussing the HIV issue; I therefore tried to be responsive and did not press her any further.

Many of my informants said they were afraid of being tested because they were worried more about the societal consequences of having HIV than about the health hazards. As indicated earlier, although there are several drop-in centers that perform free, voluntary testing and counseling, there are currently no anonymous HIV testing centers in the country. An HIV test is a mandatory prerequisite for obtaining a marriage license; however, there is no prenatal testing. Some young people said their biggest fears about contracting HIV would be familial and community rejection, not to mention bringing shame to the family. But although many said they were worried about being exposed to

HIV, most did not indicate any willingness to do anything to minimize their risk. Those who had decided that HIV came from dentists or hairdressers had found ways to put their minds at ease about these assumed modes of transmission, and those who believed it came solely from injection drug use or prisons felt that by staying out of trouble they were somehow safe. Although some people's misconceptions about the disease made them feel at ease, others felt anxiety at not being equipped with the right information to make informed choices.

STIs are prevalent among Iranian young adults, as indicated earlier, but "highly understudied," according to Dr. M. Sadeghi, a gynecologist in midtown Tehran. Most of my informants did not have personal experience with STIs, did not know of a friend who had contracted one, and could not name a single STI, and many did not even know what STIs were or how they were transmitted. The few who did boast some knowledge of STIs were often misinformed.

"You mostly get these sexual diseases from women," explained Khodi. "I know about them, sure, but it's women who carry them; so if you go with the right women, you won't get sick." Leila alluded to Khodi's statements in her concerns about STIs. "I don't know a lot about STIs, I admit it, but the one thing I do know is that women suffer from these diseases more, that it's tougher on us," she explained. When I asked her how she thought women contracted STIs, she responded, "You don't necessarily get it from an infected person; sometimes you get it from bacteria, just from interacting with someone else. But I guess there are certain things you can do to curb them, right?" she asked. Although Leila was worried about women being more susceptible to contracting STIs, she revealed that she doesn't take any measures to protect herself.

"Look, I don't know much about STIs, but I heard they come mostly from outside the country, and if you are strong, athletic, and eat well, like me, you won't get them," said military officer-in-training Hossein. He was confident that he was not at risk for STIs because of his lifestyle. Although he told me that he engages regularly in unprotected sex with multiple partners, he added that because he took care of himself he was not worried about being at risk for contracting an STI.

Most of my informants indicated that they had virtually no knowledge about STIs and could not even explain how they were transmitted.

A few informants alluded to urinary tract infections and having to treat those with home remedies, but this issue was largely not discussed among the young people with whom I interacted. Many were concerned about HIV or pregnancy or both, but very few reported being concerned about other STIs, and even fewer reported having firsthand experience with any STIs. My informants also indicated (and I observed) that no information is distributed about STIs and no public education campaigns refer to them. As indicated earlier, this lack of awareness highlights a need for further research into this area that has virtually been ignored. Few of the sex education campaigns of the past referred to STIs, and the ones being designed for the future do not refer to them either. There is also currently, to my knowledge, no qualitative research being conducted in Iran on this important area of concern.

Many of my informants noted that their friends were their primary sources of information about sexuality, although some informants reported receiving information from billboards, advertising campaigns, and public television and radio broadcasts. During the summer of 2007, I too saw many television specials about HIV, heard radio stories about STIs and HIV, and saw several billboards that addressed them. Although they did not refer to condoms or condom usage, some information is now being distributed through public avenues, which is a notable shift.

"Everything I know, I know from my friends," said Hatef. "Before my friends, I didn't know anything about sex; they explained things to me. At first I didn't believe the things they were saying, but then I learned that they were right, that's how it really was." Salima, a twenty-four-year-old painter whose paintings I observed at Tehran's Museum of Contemporary Art, also described her friends as being her primary source of information, and the only forum in which she felt comfortable asking questions about sex. "I think there are so many things about sex that are mysterious," she said. "There were so many more things in the beginning that I just didn't know and I had to learn on my own from my friends. But thank goodness for my friends; they are the only people I can speak comfortably about sex with." Reraj and Shireen indicated on separate occasions that their friends relied on them to transmit their knowledge about sex and sexuality. "My friends at school depend on me for their information about sex," noted Reraj proudly. "It's hard 'cause I don't know that much either, like in medical school they don't teach us how to turn a girl on, but my buddies think that I have all the answers, but I don't!" Reraj said he often felt pressure to disseminate information he did not have, and noted that more extensive sex education in schools would help young people not to rely exclusively on word-of-mouth for information. Shireen agreed with this, describing that she was the member of her group of girlfriends who was responsible for giving the women information about sex, and often for obtaining contraceptive materials. "I don't like having to play this role necessarily, but I'll do it," she said. "It's just that I don't have a clue about a lot of this stuff, and to tell you the truth, sometimes I have to make stuff up. I know that this isn't good, but what can we do? It's not like we have proper sex education."

Although most of the information about sex and sexuality is transmitted through word of mouth, some of my informants said they received some information from television programs, especially those transmitted by satellite. "If I really want to learn about sex, I like to do it from the television; I always have," explained Khodi. "When I was a kid there was this program called *Tooti-Fruitie* and the women in this show would take off their clothes. That's how I first started learning about the female body. Now I watch Persian Music Channel and I listen to your American rap. That gives me all the information I need to know about sex, *mifahmi* [do you get it]?"

Nilufar, a twenty-year-old university student, also described television programming as a primary source of information about sex, although she referred to domestic television programs. "A lot of the information I get about diseases like AIDS is from this television program hosted by a doctor on Channel 2," she explained. "The other night there was a special in which they were talking to AIDS patients—you know, people who have AIDS—and the people on the show were sad and embarrassed and stuff, but that was the first time I ever saw someone who has AIDS." Several other informants indicated that in the two years since 2005 there had been an increase in programs about HIV/AIDS on *Seda-o-Sima*, the Islamic Republic radio station. This development—of public television and radio stations now talking about sex, STIs, and HIV, topics that previously would have been considered taboo—alone is an indicator of the depth of the shift in ideas and attitudes about sex and sexuality.

Asana and Saara also noted that for them television programs were useful avenues for information, especially the interactive programs broadcast from Los Angeles that people from around the world are able to call into and ask questions about a variety of issues. "She doesn't really talk a lot about actual sex, but Dr. Farnoody's show is a good place to learn about people's emotional problems," explained Saara, referring to the California-based Iranian psychologist who has her own show on one of the more popular Iranian stations in Los Angeles. "Yeah, and you can call and ask her for relationship advice," added Asana. "She is great, we all love her, but she doesn't educate us on a lot of aspects about sex," interjected Saara. "That's what we need, a sex education channel that we can call into! Can you set that up for us?"

Minimizing Risk

The family planning program in Iran has been hailed as a role model for other countries. It has been greatly successful in producing a decline in births from more than six children per woman in the mid-1980s to 2.1 in 2000.[11] Additionally, the rate of contraceptive use rose from 37 percent in 1976 to about 75 percent in 2000. This included a rise in rural areas from 20 percent in 1976 to 72 percent in 2000, and in urban areas from 54 percent to 82 percent.[12] This success has come at great cost to the government, however. Prior to 1989 there had been no specific budget line for family planning activities in Iran. Between 1991 and 1992 approximately thirteen billion rials (roughly US$1.5 million) were allocated to the program. By 1993 the budget had grown to 16.8 billion rials (roughly US$2 million).[13] In 2000, the Ministry of Health and Medical Education provided 75 percent of all family planning services.

It is important to note that most of the efforts to improve the family planning program in Iran have taken place in the last two decades. Immediately following the revolution, much of the family planning system from the old regime was disintegrated. The new government adopted a policy advocating early marriage and large families, reducing the minimum legal age for marriage to nine years old for girls and twelve years old for boys.[14] In addition to this pronatalist position of the government,[15] the war with Iraq fueled the desire for a growth rate because the Ayatollah Khomeini was pushing to bolster the ranks of "soldiers for Islam," aiming for "an army of twenty million."[16] Additionally, the previous family planning system was denounced as part of the Shah's Westernization efforts. During this period, the rate of children per woman jumped from 3.6 in 1976 to 7.0 in 1986.[17] Even though contraceptive use was not illegal (as long as it did not hurt the mother or child), did not include abortion, and was often not opposed by married women or their husbands, many suppliers of contraceptives were closed. Those that were not closed quickly ran out of contraceptive supplies and replacements were not procured, leading to shortages. IUD and sterilization methods were officially suspended until 1980, when Dr. M. R. Moatamedi, a major advocate for reproductive health and rights, requested and received a fatwa from Ayatollah Khomeini allowing contraceptives to be used as long as they did not expose the couple to harm. Sterilization was still under much debate after this fatwa and was therefore not made available. Ayatollah Khomeini issued a statement in 1985 saying that any devices that did not harm women physically or make them sterile were permissible.[18] The universal rationing system that was introduced as a means to provide equal access to basic necessities also encouraged higher fertility rates. The rationing system included everything from property ownership to basic food items to modern consumer goods, which were distributed on a per capita basis, so larger families were entitled to a bigger share of both basic commodities and modern consumer items.[19] Families with more than five children, for example, were given a free plot of land.

It was not until December 1989 and early 1990 that the government officially changed its position regarding family planning, although in 1988 free contraceptives were made available through the primary health care system, but only to married couples. The new plan was deemed the National Birth Control Policy and included an intensive campaign to persuade the public, through newspaper reports, television spots, and Friday prayer speeches, of the need for family planning.[20] The policy was supported by a three-day seminar on population and development held in Mashad in September 1988 at which it was announced that the population growth rate was too high and the fatwa regarding family planning was reiterated. In December 1988, the Supreme Judicial Council declared that "there is no Islamic barrier to family planning."[21]

By 1986, the Iranian population had reached nearly fifty million, an increase of fourteen million in the span of a decade.[22] The family planning program had three declared goals: (1) to encourage women to space their pregnancies three to four years apart, (2) to discourage pregnancy among women younger than eighteen and older than thirty-five, and (3) to limit family size to three children.[23]

In 1990 the Birth Limitation Council was created by the Council of Ministers. The Birth Limitation Council was given the duty to increase contraceptive use among married women and thereby decrease the fertility rate. This meant instituting a massive campaign of education programs (including the construction throughout the country of billboards with slogans such as *bache kamtar—zendegi behtar,* or "fewer children—better life"), increased access to contraceptives, a wider variety of contraceptives, and research on aspects of family planning services. In 1991 a separate Directorship of Population and Family Planning was established to oversee the delivery of family planning services within the primary health care network. The system included supplying all forms of modern contraceptives free of charge to married couples only.[24]

In 1993 the Family Planning Bill removed most of the economic incentives for having large families. Many of the allowances to large families were canceled, as well as several benefits for children, so that only the first three children in a family were subsidized. The bill also included such measures as guaranteed maternity leave for female workers and other privileges in the labor law, cutting the subsidies for day care for female employees, and cutting subsidies for health insurance premiums for the fourth child and any additional children.[25] As part of the second social, economic, and cultural plan of the Iranian government (1994–1999), the family planning program was fully integrated into the primary health care system.

In addition to allowing typical methods of birth control (such as the pill and the ring), Iran also allows for both tubal ligations and vasectomies. In 1992, the pill was the most frequently used method (64 percent of couples who used contraceptives relied on the pill), followed by the IUD in urban areas (21 percent) and tubal ligation, or tubectomy, in rural areas (18 percent). Also in 1992, 57 percent of modern contraceptives were supplied through public hospitals, health centers, and pharmacies.

However, in 1996, 30 percent of pill users did not know how to use it correctly.[26] Failure of the contraceptive in use was the most commonly cited reason for unwanted pregnancies in the 5.2 percent of married women between the ages of fifteen and forty-nine who were pregnant in 2000, which showed that some educational work about contraceptive use still needs to be undertaken by the government.[27]

There is no doubt about the effectiveness of the Family Planning program in Iran. There is, however, some doubt that the government will be able to continue to afford such an extensive program. This ability is questioned because within the next ten years the number of reproductive-aged women will grow by more than 20 percent. Iran, however, has been hailed as progressive in its family planning system, particularly relative to other countries in its region of the world. One of the Middle East's largest condom factories operates in Iran, and it is in the process of expanding its services to help couples with emergency contraceptive needs.[28]

Although Iran must be applauded for its efforts in the family planning arena, the many unmet needs of an increasing portion of Iran's population must also be acknowledged. None of these services are offered to unmarried young people, and many married women feel uncomfortable demanding information or resources on family planning out of fear of social stigma. Officially, statistics show that only about 7.6 percent of all women have an unmet need for family planning in Iran,[29] but my qualitative research shows that this number is higher than official statistics indicate because many unmarried young women are hesitant to come forward about their need and desire for family planning resources out of fear of stigmatization and punishment from the morality police or their family members. They would prefer to avoid pregnancy but are not using any form of family planning.

For many young adults, the ways in which they choose to grapple with the risks of pregnancy and disease often put them at high risk. The false sense of security they create for themselves by using either *coitus interruptus* (the pullout method) or anal sex, or just "being sure of your partner," has in fact often made them more vulnerable to disease, and has reduced the likelihood of them going to visit a physician for regular testing or for protection. Less than 10 percent of my informants indicated ever using a condom, and for this 10 percent, condom usage was not 100 percent of the time. When I asked the men why they so seldom used condoms, their responses included, "I don't need them because I'm sure of my partner," "They are hard to get," "They are too expensive," "I don't know how to [use them]," and "It's just too awkward." When I asked the women why fewer than 10 percent of them used oral contraceptives, their responses included, "It makes me fat," "We can't get them, we're not allowed [to buy them] if we're single," "It makes me moody," "I don't know where to get them," and "I'm too embarrassed that someone in my family will find them."

Many of my informants felt shy and awkward when discussing condoms and condom usage. This was especially true in focus groups. When I asked the participants in one of my first focus groups why they don't use condoms, the room went silent for several minutes. Finally, a nineteen-year-old man bravely started to speak. He alluded to multiple issues that were later described in more depth by many of my informants. "Look, people don't use them so much here. It's not an easy issue to talk about here, as you may have noticed," he said, looking around at the other members of the group. I asked him to continue.

Well, it's just that it's not part of our culture. Also, remember, a girl who *khodesh ra mifrooshe* [is willing to sell herself] for ten tomans or less obviously doesn't value her life that much that she would actively go out and buy condoms. First of all, they aren't cheap, from what I hear; and then it's just that the thought probably wouldn't enter her mind. If she is the type of person, and I've met these kinds of people, they go with, like, two guys in the morning, two guys in the afternoon, and two in the evening. You think a girl like that, with a million guys on her mind, is going to go out and buy condoms? You see what I'm saying? There is only one thing on their minds. . . .

Although this particular young man conflated many of the issues that other informants would later tease apart, he did provide an introduction to the way some young people think of condoms. This young man and several others seemed to view condoms as something dirty that only certain types of "bad" women would use. Therefore, by not using them, and in many cases refusing to discuss them, they distinguished themselves from "those kinds of people."

Gypsy alluded to this theme as well. "You see, using condoms in Iran is different," he began.

With your girlfriend, you can't use condoms; it's, in a way, like, well, you know, weird or dirty, you just can't. Like for example, let's say you are going to take her virginity; well, like you know if it's her first time, or something, well that's different, a whole different thing. You just can't use them. Like I said, I sometimes use condoms, but with a girl who I started out not using condoms with, I'm not going to all of a sudden start using condoms again, you know? It's just, it depends on the type of girl you are with.

Gypsy's response to this issue surprised me. The concept of condoms as dirty was repeated. Sharare, one of my key informants, who often reminded me that I was bringing up a sensitive topic in a culture that was not used to discussing contraception and family planning so openly, said, "Let me tell you that condoms, that the condom issue *hanouz ja nayoftadeh* [has not fallen into place, that is, has not been accepted] here in Iran. People really don't like it." I asked her what she thought the reasons for this might be. "They don't like how it feels, or it's not a good option," she began.

The condom hanouz ja nayoftadeh, that's one issue, but another issue is that you would have to go and buy the condom from the pharmacy, and well, you have seen yourself that Tehran can be a very small place and people know each other. So the kids, my friends too, are afraid to go to the pharmacy and buy condoms, or even pills, because they think they might see someone they know, or the pharmacist may tell their parents, or something like that. The main thing is that it's hard; it's hard to buy them and hard to use them. Our life here is hard; why add this to that?

Sharare stressed that because condoms were not a culturally accepted phenomenon, many of the women she knew and interacted with were not comfortable discussing condom usage even among their friends, let alone with their partners. Nazgol, a nineteen-year-old student at Azad University in Tehran, alluded to this when discussing her lack of condom usage with me. "Look, it's not like I actively *don't* want to use them— you know, *them*." Throughout the interview she avoided even saying the word *condom*, which goes by its English name rather than the Persian

slang word *caput*. "It's just a matter of I don't want to be the one bringing the issue up. I don't want to have to talk about it, it's just not me,"
she explained. Azita seconded Nazgol's statements. "Look, those things,
condoms, they are just *khashen* [awkward, uncomfortable]." She made a
face. "They are gross, and icky. Not the kind of things that 'good Iranian women' bring up."

Shahab, a twenty-four-year-old salesman from the northern part of
Tehran, commented on this phenomenon. He had spent part of his life in
the United States and moved back to Iran in 2001 to work in the family
business. "You know, if you ask me, Iran is going to end up with a really
high AIDS rate, 'cause no one here uses condoms," he began, lowering
his voice when saying the word *AIDS*.

It's strange; it's like they get offended if you even ask or try to use one; they
say, "Who do you think I am, a prostitute?" or like "D'you think I'm sick or
something?" or "Don't you trust me?" Yeah, trust is a big thing here. But how
are we supposed to trust these women? There is this one girl, OK? She wants
to sleep with me, but over the past two months I have seen her ten times out
with probably ten different guys! Can you believe it? Like it's becoming a joke
at this point. Yesterday I went for lunch at this restaurant in the middle of
town. I had taken this client there for lunch, and then as soon as I sat down,
she sat down at the table next to us with yet another guy! Her eyes caught
mine, and we both actually laughed. Am I really supposed to trust a girl like
that? For fun or dating, OK. But to have sex without a condom, no way!

Shahab preferred to use condoms with women he didn't know, but
with his steady girlfriend, they had never used them. Two of my other
male informants also noted that they "sometimes" used condoms, especially with women they didn't "know" or "trust." "Usually when I have
a steady girlfriend, I don't use them," explained Hossein. "But if I decide
to go out one night and I see some girl, someone I don't know too well,
if it's like this, then maybe I'll use [condoms]. But even then I can't say
I do that every time. I know it's really bad, but yeah, that's the truth,"
he admitted. Hossein's friend Massoud, twenty-four, an air force pilot
in training, said that he too uses condoms only when he is at a party
and drunk and about to sleep with someone other than his girlfriend.
"When I was younger, I started having sex when I was like thirteen

or fourteen, and back then we didn't know what condoms were, so that wasn't my fault. But now, well, I guess I'm just not used to them, but when I'm pretty drunk I use them." I stopped taking notes and looked at him. I found it odd that he would remember to use condoms only when he was drunk, because most young people I knew in the United States claimed they would forget to use a condom when alcohol was involved.[30] "When you're drunk you use them?" I asked incredulously. "You bet," he said smiling. "So when do you *not* use them?" I asked. "When I'm not drunk or when I'm with my girlfriend," he responded. Massoud then began describing his girlfriend, but left me confused until our next interview, when he explained his reasoning further. Later he told me that the reason he uses condoms when intoxicated is that when he is sober he is able to control himself to the point where he can *tamoom nemikonam* (Persian for coitus interruptus; literally means "I don't finish"). When he is drunk he does not have the same level of control.

Many of my informants also indicated that the process and price of obtaining condoms were simply too cumbersome and high. If one is unmarried, stigma, gossip, and chastising pharmacists make it difficult to purchase condoms, and many drugstore salespersons do ask for proof of marriage license before selling the condoms (although it is not strictly illegal for unmarried people to purchase them). For young people who are married, it is legal to purchase condoms, but for many, especially the women, the price is simply too high (both monetarily and with regard to potentially tarnishing their reputations, as some women say that purchasing condoms, even as a married woman, will do). In countries such as the United States, where there is significantly less stigmatization attached to purchasing condoms, and where they are distributed for free on many college campuses, young people are still hesitant to procure them; in an environment such as Iran, where premarital sex is punishable and tarnished reputations carry the significant weight of social exclusion, purchasing condoms is nearly impossible for unmarried young adults.

Two of my female informants said they preferred not to buy the condoms and saw this as "a man's job." Rhana, a twenty-three-year-old housewife who has been married for two years, believes that "it's really something the guy has to buy, not something that I am supposed to deal with. I don't think women should have to worry about these things, because it's one of those things where a girl just has to ask if the guy has it or not." I then asked her what would happen if a young man did not have a condom. "Well, then you just have to be going with a guy you trust, like your boyfriend or husband," she answered nonchalantly. This response corresponds with many of the comments made by young men, that being "with people you can trust" is a risk-reduction measure. Naghmeh, who preferred condoms to other methods of family planning, echoed Rhana's sentiments. "Well, condoms, I guess we sometimes use them, but we really don't like them," she complained. When I asked her what she didn't like about them, she talked about the process of purchasing them. "It's really something that he should do, not me. I hate doing it, but I sometimes have to, and let me tell you, Pardis, it's a hard process." She lowered her voice to hushed tones. I asked her if she bought them at a local drugstore. "No!" she exclaimed. "Not a drugstore around here, but one in the southern part of town, where no one will see me!" I found this interesting, given that she is married. I couldn't exactly understand why she was embarrassed to be seen buying condoms. "Because I'm the *girl*!" she shouted. "It's not supposed to be my job, but I do it. I go there and there is always a different selection. But I tell you, you never know exactly what you're going to get when you open the box." "Really?" I asked. "Yes, I mean sometimes they are good, but sometimes you get ones that are studded or have strange patterns on them, and those ones I don't like at all. I hate them, actually; they make me feel dirty and are superuncomfortable." Naghmeh again expressed the sentiments of many of my married female informants who felt that using condoms, buying them, or in some cases even discussing them made them feel "dirty" or like "bad Iranian women."

Saara also reiterated Naghmeh's feelings, that she did not want to risk being seen by family members or gossiping friends while purchasing condoms at the drugstore, especially because of her single status. "My whole family goes to, like, the three main pharmacies in this neighborhood," she said. "Can you imagine if I was caught by my parents or someone found out that I was out buying condoms?! I'd be thrown out of my parents' house, that's for sure!"

I found it interesting that although the women did not like discussing condoms with other women or with their partners, many of the young men preferred to purchase their condoms from female pharmacy attendants. "I find it's really tough to make myself walk into a pharmacy and buy a condom, which, by the way, isn't cheap," explained Khodi. I asked him what he found to be the most difficult part of the process. "To tell you the truth, I would prefer if there was a woman behind the counter. I feel like that might make it easier," he responded. I was surprised by this and asked him to elaborate. "Well, I'm just more comfortable discussing this stuff with women, like you," he said. Gypsy reaffirmed Khodi's statement. "Well, of course, if there is a woman behind the counter, I feel much more comfortable going up and getting a condom," he explained to me. When I asked him why he felt this way, he said it was because "she doesn't look in my eyes, just gives it to me, you know? If it was a man behind the counter, God help you. The man will make fun of you, hassle you, and ask you a million questions. You'll have to bargain with him." He pulled a crumpled condom wrapper from his bag and handed it to me. "And then sometimes they give you cheap Chinese condoms, stuff that breaks easily, stuff that doesn't feel good. So then maybe I'll ask the guy behind the counter, give me a different one, like a ribbed one, and he'll just say, 'Why do you want that one?' or 'Why do you even know the difference in the first place?' followed by 'What is your story?' you know? And well, I get really put off by that."

On several occasions I went to drugstores in different parts of town to buy condoms in order to understand the experiences described to me by my informants. The condoms were usually locked behind glass doors behind the counter so the customer would have to ask an employee to unlock the doors and display the choices up close. This was a difficult procedure on my first attempt at Super Jordan, a one-stop drugstore and grocery mini-mart on Jordan Street (also called Africa Street since the revolution). I walked into the market and noticed that the condoms were located with all the "Western" goods, such as M&M's, Chips Ahoy cookies, Fruit Loops, Pantene shampoo, and Tampax tampons. All of these products were significantly more expensive than products manufactured in Iran or imported from Dubai, and they were locked behind a glass door. I walked up to the counter with confidence and asked the gentleman behind the counter for a box of condoms. He looked at me inquisitively. I quickly dipped my hand into my mānto pocket and slid my emergency fake wedding ring onto my fourth finger. I brought it out of my pocket and put it on the glass counter so that it made a clicking noise. The gentleman smiled and brought out four boxes of different kinds of condoms: ribbed, lubricated, plain, and flavored. I looked at the price and was taken aback: six thousand tomans (which converts to roughly US$7) for a box of three condoms! I chose a box of ribbed condoms and took them to the cashier. She smiled and winked at me as I handed over the money. When I got home, I opened the bag and took another look at the box. I smiled as I looked at the familiar words—"Durex: Strong and Ribbed for Her Pleasure." Then I realized, it was written in English! And Durex was an American brand! I opened the box and pulled out the instructions. It didn't take long to figure out that they were written in English, Spanish, French, German, and Arabic, but not Persian. I suddenly remembered that Iran has one of the largest condom manufacturing factories in the Middle East. So what was happening? Why were Iranians being forced to buy Western-manufactured condoms at Western prices when there was a condom factory not one hundred miles away from the city? A small amount of research led me to discover that the condoms manufactured in Iran were often exported. Rarely, if ever, were they manufactured for use domestically. That night, as I recounted my day's events to my friend Bibi, a young Iranian-American woman visiting Iran for the sumer, she was shocked. "So let me get this straight," she said. "So if a young person here is brave enough to go to the pharmacy, risking the possibility of being asked for a marriage license or seen by watchful eyes and then gossiped about later, rich enough to buy a box of condoms, bold enough to take them out and try to use them, then the damn instructions are not even in Persian?!" she exclaimed. "I know," I said. "This is a problem."

Although many believed that condoms would be too difficult to use, or that they would be embarrassing to buy or discuss with one's partner, others just didn't like them. Some said they preferred sex without a condom and resorted to other methods of birth control, which did not necessarily prevent STIs; others said they just didn't believe that condoms ever worked in the first place. One of my respondents, a twenty-year-old male, noted that "for prevention, I try not to use a lot of condoms because it lessens the pleasure of sex. I don't worry about sickness, I just worry about pregnancy, and because I don't like condoms, I try to come outside the girl." Nazanin believes that not only do condoms not work, but they also harm women. "I have heard that the condoms in Iran aren't so great. I have heard that they cause women to bleed and hurt and stuff," she told me. I asked her if she had had any experience with these condoms. She admitted that she hadn't but she had heard through the grapevine that this was true. Hatef believed that the condoms in Iran are fake, thus he need not even bother with trying to use them. "There are a lot of *dooroghi* [fake] condoms here at the pharmacies," he told me while serving me a cup of tea. "How do you know they are fake?" I asked him. "They often rip. There are so many fake ones," he said definitively. I then asked if he thought *all* the condoms sold at the pharmacies were unreliable. "Most of the ones from the pharmacies are fakes, but I guess it depends on which pharmacy you go to," he explained. I asked him the same question I had posited to Nazanin: had he had personal experience with these "fake" condoms? He told me he had never used a condom but he didn't really see the point. Finally, Reraj revealed to me that although he recommends to his friends that they should use condoms, he doesn't believe that condoms would work for him personally. "I just don't think condoms work for guys like me," he told me matter-of-factly. I asked what made him such a bad candidate for condoms. He replied that he was a "real man" and for men like him, condoms don't work. I then asked what he relied on for contraception. Similar to the women who said that contraception was a "man's job," Reraj said he believed that because pregnancy affects the woman more than the man, the woman should be on the pill so as not to bother the man. "I think it's the woman's job. Come on, let's face it, the pill is easier to use and less awkward. Admit it. It should be her job," he said.

While a select few of my informants felt that the pill was a good and easy option for family planning, most of them complained that it made them gain weight, become sensitive, have mood swings, and develop bad skin. It was for this reason that most of them revealed they were not on an oral birth control regimen, and many said they had no interest in this option. One of the biggest challenges in talking to my informants about oral contraceptives was their confusion about what this category encompassed. Informants would often indicate that they used the pill as a primary means of contraception, but I would later realize that when they referred to "the pill" they actually meant "the morning-after pill," or emergency contraception. Another major problem that my female informants faced was lack of knowledge about how to administer oral contraceptives, both birth control pills and emergency contraception, properly. Some of the women would actually create emergency contraception concoctions for themselves, and then face health consequences (such as internal bleeding or infertility) afterward.

Sepideh, a twenty-two-year-old musician and waitress at Darband (the mountainside area in the North of Tehran discussed in Chapter 2), described her experience with homemade emergency contraception. "Look, I can't get my own pills, OK? It's not as easy as you think," she said, her voice suddenly taking on a somewhat hostile tone. "Oh, but you're on the pill then?" I asked. "No," she explained. "I'm not *on* the pill, I sometimes *take* pills, you know, after sex. You understand, mifahmi? I take them maybe that night or perhaps the morning after," she said, her tone softening a bit. I then asked if she took a special set of emergency contraceptive pills or if they were birth control pills that were supposed to be taken as part of a monthly regimen. "I don't know what you are talking about. I get my cousin's pills. They come in a box with a bunch of them, and then I take a few after sex if the guy has, you know, come inside me." Sepideh did not seem worried about the fact that she was self-prescribing oral contraceptives. "Have you ever been to a doctor? Like a gynecologist?" I asked her. "Why? What for? I'm not sick, and it's under control," she responded. Sepideh alluded to a theme brought up by many of my female informants, who believed they did not need to see a doctor unless they were very sick. The idea of regular checkups or preventive medicine was not a part of their routines.

One of my earliest experiences in Iran on my first visit in 2000, an experience that has stayed with me as one of my most vivid memories, is an example of homemade contraception. I remember being awakened in the middle of the night to the shrill shrieks of a friend who had called from her boyfriend's house and was sobbing so hard I could barely understand what she was upset about. When she calmed down, she told me she was very sick and needed my help. What happened? I asked her. She explained to me that after having sex with her boyfriend, during which he failed to use their favored birth control method, of coitus interruptus, she had secretly crept into her sister's room and stolen a box of birth control pills from her medicine cabinet. Then, after a short consultation with her boyfriend, she had ingested all twenty-eight pills in the packet and was now violently ill. She begged me for advice, but outside of telling her to go to the doctor, I had very little insight into what she should now do. I did, however, take the opportunity to tell her that this was not the proper way to ingest oral contraceptives, and I followed up on this later when I explained the intricacies of family planning to her and a group of friends. Luckily she was sick only for a day or two after swallowing such a high level of hormones. She now tells me she uses her own story to educate her friends about the importance of education.

Nazanin, who earlier expressed her distaste for condoms, also expressed a dislike for being on a daily oral contraceptive regimen. "Take them every day?!" she exclaimed. "No, I prefer to take them only the mornings after I've had sex. This seems to me the best way for me," she explained. I asked her about her aversion to taking the pill on a regular basis. "Well, once for a while I was taking the birth control pill, but I didn't like it 'cause I got heavy and cranky, so I stopped and decided not to do this anymore," she responded. Nazanin seemed to feel that taking emergency contraception occasionally (hers was also a self-prescribed dose of Ortho Tri-Cyclin, a pill meant to be taken on a monthly basis) was better than being on the pill permanently.

Nazanin was not the only one of my female informants to complain of the negative side effects of oral contraceptives. In fact, most of the women I asked about them cited such effects as reasons either for going off the pill or for not starting in the first place. Naghmeh complained, "I hate the pill 'cause it made me fat! I used to be on the pill, but you know, it made me big, it made me gain a lot of weight right here," she said, putting her hands on her hips and then extending them out to the sides to indicate a growth in their size. "My bottom half just grew enormous, so I went off it," she explained. Naghmeh was able to access oral contraceptives more easily because she was married, and she noted that she had learned about their proper usage only in the mandatory prenuptial counseling course she had taken a few years earlier.

While the women complained of the negative side effects of oral contraceptives, the young men complained about women's complaints. "The pill, though it seems like a great option, is just not a viable choice," explained Hossein. When I asked him why he felt this way, he said, "because it's just not worth it, it has too many side effects, your girl gets crazy." "So you were with a girl who took birth control pills?" I asked. "Yes, I was. But like I said, there were a lot of side effects. She got frustrated and moody and sensitive. I couldn't take it. But I guess it's different for everyone, 'cause another girl I dated said she was off the pill not 'cause it made her moody but because it made her fat." Hossein added that regardless of which side effect manifested itself, he preferred not to deal with fat, cranky, or sensitive women.

Kayvan echoed Hossein's sentiments. "I don't know a single girl who was happy with being on the pill," he said. At this point I asked which pill he was talking about, monthly oral contraceptives or emergency contraception? He paused before answering. "Well, mostly the ones you have to take a lot. None of them are happy about it, mostly because of the nausea; people hate that, and the mood swings and the weight gain, you know all that stuff." I asked if these things deterred him from recommending oral contraceptives to his partners. "Of course! It's all so awkward, complicated, and difficult; it's better just to be careful, you know what I mean?" By "being careful" Kayvan meant what so many of my informants professed to be their primary means of contraception—coitus interruptus.

By far the response I received most often to questions about prevention, contraception, and protection was coitus interruptus. Some referred to this as "being careful." Others cited "being sure of your partner" in response to questions about disease prevention. This was the most popular way of preventing pregnancy and disease according to all of my sexually active informants. Even those informants who used condoms or other contraceptives did not do so when "sure of their partner," or sure of themselves in the case of young men who were confident that they would be able to "pull out in time."

"I don't take pills, I don't do anything special, I'm just careful," Leila explained to me. "Natural methods, those are the options we've been given here. So we're careful." Leila was just one of many informants who used the phrase "being careful." Saara used "being careful" in her response when I asked about her own contraception choices. "So, wait, what do you do for protection?" I asked her, wanting to make sure I had understood her correctly. "Well, I'm careful," she said shyly. "Oh, you mean the pull-out method?" I added. "Yes, I won't let a guy come inside me, that's what we do." I was a bit surprised given Saara's decision to be involved in reproductive health as a profession. "But this doesn't always work; plus there are diseases," I protested. "Well, the guys I go with aren't the type to go around with a lot of women, so it's OK," she explained. It seemed as though young women and men had created in their minds an ideal type of person that one could have unprotected sex with, and they were perfectly comfortable with this notion. Nazgol was very matter-of-fact when she told me that her primary means of prevention is "being sure of myself and my partner." When I told her this did not always prevent disease transmission or pregnancy, she just shrugged and said she felt comfortable with her family planning choice. "I am sure of what I'm doing," she told me very seriously. "Well, what prevention methods do your friends use?" I asked her. "Well, pullout. That's just how it's done here. Soon you will realize that."

Virtually all of the sexually active young men I interviewed indicated using coitus interruptus as a primary means of contraception at one time or another. This combined with being "sure" of their partners and "sure" of themselves and their own skills seemed to put them at ease. "When I'm sure of my partner, I don't use condoms. That's it really, nothing more to it than that," explained Hossein when I asked about his contraception preferences. "With this kind of thing, you just have to be careful. That's the primary means of family planning." Hossein's friend and fellow military officer in training Khodi echoed his friend's sentiments when I interviewed him alone later that day. "See, in Iran you know what we all use for pregnancy prevention?" he asked. At this point I felt I knew the answer, but I wanted to hear him give his opinion, so I shook my head. "Natural methods, you know? Pulling out. Me? I never come inside a girl; I'm good like that," he said proudly. This seemed to be a skill that men worked to perfect, and when they achieved their goal, they were not shy about boasting. I then went back to my interview with Massoud, who had told me he used condoms only when he was drunk. I remember that his main reason was that he could not control himself, or be "sure" of himself, when drunk. He also used the phrase "sure of my partner" repeatedly in our interview.

> P: So, when do you *not* use a condom, since you are saying you do use them when drunk?
>
> M: Only when I'm sure of my partner.
>
> P: How is it that one becomes "sure" of their partner?
>
> M: Of my partner? When I have some knowledge of them, when I know who they were with and who they were not with.
>
> P: How can you know and be trusting of your partner? Especially you, given that you tell me you sleep with twelve people a month?!
>
> M: Well, because I am very comfortable, and my partner is very comfortable with me, so it's all good.

Massoud was just one of many young people who indicated that being "sure" of himself and his partner was enough to keep his mind at peace.

Many of my informants attributed their reliance on coitus interruptus to their lack of knowledge of other options, and many indicated this to me at different times. "Before I met you, I had no idea what a diaphragm was," one informant told me, while others noted that they had been led to believe that relying on the pullout method was quite safe. "You can't get pregnant from doing it from behind, or from pulling out, right?" Nassim asked me. When I told her she could, she, like many other informants who were astounded at this revelation, told me, "You see, these are things they don't tell us in Iran. We talk about sex, yes, that's an improvement; but we don't talk about risk, health, and taking care of ourselves." Later that week she invited me to offer informal sex education classes for her and her female friends at her house once a week. I gladly accepted.

Abortion: The Biggest Challenge

Prior to 1973, any form of induced abortion was illegal in Iran, except to save the life of the pregnant woman, provided she was married. At no point in the nation's history has abortion for any reason been legal for unmarried women, and self-administered abortions have also been illegal historically. In 1973, article 182 of the Penal Code referenced self-induced abortion: "A woman who took or employed any kind of medication or substance resulting in an abortion except on the orders of a physician was subject to up to three years of imprisonment."[31] Under article 183 of the Penal Code, which was in place by 1974, "a medical worker or person acting as such who performed an abortion was subject to three to ten years forced labor unless it could be proved that the action had taken place to save the life of the mother."[32]

In 1976 the Penal Code was changed to

permit a physician to perform an abortion if: (a) the couple was able to provide evidence of social or medico-social grounds for an abortion; (b) the abortion was performed during the first 12 weeks of pregnancy; (c) written permission of the parents was obtained (even for married women); and (d) there was no danger to the health of the mother from the procedure. In the event that the abortion was requested on the grounds that the pregnant woman or her husband was insane, the law required written permission of the legal guardian of the insane partner. For a woman in the process of suing for a divorce, the consent of her husband was required if the fetus was legally considered to be his responsibility. In the case of an abortion performed for medical purposes, including cases in which the child would be born with an incurable disease, the physician had to obtain the endorsed opinion of two other qualified physicians. In such cases, the written consent of the woman alone was considered to be sufficient. The law also required that abortions be performed in a fully equipped hospital or clinic.[33]

After the revolution, in 1979 abortion was made illegal on most grounds (except to save the mother's life). Under the Penal Code of 1991, which was revised on the basis of a reformist interpretation of Islamic law, abortion became classified as a "lesser crime" involving bodily injury, which in turn is punishable by three to ten years in prison, accompanied by the payment of diye (blood money) or compensation paid to the "victim" or, in the case of the "victim's" death, to their relatives—in the instance of abortion, to the father of the fetus.

In early 2005, prompted by a law instated by former reformist president Khatami in 2003, the Iranian Parliament voted to liberalize the country's abortion laws. Under the proposed law, a pregnancy (for a married woman only) could be terminated in the first four months if the fetus is mentally or physically handicapped. This is said to be in accordance with recent interpretations of Islamic law that hold that a fetus does not have a soul until it is 120 days (some say seventeen weeks) old. Under this new law, both sets of parents of the married couple would be required to give their consent, and three doctors would have to confirm that the fetus is damaged.[34] These are the kind of abortion services proposed during Khatami's rule; the proposed law was passed by the Iranian Parliament but was rejected by the Council of Guardians, who reported that "it is against sharia to abort children who would inflict a financial burden on the parents after birth due to mental or physical handicap."[35] Currently all abortions are strictly illegal, except to save the mother's life or when the fetus is diagnosed with thalassemia, in which case it must take place while the pregnancy is still under three months. However, many illegal abortions are performed by doctors throughout Tehran (who risk imprisonment, removal of their medical license, and heavy fines if caught, yet continue to perform them), and unmarried young people continue to make use of self-administered medications to induce abortions (although, as mentioned, there is no research that speaks to the numbers of young people doing this). Self-administered abortions were the major complaints of physicians I spoke to in Tehran in 2004 and 2005. They argued that they often had to aid young people in emergency situations when problems arose due to these abortions.

Whenever I asked my informants what they saw as the biggest challenges or risks in their lives, most of the women, and some of the men, mentioned abortion. By 2005, this response was more common (compared to the summer of 2002, when none of the young people I spoke with had unplanned pregnancies on their minds) than the traditional version of being "caught" (by the morality police).

When I asked Rhana about her experience with private doctors who provide illegal abortions, she said it was a relatively easy process to find a doctor who would be willing to perform an abortion, and she was highly satisfied with the level of service she had received.

R: Yeah, I had an abortion.

P: And was that abortion easy?

R: Well, in terms of pain, no, it wasn't; it hurt. But other than that it was good. They did it in an office.

P: Was the office easy to find?

R: Oh yes, very easy to find.

P: And is it expensive?

R: Well yes, and it's gotten more expensive. But you know, it was OK, I
   handled it.

Although Rhana emphasized that she was happy with the attention
and care she received before, during, and after her abortion, she indicated that it was one of the biggest challenges and risks of her life. She
revealed to me later in the interview that she often worries that she will
not be able to conceive when she and her husband are ready to have children. She worries that God will punish her by making her infertile, yet
she refuses, even after the difficult emotional experiences following her
abortion, to take contraceptive pills or utilize condoms.

Two other informants (both married women) indicated that they were
so comfortable with finding private abortion doctors in Tehran that they
use abortions as a form of contraception. Sonia told me one afternoon
that after having two boys only one year apart, she was ready to stop
having children. When I asked her about her method of contraception,
she said, "Suction" (actually using the English word). I looked at her, confused, until she explained that *suction* is one of the slang words Iranian
women use for abortion. Sonia told me she had already had two abortions and was planning a third. At her announcement, the other ladies
we were dining with whirled around in their seats to look at her. "Well,
don't look so shocked ladies, I can't keep having kids. I'm not exactly
the motherly type, now am I?" she asked rhetorically. After seeing Sonia
speak comfortably about her abortion experiences, four other women in
the group told their abortion stories as well. They all described receiving the "suction" at various points in their marriages when they felt they
were not yet ready for children, either financially or emotionally.

Although it is not clear how many young women in Tehran have the
same perspective as Rhana and Sonia or have gone through the same
experiences, I did speak to seven other women who had undergone abortions (sometimes very complicated procedures) who were still not using
contraception. This was an interesting and complicated paradox, and I
often asked them why they did not use protection, especially after having
gone through the difficult experience of an abortion. They explained that
the social risks of procuring contraceptives were too high (people might
see them and say they are "bad" women, or they might be harassed by

members of the morality police), and that negotiating condom use with their partners was often so challenging that they "gave up the fight."

Women who had undergone abortion procedures performed by doctors described emotional challenges (suffering from guilt and often fighting with their husbands, who are sometimes reluctant to sign paperwork agreeing to their wife's abortion) and physical challenges (there are still health risks, especially for late-term abortions). The young women who did not have access to expensive doctors (for financial reasons or because they were afraid due to their unmarried status) described the challenges they faced as being much more pronounced. Ten of the young women I interviewed described the difficult choices they grappled with when facing an unwanted pregnancy. Some of these women were unmarried and from prominent religious or political families; they experienced great levels of trepidation when discussing matters related to abortion.

"Abortion is super high here, but let me tell you, there are more illegal abortions, I mean self-abortions, and they [women] do them in strange ways," explained Mandanna, a twenty-four-year-old English teacher. "Like right behind the mosques, the Haram e-Imam Reza [Holy Shrine of the Eighth Shi'ite Imam Reza in Mashad], even! Just back there, there are places that sell various abortion stuff like pills or shots or other things, and sometimes the mullahs go there and buy them and give them out to their women." Mandanna stopped and looked at me as if waiting for me to say something. She often would use the language of conspiracy, taking every opportunity she had to blame things on religious figures, and I often wondered if she was serious in these accusations or if she was half-joking. She hated my skepticism, so I had learned to keep my mouth shut and let her speak. When I didn't laugh or make any comment, Mandanna continued.

Otherwise, the young people themselves go and buy them. And there are these shots they use for cows, for animals, to induce cow abortions, and they give these to the women! I'm serious, Pardis. I know people who have used them. And it's like the shots: they use these so that the girl aborts quickly, but the problem is that it's not that simple.

Mandanna sighed and looked at me. Her face was usually cheerful and her lips naturally curved into a smile, but when discussing this topic she became quite serious and morose. It wasn't until a year later that I found out that one of her cousins, a young woman she was very close to, had employed this method to get rid of an unwanted pregnancy, and now faced serious health problems. Ever since then, many of Mandanna's friends had become more apprehensive about these kinds of abortion methods.

When I asked Mandanna about the use of doctors for abortions, she explained that doctors didn't always perform abortions in the most medically safe way. "Well, sometimes the doctors have come to the girl's house to perform the abortion there," she began, her eyes darkening as she spoke. "The doctors will come and then they have to do it on a bed, and there aren't any really safe health resources there. They have a bed, but it's not so sterile. They have nothing at their homes sometimes, and if something goes wrong, well, there is nothing anyone can do about it," she explained. When I asked her about the possibility of going to doctors' offices or clinics for these procedures, she told me she didn't know of anyone who had gone to a doctor's office for an abortion, because it was too expensive and because they had heard that increasingly doctors are not wanting to risk their reputations to perform these illegal operations. (Even though they are sometimes performed in private homes, walls have eyes, and watchful neighbors regularly turn one another into the morality police.)

"Here it's hard to get rid of the baby," began Leila. "Well, I mean you can get rid of it, like I did, but it's tough and you have to go to scary places. Many doctors don't do it, and you can't tell your parents. Basically, it's difficult to find information on what to do to get rid of it." Leila then described to me the process she had gone through, which led her eventually to procure an injection (the actual composition and ingredients of which she still doesn't know) from a black market dealer who brought it to her boyfriend's home one afternoon. Leila told me she is from an extremely religious family and her father was a famous cleric. She noted that to this day she feels conflicted about her decision, but her parents have no knowledge of the difficult events that transpired in her life during the summer of 2003. Leila was hesitant to tell me her story, but then decided she wanted to "get it out" and talk to me about it. "First, when we found out I was pregnant, well, my first instinct was to kill myself," she started. "I mean, given who my father is—oh, and by the way, he would kill me if he ever found out," she cautioned, leaning into me so that her voice was almost a whisper. "Well, so I found out I was pregnant last summer, right? And so, well, we faced a bad situation, my boyfriend and me." Leila shifted in her seat as she told the story, stopping toward the end to wipe a tear from her cheek.

Well, it was difficult, but we went to a few doctors. When they saw my name, they refused to do it. It was terrible, everywhere we went, the doctors refused me, maybe 'cause of my dad. Anyways, things were getting desperate, most of the doctors we knew had turned us away, and other doctors who had been recommended to us we couldn't afford. Mind you, I was totally uncomfortable asking for money from my parents. Well, anyways, finally I turned to my friends to ask for advice. Some of them told me that there are these pills or injections that you can get from Nasser Khosrow Avenue, you know, behind the big mosque outside the *bāzār-e-shahr*? I was embarrassed to go down there and buy stuff, so I sent my boyfriend to check it out. He took one look at the alleyway and refused. We decided to call someone to deliver the stuff to my boyfriend's house one day, when his parents were out of town visiting Shomal. So, some guy on a motorbike came and delivered a mysterious shot. My boyfriend injected me with it and I became very ill. I was sick for days. When my parents called asking me where I was, I told them I had gone out of town with my friends. It was terrible.

Leila spent seven days hiding and resting in her boyfriend's bedroom. She recalled her experience with a great deal of sorrow. She told me that the worst part of it was not the sickness she felt after the injection but rather the sense of guilt that has plagued her to this day. She felt horrible about lying to her parents, and had a great deal of anxiety and fear that what she had done to her body would have long-term consequences. Leila told me that many women of her sister's age (early thirties) who had used these methods to end unwanted pregnancies now faced problems of infertility. She recounted the story of her best friend's sister, who at twenty-seven was ready to have her first child, but because she had used abortion-inducing drugs, she believed she would no longer be able to conceive. Her friend's current husband, who could not understand the situation, was now filing for a divorce, claiming that an infertile woman is a "damaged good." "This is my biggest fear," Leila said as her eyes began to fill with tears. "That one day, I will want that baby back."

It is unclear what the market for animal abortions is like, but it seems as though selling these concoctions on the black market has become very popular. One afternoon in the summer of 2004, I decided to attempt to purchase one of these shots from Nasser Khosrow Avenue, the alleys of which, I had been told, were filled with black market goods, specifically pharmaceutical concoctions. I took down the address of the alleyway that was known to sell "solutions to pregnancy problems," as one of my informants described it. That afternoon I walked around until I found the exact alleyway, marked by a man selling candy and chocolates at the entrance. I walked up to the candy seller and spoke to him just as I had been instructed to by my informants. "Hello sir," I said, looking over my shoulder to make sure no one was following me. The man looked up from his newspaper and nodded. "I have a problem that I want to get rid of," I said quickly, trying to speak in correct Persian so that none of my slight American accent would come through. The man looked at me for another instant, then turned his attention back to his paper. *"Khahesh bokon* [Say please]," he gruffly mumbled. I was insulted and nervous about being followed as I stood in the alleyway with beads of sweat running down my neck and palms. "Please," I added. "Today, go to the third gentleman on the left. He has lollipops out in front of his *dakkeh* [small standlike shop]," he said, again not looking up from his paper. I thanked the "candy man" and went looking for the man with the lollipops. He was relatively easy to spot because the candies he sold were wrapped in bright colors. When I walked up to the stand, the man was sucking on one of his own lollipops and filling in a crossword puzzle. "Hello sir, *khaste nabashi*" (which literally means "I hope you aren't tired" and acknowledges that the person spoken to is hard working). I began again, wondering if he would have the same attitude as the candy-selling bouncer at the entrance to the alley. "Hello, khawharam [my sister]," he said brightly. "How can I help you?" I took a deep breath and once again checked to make sure no one was around me. "I'm pregnant and I want not to be," I quickly said, trying to be as convincing as possible. "No problem, sister, just wait a moment," he replied calmly. I waited for what seemed like an eternity until the man came back with a bottle of pills and what looked like a vile of liquid. "Do you prefer the pills or the injection?" he asked me. At this point I wasn't sure what to say. I hadn't really thought it through because I just wanted to see how easy it was to obtain these goods. "The pills," I found myself saying. "Very good then," he said, taking out a few pills from the bottle, putting them into a smaller bottle, and handing them to me. "That'll be thirty tomans [shorthand for thirty thousand tomans, equivalent to US$32], please," he said, handing me the smaller bottle, which I quickly put into my purse. I handed him the money and left. I was once again surprised at how easily a woman could buy these unknown pills (or liquid injections), and how little information about their substance was provided.

During my time in Tehran in 2004 and 2005, I interviewed six women who within the preceding few months had received abortions. For three of them, this was not their first experience with abortion; one of them had already had four. However, all six of the women with whom I talked about their abortion experiences were quite lucky in that they were all able to see expensive doctors in the northern parts of town and thus received more adequate medical care than did my other informants who could not afford these services.

Farnoush, a twenty-three-year-old mother of one, was one of the first young women to ask me to assist her in attaining an abortion. Her friend Mahnaz, a mutual friend of ours, called me one afternoon in the summer of 2004 and begged me to come to Farnoush's house. I told Mahnaz I was busy working and that I had made dinner plans with Mojdeh for later that day. "No problem, Pardis. Farnoush and I will meet you at Mojdeh's in two hours. See you then." Before I had a chance to tell her that she should probably clear it with Mojdeh, she had already hung up the phone. When I arrived at Mojdeh's house, I found Farnoush in tears. "Thank God you're here, Pardis," Mahnaz said, rushing to me and taking me to Farnoush. She was crying so hard that her mascara and eyeliner, which were usually impeccable and highlighted the yellow and gold specks in her eyes, were now running down her cheeks, forming lines at the corners of her mouth. These lines served only to further accentuate her already full lips, which now trembled as she tried to speak. "Pardis jun, you are the only person who can help me," she sobbed. I sat down and put my arm around her. Farnoush attempted to calm herself before speaking again.

"I . . . I . . . I hate my husband, you know," she stammered. "And now I'm pregnant again, and I didn't even want the first one, but I really don't want this one; all I want is a divorce." Mahnaz sat down across from me and shook her head at Farnoush. "She is so stupid. She has been having problems all along with her husband, and then decided to get pregnant to help bring them closer together. Now it's only driving them apart," Mahnaz scolded. I put down my glass of pomegranate juice and offered Farnoush some tissues. "I don't want this baby; I want to have an abortion, I want to get rid of it. Can't you help me?" begged Farnoush. I didn't know what to say. "I can try as best I can to help you," I said. I barely had a chance to speak before Mahnaz stepped in again. "But Pardis, it's complicated; she's almost four months pregnant," cautioned Mahnaz. I looked from Farnoush's face to her stomach. I had never noticed before but she was actually starting to show. "Is this true?" I asked. Farnoush shrugged. "I think so, I'm not sure, four or five. Either way, I know it's late, but I absolutely can't go through with the pregnancy, and I can't go through the abortion alone. Please help me. My husband isn't speaking to me. He isn't even here, he's in Dubai. I know I have to get his permission, which will be hell, but after that. . . . " Her voice trailed off. "What would you like me to do?" I asked. "Don't you know some good doctors? With all that research you do, I'm sure you know someone who can help me, right?" she asked. I thought for a moment and then remembered a certain doctor who had been highly recommended to me and whom I had interviewed only weeks before. "Yes, I know a good doctor," I told Farnoush. Her face completely changed and her heaving sobs finally slowed. "I will give you his number," I told her. Farnoush then threw her arms around me. Mahnaz gave yet another disapproving stare; she always voiced her opposition to abortions, saying that pregnancy was a gift from God that should not be disrespected. "And I will pray for you, Farnoush. God be with you and give you strength to get through this," whispered Mahnaz.

The next day Mahnaz called the doctor I had recently interviewed and set up an appointment for two days later for an abortion for Farnoush. When Mahnaz took her in, the doctor took one look at her stomach and drew in his breath and seemed hesitant. Farnoush burst into tears yet again. The past few days had been torture for her. She had gotten into a fight with her husband, who was furious at her and now calling her a murderer. During the Khatami era, it was common law that a married woman could get an abortion if she could prove that it would save her life or the life of the fetus; however, she needed the signature of her husband, her physician, and two attending nurses or physician's assistants. Her husband was reluctant about signing the necessary paperwork. She had been going to mosque every day (a practice she told me she hadn't done since she was in middle school) to pray for the strength to endure the difficulties of the procedure. The doctor put his arm around her and escorted her into the room where the procedure was to take place. It is unclear to me what type of abortion was performed on Farnoush. She later told me that the doctor told her to rest and to come back the next day for more care and examination.

When I came to visit her after Mahnaz took her home, she was wailing in her bed. Her five-year-old son ran to her bedside. "What's wrong with my mommy?" he asked me. "She's just not feeling well today," I told him as Farnoush brushed aside a tear and reached out her hand to bring her son closer to her side. "Grandma is going to take care of you and mommy for a few days," she told him. A few hours later Farnoush's mother arrived to take care of her daughter and grandson. Farnoush's mother was very supportive of her daughter's decision and had offered to take care of her in her husband's absence. She thanked me and Mahnaz immensely for our support and sent us on our way. Three days later Farnoush had recovered and was her old self. She had healed beautifully, according to her doctor, and her final visit to the doctor was scheduled for the following week. She was smiling radiantly the next time I saw her, a week later at a party.

"Thank you, Pardis," she said, hugging me. "Everything just fell into place after all that mess. The doctor was so nice, and now my husband thinks I was so brave to go through all that. Things just might get a bit better," she said, drinking a double shot of vodka in a toast to her own health.

It is unclear how many women are receiving abortions in doctors' offices, and how many are electing other solutions to the problem. One thing that is clear from the casual conversations I had with young women regarding abortion, as well as from insights from doctors, is that many young people are choosing this method to end unwanted pregnancies, and they are now suffering tremendously from it on an emotional level, and often even on a physical level. The most glaring problem is the criminalization of abortions, which needs to be addressed given the rising number of unwanted pregnancies.

Other Health Challenges: STIs

Although many young adults were unaware of what an STI is, let alone the names of STIs and their modes of transmission, a few of my informants admitted to having been diagnosed with what they later found out was an STI, while others described friends who had had this experience.

"It was so painful," recalled Laleh, describing her first urinary tract infection (UTI). "It was only a year after I was married that I got these horrible pains when I wanted to go to the bathroom! Then I would get stuck in there for hours." Laleh and her group of friends regularly referred to their UTIs, or "burnings," as they called them, as their worst STIs. Whenever I asked them about their experiences with STIs, they could only talk about these "burnings." "That's the worst disease you can get from sex, and for the longest time I didn't know it was from sex. I just thought I ate something or it was my clothes," said Laleh. "It wasn't until two years and three burning episodes later that I realized I had an STI." As Laleh described this in front of a group of six or seven young women, many of them nodded, indicating that they had experienced this as well. "It's really the worst," added another young woman. "You feel as though God is punishing you for enjoying too much sex."

My friend Shadi, a twenty-three-year-old housewife, introduced in Chapter 1, described her experience with gonorrhea, or *souzak*. "Yes, I know what STIs are, unfortunately," she told me. "I didn't for a long time, but then I found out I had one; this is before I got married" she said stopping to look at my face for a reaction. When I showed none, she continued. "I had souzak. I don't know what you call it in English, but that's what I had, and it was terrible." She stopped again and looked at my tape recorder, then at me. "Would you like me to turn it off?" I asked her. She paused and then shook her head. Readjusting her headscarf, she continued. "I trust you," she said before continuing. "It was sad, but luckily my mom supported me and took me to the doctor to get it taken care of. I was really fortunate, because it happened and got taken care of before I got married, so I never even had to tell my husband," she explained. Shadi seemed relieved that the process was over, but still somewhat scarred by the experience, because she switched topics after this short explanation.

Two of the young men I interviewed also indicated they had experiences with other STIs, one through his own struggle with genital herpes, and another through his friend's fight against hepatitis. Both young men did not know about STIs before these infections, and both reiterated that it is something that should be talked about in schools and with other young adults. Seppand, the university student whose first sexual encounter in a car was so vividly described in Chapter Four, later told me that he had contracted genital herpes from another girl (he referred to her as a prostitute) whom he and his friends had picked up in his car.

"Yes, I know the name of an STI: herpes. How about that one?" he said with a biting tone. "You wanna know how come I know that one?" he angrily asked. I nodded. "Because I have it! Forever, apparently, but I don't let it ruin me." "How did you get it, do you know?" I asked him. He leaned in toward me, took my digital recorder in his hand, and began talking into it in a hushed voice, his lips millimeters away from the device, as though it were a microphone. "From a jendeh [slut], that's how. That's how I got it. We picked her up, and she was good, and we took turns with her, but as far as I know I'm the only one who got sick." I asked him if he was sure it had been this particular sexual encounter that had exposed him to herpes. "Of course! Duh! Everyone knows you get these diseases from whores! My cousin says I got what I deserved." I started to point out that these "whores" must have contracted the disease in some way, because women are not walking disease carriers, and that this was a problematic way of looking at women, but I stopped when I realized he probably did not want to hear my rhetoric. "How did you know you had herpes?" I asked. "Cause my [dick] broke out in these sores, you know? At first I thought it was acne. When my brother saw it he said it was just acne or a rash, but when it persisted, I finally went to a doctor at school," he said, motioning to his penis. "It wasn't great. The doctor told me I had committed a sin and this disease was my punishment. I think he was stupid, but I'm still dealing with it."

Saman, the university student who in Chapter 5 told of his experiences being caught by the komite, told me about how his best friend from school contracted hepatitis from a girl they knew from school. "To tell you the truth, I do know about STIs because my best friend has hepatitis," he said. "He slept with this girl from school who was kind of slutty, and we think that's how he got it. Hepatitis is an STI, right?" he asked. "Yes, it can be passed along sexually or through intravenous drug use," I answered. "Well, yeah, he doesn't put needles in his arms, so he definitely got it from her; but there aren't any real visible signs, right?" I debated whether or not to launch into a full description of the different forms of hepatitis and their symptoms. "To tell you the truth," he said, before I could make up my mind, "I don't know much about hepatitis or other STIs. It's really bad. You should come talk to all of us, or there should be a way for us to find out about this other than from our friends." I nodded, told him I would always be available for information, and referred him to one of the drop-in centers nearby. I also fished a pamphlet about sexual and reproductive health out of my bag and handed it to him. "Another thing I have to admit," Saman added, interrupting me as I was describing one of the clinics in his part of town, "I don't even know how to protect myself from it. I have the fear of God, seriously, that I'll get one of these diseases, but I don't even *do* anything about it."

FAMILY PLANNING AND PUBLIC HEALTH EFFORTS have been very successful among the married population in Tehran, but rates of HIV, STIs, and unwanted pregnancies are on the rise because unmarried youth do not have access to information or risk-reduction resources. This is due in part to the regime's restriction of sex education for unmarried youth, but it can also be attributed to the lack of discussions about sexual health in the general youth population. Although youth have succeeded in causing a societal shift in attitudes toward sexual and social behaviors, discussions about risk and health are not taking place among unmarried young people. Parents, providers, and counselors are working to address these problems and to provide information and services to more youth. My extensive discussions with young people and health care providers illuminated three issues: (1) the need to bridge the gap between providers and young people, (2) the need to find new ways of distributing information to young people (such as the Internet and satellite television) that takes into consideration their concerns about both the social and viral risks to which they are exposed, and (3) the need to find ways of distributing resources to this underserved population. The perspective offered by providers, coupled with young Tehrani voices about sexuality and sexual health, are combining to produce a picture of how Iranian society views sexuality and sexual health, and of the disconnect between young people and providers that is occurring in contemporary Tehran as a result of changes in Iran's sexual culture.

7   The Adults

C HANGING PARENT, teacher, and health care provider perspectives are perhaps the most significant evidence of a shift in the societal conversation about sexuality and social relations, and of the changing social and sexual culture. It is important to note the ways in which parents' perspectives toward their children and toward sexuality and social relations have changed. Although not all parents support their children's behavior and their involvement in the sexual and social revolution, a significant number of parents with whom I spoke had changed their point of view in the last decade and are now more open to the behavioral and attitudinal shifts taking place in their children. During the summers of 2005 and 2007, I had the opportunity to interview twenty-six parents (some the parents of my informants, others, parents whose children were not part of the study), and although this is a small sample of people, I believe that the responses of these parents reveal the changes I have noted in the preceding chapters. Most of the parents with whom I spoke expressed distaste toward the regime and saw themselves as mediators between their children and the state. Similarly, of the thirty health care providers I interviewed (including doctors, health counselors, social workers, mental health care providers, and health workers at drop-in centers and harm-reduction clinics), all but one indicated that they supported the shifts in the sexual and social culture that are occurring among the country's youth, but they were concerned about the potential health risks that would accompany this shift. Many of the health care providers were accepting of youth engaging in sexual behaviors not sanctioned by the regime, and they indicated they always wanted to make their services available to the young adults, especially to unmarried young people, whose access to risk-reduction resources and information is limited. I was pleasantly surprised to see the number of "adults" (including parents and providers) who were fighting for more rights, services, and education for the young people. That so many parents and health care providers are accepting their children's participation in premarital sex and the risks that accompany it, and that they are fighting for these young people's rights, indicates that the changes that have been taking place have taken hold in parts of society outside of the youth culture. This chapter explores "adult" perspectives on youth to point to ways in which the sexual and social revolution enacted by the youth has resulted in a broader shift in viewpoints and attitudes in Tehran.

Parents

Overall, the parents I interviewed characterized themselves and their friends into three main groups: (1) parents who were in denial or did not know or wish to acknowledge their children's sexual and social behavior, which they considered immoral; (2) parents who were concerned about their children's well-being and mental and physical health growing up in the current environment, and who wanted to be a friend to their children and talk openly and be supportive of changes in their lifestyles; and (3) parents who themselves had begun to embody many of the changes in social and sexual culture and who looked to their children to learn about changes in fashion or to procure alcohol. Many of this third group of parents often played host to elaborate parties for their friends and their children's friends. Although I did not have the opportunity to conduct in-depth interviews with as many parents as youth (I interviewed only twenty-six parents—some as couples, meaning I interviewed mother and father together, and some as just one parent), I did observe many of the parents' interactions with my informants, and frequently asked my informants about their relationships with their mothers and fathers. I also observed and participated in a lot of parties and gatherings hosted by my informants' parents, where I had the opportunity to conduct brief informal interviews with the parents. As with the majority of the young people I interviewed, many of the parents with whom I spoke would consider themselves members of the secular middle class.

As indicated by the three categories just listed, certain parents were very strict and closed-minded and imposed harsh punishment on their children if they were caught doing things that were considered morally questionable (such as dancing, drinking, dating, and male-female socializing). As several of the social workers I spoke with noted, these kinds of parents did not inspire trust in their children and encouraged lying and deceit. It also seemed that this group of parents (who formed the minority among those I interviewed) was often in denial about their children's behavior; they would tell me that their children never attended parties and would not even consider premarital sex, but when I interviewed their children I found that not only were they engaging in a large amount of partying, but they also had had several sexual partners and were not yet married. Although four of the parents I interviewed fit into this group of "parents in denial," a large group of parents were empathetic with their children and aimed to provide an open forum for discussing many morally challenging issues, such as sexuality, contraception, and relationships. The majority of the fourteen parents with whom I spoke fell into this category and identified themselves as mediators between their children and the state. There was also a group of parents who themselves enacted many of the behaviors of their children and enjoyed being social, attending parties, and breaking many of the Islamic rules in regard to drinking and dancing. There were many different kinds of parents, and although many of them did not fit neatly into the three categories described earlier, the shift in attitude among the majority of the parents I interviewed, and their support of their children and the changing youth culture, indicates a societywide shift.

When I began my research in Iran in 2000, the majority of my informants told me that their parents were not open to their sexual and social revolution. They indicated that most of their parents had no idea about their social and sexual activities, and found out only when the young people were caught by the morality police. "You have to be careful here," explained Hossein in July of 2000. "I mean we have to hide our partying not just from the Islamic Republic and their goons, but also in the house; families are strict about it. My family would kill me if they knew what I did every night, so it all has to be in secret." Saara and Asana concurred with Hossein's assessment when I interviewed them in 2002. "My dad is the worst," began Asana. I nodded in agreement, remembering observing her interacting with her father. She was so afraid of him that when she heard him coming home, she grabbed me, ran to her room, and closed the door. Her mother was sweet and very hospitable, but her father would always ignore me and refer to me as "Asana's AIDS friend." "He is horrible and he would kill me if he knew I even came to our dance class! I have to hide everything from him," Asana remarked. Her friend Saara agreed with her and talked of her own experience with her family. "Yeah, and, well, it's difficult for me because, like she said, I too have to lie to my parents. That's hard; I don't like to lie, and I don't like to lie to my parents either." By 2007, both Asana and Saara described very different relationships with their parents. Both of them indicated that their parents now accepted their current boyfriends, a definite shift in parent-child relations.

Many young people indicated their distaste for lying and the breeding of mistrust with family members, but many of them also said that when it came to their parents it was a necessity. "Some of my friends say it's a matter of life and death," said Gypsy. "They have to lie to their parents about their sex lives because they don't want to be killed. I'm serious, you don't know religiously fanatical people, but they will kill their kids if they find out what they do!" It seemed to me that Gypsy's example was a bit over the top, but several of my other informants who were from religiously conservative families concurred with his assessment. Also, it may have been coincidental but it was three days after my last interview with Gypsy in the summer of 2002 that the young woman was publicly executed on orders from her grandfather (see Chapter 4).

When I interviewed two sets of parents from Tehran *Pars*, the eastern part of town, they both indicated that they believed their children did not participate in the changing sexual and social culture that was occurring on the streets of Tehran. "Yes, there are many changes taking place among the youth of Tehran today," said Mr. Behroozian, a fifty-five-year-old writer and father of two young women (ages twenty-one and twenty-three). "You go out in the streets today and you see that many women walk around looking like prostitutes, kids are going to parties right and left, and women are having plenty of sex before marriage." His wife nodded in agreement. When I asked him what he thought of the changes taking place among the youth, he seemed sympathetic. "Yes, they are doing a lot of *kesafat kari* [dirty activities], but it's their right! This regime may have done it to them, but that doesn't make it right." I then asked him what he thought about his daughters' social activities. "I raised my children right," he said emphatically. His wife remained silent but continued to nod in agreement. "They don't do anything they aren't supposed to do. They are *dokhtareh khub* [pure and good women] and don't go around to parties or have boyfriends. When it comes time for marriage, I will choose their husbands for them." As I jotted down what he told me, I remembered interviewing his two daughters only three weeks earlier. Both of them had told me they regularly attended parties, and both had had at least two sexual partners although neither was married. When I later asked them how they got away with going to parties or having a boyfriend without the knowledge of their parents, they both told me they lied to their parents and covered for each other. "When I'm going to go to a party, I tell my dad I'm going over to a friend's house to study, and then I get ready there," the twenty-one-year-old daughter told me. The other daughter explained that when she wanted to see her boyfriend, she asked her sister to tell her parents she was working late (she was a travel agent). It is possible that their parents knew what was going on and chose to ignore it, but it was also imaginable that the young women did an excellent job of covering their tracks so that their parents would not discover their whereabouts.

Many of my informants complained of harsh punishment from their parents and admitted to lying to them out of fear of what that punishment might entail. "I think if I were caught by the komite and held in jail overnight, I would kill myself," said Saara very seriously. "It's not that being in jail would be that bad, but it's just that I wouldn't want to go home after that; my parents would be so angry with me. I think it would be better at that point to stay in jail than to go home with my family." Shahrzad explained that if she were caught by her parents in the company of a young man, she would be disowned. "I'm serious, Pardis. You don't even know, my mother does not accept relations between boys and girls at any age!" she exclaimed. "When my sister was almost thirty she was hanging out with her boyfriend and my mom caught her. My mom actually kicked her out! She hasn't been home in a year, and that makes me really nervous." She frowned.

Although during the summer of 2000 and 2002 the majority of parents were in denial, by 2007 the majority of parents (both those with whom I spoke and those who were described to me by informants) could be categorized into the group who were trying to be understanding and supportive and who saw themselves as mediators between their children and the state. This shift in the number of parents who now accepted and supported many of the behaviors they would previously have deemed wrong or immoral is an important indicator of the far-reaching and broad societal effects of the sexual and social revolution. It is not clear whether this change in support and perspective among the parents happened gradually or was a result of shifting behavior among the young people on a large scale. Some parents said they had "no choice" but to accept and support changes in their children's behavior if they didn't want their children to run away or be hurt. Others indicated their distaste for the regime and the need to help their children navigate what they saw as a difficult environment. However, evidence of the parents' assent to and support of the sexual and social revolution can be seen daily as they drop off heavily made-up daughters, or sons with piercings and tattoos aplenty, at school; host gatherings for their children; or come to their children's defense when picking them up from a night in jail or being scolded by members of the morality police or harsh teachers. Every day, evidence can be seen in Tehran of parents supporting their children's social behaviors, and this is an important indicator of shifts in their thinking. Whereas at one time young people were afraid of their parents finding out about their partners, today they take boyfriends and girlfriends to family parties; whereas once young people used to hide their piercings, makeup, and tattoos from their parents, who would have kicked them out of the house, they now show off their style to their parents, who often give them money to support their shopping habits.

Although the exact reasons for this attitude shift in many of the parents are not clear, during the summers of 2005 and 2007 many of my informants described good, strong relationships with their mothers and fathers, and I was able to observe many instances in which parents actually facilitated and participated in social gatherings. When I asked my informants and the parents with whom I spoke about the reasons behind shifts in parental outlooks, the answers varied. "Many of us don't agree with this regime and we feel guilty, that it's our fault that the kids have to grow up in an environment like this," said Mrs. Gooya, a factory owner and the mother of a teenage daughter and a twenty-one-year-old son. "We defend our kids and we want to be there for them because it's not right that they have to grow up like this." Another mother described defending her son against harsh schoolteachers who wanted to cut his hair. "My kids should be my business," she said. "If I think his hair is too long or he doesn't have an appropriate haircut, that is up to me and him and not to his teachers. So when they wanted to cut his hair, I screamed at them and pulled him out of that school! It's not right the way they want to be so mean to our children. Their childhood is being taken away from them." At least ten of the parents I interviewed relayed stories of defending their children at school or against the morality police in the street, or even of getting their children released from jail. "If my kids are caught, I go and get them and pay whatever price needs to be paid to get them out," said yet another mother who has three children between the ages of eighteen and twenty-three. "I go to the jail, make sure they are released, and then bring them home and make them a nice warm meal. I don't even care what the crime is. I know my children don't deserve the treatment they get in jail." When I asked her if she punished her children for being caught partying, drinking, or being out with a member of the opposite sex, she shook her head firmly and said, "They are young, this is what young people are *supposed* to do! This regime just doesn't get it, so we have to help our kids out."

Five of the mothers with whom I spoke indicated that they supported their children's decisions to have partners before marriage, and all of them spoke of the need to broaden horizons in this arena. "Yes! Young people should date; why not?" asked Mrs. Farzanpoor, a social worker and mother of three daughters ages eighteen, twenty, and twenty-seven. "Having a few boyfriends before marriage is no problem. I encourage my daughters to do so." I was surprised at the number of times I heard variations on this same sentence from mothers, and even from older women who did not have children themselves. Many members of the Iranian-American community in California (the largest community of

Iranians outside of Iran) were not yet open to their children's dating patterns, and this openness was not as prevalent in Tehran in 2000 when I began my research there. Thus I saw the new openness as evidence of the spread of new views on sexuality. Whereas young women used to have to hide their boyfriends and purchase hymen reconstructions, today many are bringing their boyfriends on family vacations and talking to their parents about their sex lives.

"For me, for us, me and my sister, my mom took the approach of wanting to be our friend, so she talked to us like a friend," described Taraneh, a twenty-two-year-old musician. "She wanted to help us so she always asked us if we were OK with our sex lives. But I know that some women are unfortunate, and they go out and can't talk to their parents if they have a problem. This is sad because we as kids need parents and guidance. I'm so thankful for my mom." Other informants also indicated that they were able to talk with their parents about a variety of issues. "My mom is really great and she talks to me about everything," said Nazanin. "I remember one day when I was young she picked me up from school and I told her my stomach was hurting. That day she talked to me about menstruation and it was great because I didn't have to feel awkward about it like many of my friends did."

Two of my male informants also indicated that they routinely discussed sexual issues with their mothers. "It's great because I can talk to my mom easily about sex," explained Seppand. "I tell my mom about the women I'm dating and she gives me advice on them. She even tells me to bring them home sometimes!" he added. Khodi too noted that he turned to his mother for relationship advice and support. "It's called family support, and it's very important. Like if you want to be with a girl and then if you decide you want to marry her, your family can be really helpful and tell you whether they think this will be a good thing, and then they can support you and help you in your marriage." Khodi felt that family support was instrumental in his decision-making process. Nazanin also noted that both her parents were supportive of her, and this support gave her a sense of security. "I'm not so scared of being caught by the morality police because I know my parents support me. They always tell me that, so if one day I get caught I'm not scared because my parents are behind me and they will come get me out of jail and take me home." Nazanin emphasized that sometimes the morality police use young people's parents to threaten them but if young people have strong relationships with their parents, this line of threat and punishment does not work.

In talking with several of my informants' parents, it seemed that many of them in fact supported their children's social movement and encouraged them to continue their partying and to resist the harsh social rules imposed by the regime. "Look, we don't agree with this regime, so if this is our kids' way of getting back at them, then so be it. That's fine by us; let them party, let them not wear headscarves at all! I hate this outfit. I encourage my daughter to push the envelope," said one mother as she was hosting a party for her daughter. Many parents advocated social gatherings and offered to host parties and even bribe members of the morality police so that their kids could "party in peace," as the father of one of my informants put it. On several occasions I attended a party and found an informant's parents there, serving alcohol and drinking and dancing themselves. "Screw the Islamic Republic; our kids need happiness in their hearts, and this is the best way to get it," shouted an informant's father at one party I attended. He handed me a drink and ushered me over to the dance floor. "Go on! Have fun, and remember, screw the Islamic Republic." He raised his eyebrows, opened his eyes wide, swayed his hips, and shook his shoulders to the music.

The third category of parents, those who engaged in many of the same behaviors as their children, seemed invested in the sexual and social revolution themselves. These parents spent many evenings per week at parties, drinking alcohol (with and without their children). Four of the mothers with whom I spoke indicated that they enjoyed putting on style the way their teenage daughters did, and they saw themselves as part of the sexual and social revolution as well. These women also wore heavy layers of makeup, tight māntos, and pushed-back headscarves, and they attended dance classes and sometimes parties with their children. "Yes, we like to party too!" said one young mother of two teenage boys. "I mean, we want to have fun like our kids!" her friend (also a mother of two) added. As I spent time at beauty salons and in gyms and dance classes, I often met mother and daughter pairs who were giving each other style tips and updates. "No, mom, those headscarves aren't in fashion any more; you have to wear the translucent ones," said one young woman to her mother in a scarf shop in bāzār e-Safavieh one afternoon. Her mother quickly put away her out-of-fashion shawl in favor of a transparent rusari, as her daughter had suggested. She added a coat of lipstick and looked to her daughter for approval. "Now you are in style," her daughter said triumphantly.

It was also not uncommon for parents to host large gatherings for parents and children to attend together. I remember one party I attended with Azita and her parents where her father continued to fill our glasses with vodka. Halfway through the evening I looked across the crowded apartment-turned-disco to find many of my informants dancing to techno music with their parents! At one point Ali Reza's father (the host of the party) uncorked a bottle of champagne and started pouring it all over his head. As Ali Reza caught my eye, I could not help but stifle a laugh. He smiled, shook his head, and said, "I know, our parents are crazier than we are. Where do you think *we* get it from?"

A Parent with Many Children: Mrs. Erami

One of the female teachers who taught courses on health, puberty, and relationships at a local high school tried very hard to get her students engaged in a discussion of the social and sexual issues they were grappling with. In the end, however, the students refused to talk to her. The first time I met this teacher, Mrs. Erami, I too was afraid to talk to her, let alone tell her about my work. She was wearing a large, loose mānto and a maghna'e, and over all of this, a black chādor that was held by her teeth so that only her eyes remained visible. I was at the Ministry of Education doing research on the sex education curriculum, and she had come to discuss with the Minister her lack of progress in gaining the youths' attention. "They are terrible," she told me that day. I was very uncomfortable in her presence; I had forgotten to remove my passion pink nail polish. I made a fist to hide my nails as I spoke with her. "The kids?" I asked. "Yes, them," she said harshly. "The young girls. They are so difficult, I can't get them to talk to me, but I know what they are doing and what they are *not* doing. I had a teenage daughter myself, and I know that they are having a lot of sex, but not doing it right. I just can't get them to talk to me about it." She released the chādor from her teeth so she could talk but held it tightly in her right hand. "You do this kind of work, right? I have heard about you. Do you think you can help me figure out how to talk to them?" she asked. I then remembered my informants who had complained that they were uncomfortable discussing their personal sexual issues with *chādori* (conservative) women who did not speak their language. "Well, you have to speak to them in their own language," I relayed to Mrs. Erami. After a long moment of silence, she nodded and smiled and offered me some tea, although I was afraid to take it lest she see my painted nails.

This was the beginning of what became a close relationship between Mrs. Erami and me. We worked together throughout my time in Iran to reform the sex education curriculum and make it more appealing to the youth. We often spent hours comparing notes about what she had learned at the Ministry of Education and what I was working on with the young people. She brought me rough drafts of three pamphlets that the Ministry was working on to talk about puberty, family relationships, and maintaining good personal health. These pamphlets were very progressive and the result of much work, but Mrs. Erami often told me that the Ministry continuously faced harsh criticism from other Ministries and members of Parliament for becoming too "modernized." We routinely discussed ways of getting around bureaucratic obstacles and eventually pulled together a group of people interested in these same issues to meet once a month. Since I left Iran, Mrs. Erami has told me that the group continues to meet and is continuously strategizing on how best to get the pamphlets to the young people and how to present the education reforms they were after in a way that was palatable to Parliament.

During one of my visits to Tehran in 2005, Mrs. Erami invited me to her home for lunch. It was then that she told me the story of her daughter who had run away from home three years earlier. "Next month it will be three years that we have not seen or heard from our daughter Fatemeh. Her twenty-first birthday was last month." I looked at a framed picture of her daughter that hung on the wall. Mrs. Erami's eyes welled up with tears as I asked about her son. "He, he too has left us, but at least he writes and calls once in a while," she said, tears streaming down her face. It turned out that her son had told his mother he was gay, and this had prompted her husband to throw their son out of the house. Her daughter had been, in her mother's words, "one of those chaytoon [mischievous] women" who ran around with young men. Mrs. Erami would frequently catch her daughter at local squares and meeting spots and scold her for her disobedience. One day her daughter had come home and declared that she now had a boyfriend. After her mother had slapped her and called her a prostitute, Fatemeh had packed her bags and not returned since. One year later Mrs. Erami's husband passed away and she was totally alone in her home. It was then that she decided to dedicate her life to understanding and helping other young people learn about sex. Although Mrs. Erami was very religious, she was very open to discussing secular ideas about sexuality and remains to this day a campaigner for sex education reform within the Ministry. Throughout my time in Iran I would often go to her with the data I had gathered and talk through some of my findings. Together we would sit down and analyze some of the behaviors of the young people, trying to reconceptualize risk as they saw it. We would then inevitably try to come up with a strategy to reach out to them. To this day Mrs. Erami is working within the Ministry of Education to create a sex education program that will be acceptable to members of the regime and at the same time appeal to the young people.

Working With and Within the System: Health Service Providers

During my time in Iran I located several drop-in centers—most of which were organized, managed, or funded by the government—where young people could receive free counseling about sex, drugs, and harm reduction.[1] Most of these centers were utilized by young married couples who had taken their mandatory prenuptial counseling courses at these sites. The existence of these centers, their funding by the government, and the openness of the personnel who staff them are evidence that shifting attitudes have resulted in the development of a new infrastructure to serve urban youth. The many adults who work at these centers are all very open to discussing premarital sex, sexual behaviors, homosexuality, and harm reduction. I was constantly impressed by the amount of energy and effort dedicated by so many members of the older generation to push for a more open dialogue about sexuality and to be a part of the changing sexual culture. It is unfortunate, however, that there seems to be a distinct gap between the providers and the young people they are trying to serve. The young adults are skeptical of the providers or uninformed about this option, and the providers are frustrated at only interacting with the young people when it is "too late." Nonetheless, the centers and the services they provide are a good place to start, and the fact that members of the older generation want to participate in the unfolding conversation is in and of itself a telling sign.

Throughout Iran there are many centers set up in urban areas that call themselves *triangular clinics*. Tehran is home to five such centers, three of which I visited routinely throughout my time in Iran. According to the Ministry of Health and several key health personnel at the clinics, these centers are called triangular clinics because they provide three kinds of services: (1) testing and treatment for sexually transmitted infections (STIs); (2) HIV/AIDS testing, treatment, counseling, and housing; and (3) harm-reduction materials such as clean needles and methadone maintenance. They also serve three groups of people: (1) drug users, (2) prostitutes or sex workers, and (3) ex-prisoners.

These clinics, which look a lot like hospitals and psychiatric treatment wards and are located primarily on the northern and southern outskirts of the city (sometimes an hour out of town by car), are overcrowded and underfunded, according to the staff. According to Dr. Roozbakhsh, head of one of the clinics, most of the clientele come from the lower classes and the poorer parts of town. When I asked him why this was, he told me that the triangular clinics have become a last resort of sorts. "Those who can afford not to come here don't," he explained. "If you can afford a private doctor, that is where you are going to go, because as you can see, here is not exactly a nice place to hang out." He motioned toward the overcrowded waiting room filled with wailing women in chādors who had just been told they were HIV positive, and convulsing men who were injection drug users begging for more methadone or needles. The clinic was small and consisted of two floors, with a waiting room on the ground floor and two counseling rooms, two testing rooms, and overnight rooms upstairs. The latter were also overcrowded, with HIV positive patients who were estranged from their families and wanted to live at the clinic. The rooms were hot (there was no air conditioning in the middle of the summer) and the white floors and walls were dusty from the crowds coming in and out of the clinic.

When I asked Dr. Roozbakhsh to describe the patients who had tested positive for STIs, he told me that "so many, many people in Tehran have STIs because they are having a lot of sex but without any information on it." He walked over to his desk and pulled out a large box of condoms. "It's because they don't use these. And they are afraid to come and get them from me, but I would give a condom to anyone who asked for one; they shouldn't be afraid. I am open to ways in which the times have changed. I know kids are having more sex now, and more power to them, they just need to be protected." I then asked him to describe the demographics of his patients who had tested positive for an STI. "Most of them are from the pāyin shahr [downtown], and most of them are unmarried," he said. "Why the downtown youth?" I asked. "I thought the unmarried youth having sex were mostly uptown kids." He replied, "Kids will be kids. Everyone is having sex, but it's the poor kids who end up in here." I asked him why. "Because the rich kids either can afford doctors or have figured out how to prevent or treat the disease. Oh, but another thing you should remember is that the poor kids tend to come from more religious families, so they have the sex, but then they feel guilty about it so they come and get tested. So more poor kids come for testing, so more are diagnosed. I think that's what you call a public health phenomenon." He rushed back into a testing room to attend to a line of patients forming outside his door.

This notion of young people from the lower classes who are more religious being more likely than well-to-do kids to be diagnosed with STIs is not unique to Iran. Young people living in highly religious communities in the United States and other parts of the world face this same paradox. For example, as shown in the film *The Education of Shelby Knox*, the town of Lubbock, Texas, which is home to many conservative religious groups (many of whom are lower or lower-middle class) also boasts the highest teen pregnancy and STI rate in the United States. Many Tehranis say that the young people from pāyin shahr seek to emulate the sexual and social behaviors of the secular middle- and upper-class youth but without the education or access to online communities in which they can discuss their issues. Dr. Mehran, one of the leading HIV specialists in Iran and the only female physician to run an HIV center, agreed that young people in the lower parts of town, whom she described as being poorer, were often more at risk for STI and HIV transmission. "It's actually the kids from pāyin shahr who are more susceptible to these diseases, because they just have no idea about the risks they take," she told me one afternoon. Dr. Mehran's center is the largest testing and treatment center for people living with HIV/AIDS. It is housed in Imam Khomeini Hospital, one of the nation's largest, fully publicly funded hospital chains. This center provides free HIV testing, free condom distribution, and a twenty-four-hour hotline for questions on HIV and STIs, and it conducts research on HIV. According to Dr. Mehran, the vast majority of her patients are unmarried youth, most often from lower-class families, who come in for testing and counseling. "You work with people eighteen to twenty-five, right?" she asked. I nodded. "Look, times have changed. There is a new farhang [culture] out there now, one in which having sex before marriage is just a part of life, and we have to open our eyes. I think that herpes, HPV [human pappillomavirus], and even HIV are highest among people right in your age group," she said. Her two assistants looked at her in surprise. "I know that some people think HIV is a problem of men who are older and drug addicts; well maybe that used to be the case, but not anymore." I asked Dr. Mehran why she thought so many young people who were from the lower classes frequented her center. "I'll tell you why. It's because, and it's mostly young unmarried women too, take note of that." She waited for me to write down what she had said before she continued. "These are the women who come to me because they are the ones who are worried about virginity issues and possible impacts on marital issues. Young people from poorer classes tend to be more religious, and they are more scared and more guilt ridden, so they come to me." Again she paused to wait for me to finish writing. "Plus, there is a lot of sex between classes, and then the lower-class ones end up here. Remember, some of the more educated, more well-off ones will go to expensive black market doctors or get their information online. Plus, there is a lot of prostitution, or different forms of prostitution, with women dating men of higher classes and the opposite, but mostly the women, and then they end up coming here because they have nowhere else to go." She sighed.

As Dr. Mehran was talking, a young man walked into her office and then blushed when he saw us engaged in discussion. "I didn't mean to interrupt Khānum [Madam] doctor," he said sheepishly. "It's okay, my son," Dr. Mehran responded. "How are you feeling today?" "Better than yesterday, but it's hard and I still need to find a job," he responded. "Okay, my son. Don't worry, we'll find you a job, maybe cleaning or something here at the hospital, but don't worry about these things today." With that he nodded and left the room. When he was out of earshot, Dr. Mehran asked me, "Did you see that young man?" I nodded. "He is HIV-positive and his family has disowned him because they are very religious. He now lives here at the hospital; lots of them do, but we're running out of room. The problem is that we as service providers and the sex educators are failing. We, the providers, need to do more prevention and less treatment. But a large part of prevention is education, and the problem with many of our sex educators, especially the ones educating the young people, is they don't know how to talk to the young people. We need to figure out what appeals to them." Dr. Mehran indicated that there was a great need to do further research on HIV and STI transmission patterns, and a dire need for a knowledge, attitudes, and practices (KAP) study among the young people, whom she says account for a large percentage of the infected population. "The problem with these diseases, and especially HIV, is that we know so little about them here in Iran," she said during another interview several months later. "For God's sake, we don't even know how many people in this country are infected, have died from HIV, and what the primary mode of transmission is!" I then asked her about the results of the research that was conducted at her center. "According to our data, we estimate that about sixty thousand people in Tehran alone are HIV-positive. Of these people, 45 percent contracted the disease through unprotected sex, 50 percent through injection drug use, 3 percent through blood transfusion, and 2 percent through mother-to-child transmission." Dr. Mehran emphasized that these were all estimates, but she and her team were in the process of beginning a study to compare transmission rates due to drug use with those for unprotected sexual encounters. It was her hypothesis that the number of people who had contracted HIV through unprotected sex would soon outnumber those who had transmitted it through injection drug use.

Dr. Hosseini, a forty-five-year-old infectious disease specialist from Mashad, runs a camp for HIV-positive Iranians and their families. In the summer of 2007 I had the opportunity to visit this camp and spend time talking to Dr. Hosseini about his views on the youth in Tehran. "We have a serious situation on our hands," he began as he ushered me into his office and offered me a seat. He got up from his desk so he could pace the room as he spoke.

Young people in Iran are up against a lot. They are tired and don't have an outlet to express their frustrations with the bad economic situation, which has left many of them educated but unemployed. And they certainly have no venue to express their frustration at having to grow up with so many social restrictions. So what are they doing? They are turning to extreme social behaviors. They are doing drugs, many of them, which puts them at risk, and they are having a lot of high-risk sexual encounters. Don't get me wrong, I'm not judging them; in fact, I say good for them for doing what they want in the face of all this! But I just want to make sure no one gets hurt.

Dr. Hosseini then told me that he had been conducting a study to see what young people know about HIV and harm reduction. He relayed that after two years of his KAP study he had found that many people know about condoms as a means of contraception and protection from HIV; thus their knowledge is high but their attitudes and behaviors need to shift. He added that people's knowledge and attitudes about sex education have changed, but behavior has not, which concerned him. "We have come a long way," he explained. "The young people now know the condom— which many of them didn't acknowledge even four years ago. They are willing to hear about it, talk about it, but they are not yet willing to *do* anything about it. In terms of KAP—knowledge, attitudes, practices or behaviors—we are stuck between changing attitudes and practices." Dr. Hosseini also added his frustration that many young people do not seem to utilize the services that he and his colleagues worked so hard to establish, such as drop-in centers and counseling groups. "There is a disconnection between us and the youth; they still don't trust us older people," he said. "But I think that things are changing in many ways.

First off, the government now lets us do condom promotion and HIV awareness outreach. They are even funding us! This is success! And as far as the youth, well just last week a group of eighteen-year-old college students came to one of the drop-in centers I work at after their soccer practice. They told me they had come to be tested for HIV. The dialogue is starting to occur, and that shows progress!"

June 16, 2005
"Have you lost your way, young lady?" asked one of the seven men who were loitering on the four dirt-covered steps leading up to the front door. "No, sir," I replied, my voice quivering. As I walked through the door, the room fell silent as the fifty or so men who lined the walls and columns of the smoke-filled waiting room stopped what they were doing and turned to look at me through half-closed eyelids. I tried to stifle a cough as my lungs filled with cigarette smoke. I nearly tripped over a half-awake older male addict who was lying on the floor. Some of the men tried to walk toward me, but as they stepped away from the walls, they began to sway and swagger and turned for assistance to their friends. Suddenly the silence was pierced by the shout of one of the clinicians, who called for the next "client" to enter the methadone-dispensing room. I tried to make my way through the crowd, but I was very uncomfortable as the men walked toward me. Finally I heard a familiar voice. "This is no place for a lady," he said. I bit my lip to hide the trembling as I reached out to shake hands with Dr. Nasser, head of the clinic.

After spending a few minutes with me in the male-filled waiting room, Dr. Nasser ushered me into his office, where I met the first and only woman at the center: his secretary. (Most of the clinic's patients are men between the ages of sixteen and forty, and in my three visits to this clinic I did not see one female patient.) "It's nice to see another woman in here," she told me. "Yes, well, it's nice to see you too," I replied, letting out a sigh of relief that Dr. Nasser's office was located above the clinic and away from the comments and stares of the male clients.

On that warm afternoon in the summer of 2005, I made my way to Persepolis, one of the largest and newest harm-reduction centers in

Tehran. It provides a range of services, from HIV/AIDS and hepatitis C testing to methadone maintenance therapy. According to Dr. Nasser, they dispense roughly ten thousand tablets of methadone per day and distribute up to five hundred clean needles per day. Dr. Nasser (who insists on being called Dr. N), who runs the needle exchange, harm-reduction, and methadone maintenance program, had a harrowing estimate of the breakdown of HIV positive patients. Although the mandate of Persepolis is not necessarily to treat HIV-positive or STI patients, Dr. Nasser has been conducting research on HIV and hepatitis C prevalence among the drug users who utilize the center's facilities; he is especially interested in researching high-risk behavior among Tehrani youth and is seeking to bring harm-reduction services to universities and schools throughout the city. Out of a random sample of nine hundred street drug injectors ages fifteen to sixty-five, Dr. Nasser and his team found that 25 percent were HIV-positive, and 75 percent had hepatitis C. "We are sustaining them and trying to help them," he said "But we can't really treat them. We have outreach workers and a counseling group for people living with HIV/AIDS, but we are highly understaffed and overcrowded." We pushed our way through the smoke-filled waiting room that takes up most of the first floor of the clinic. As he took me into the room where the methadone is dispensed, the young men in the waiting room began to stare at and follow me. As they made inappropriate comments to me, Dr. Nasser shuffled me (and the two male journalist friends who had come along with me) into his office and closed the door. "This is no place for a lady," he said to me again. "So you don't really serve women?" I asked him half-jokingly. "We would like to serve more women, we would like to serve more people, if you can believe it!" he said enthusiastically. "There are so many people we can't reach, but we want to, and we want young people to come here to learn. We want to do prevention and education. But you see, we need money," he said, lowering his voice. When I asked him if he gets some amount of money from the government, he shook his head but quickly added, "But we did get a fatwa passed promoting harm reduction!"

Persepolis and many other needle exchanges in Tehran cater mostly to men. But in June 2007 I had the opportunity to visit *Khaneh-e-Khorshid* (literally, house of the sun), a harm-reduction and drop-in center just for women that had opened its doors earlier that year. Khaneh-e-Khorshid is located south of the railroad tracks in one of the southernmost parts of town. It is also just a few miles from Shahr-e-No, a somewhat run-down neighborhood near the tracks that is known to house commercial sex workers. Khaneh-e-Khorshid, a privately funded nongovernmental organization, is open every day from 9 A.M. to 4 P.M. and provides a wide array of services for the women who frequent the center: a warm meal at lunchtime every day, showers, bathrooms, feminine hygiene products, undergarments, oral hygiene care, child care services, and most important, education about risk and harm reduction. Women at the center can also volunteer to be trained to become outreach workers (which twenty-five of them have done) so that the services and education are taken into the community by members of the community. "We treat them with respect and kindness," said Mrs. Monshi, a family practitioner and head of the center. "We give them whatever they need. For some of them it's a bath; for others, I just brush their hair and give them counseling." When I asked if they distributed clean needles, she nodded and showed me a package that included clean needles and other injection paraphernalia (such as cookers and armbands). "But we don't have methadone maintenance therapy," she said. "Once a week we have someone come, on Wednesdays, to provide the women with methadone, but he doesn't always come, and there are more women who need it, and on a more regular basis than we can serve." She distributed cups of stew to the women who had gathered in the inner courtyard of the clinic. "We have more women here than we can serve, but that's our fault," said Mrs. Amini, a social worker at the clinic. "We don't have enough money even to begin to be of service to all the women who should be coming here but aren't, but no one wants to fund an organization that is helping unwanted women. But we understand why the women are doing what they are doing. A failing economy, huge life pressures, a difficult government, few outlets for recreation or activity. It's understandable why a lot of young women turn to sex and drugs. But we get the really troubled ones here, and we are happy to serve them, but it's the other women I worry about, the ones who are bringing on this sexual revolution; they don't end up here, and while I'm glad to see and hear about women taking control of their bodies and sexualities, good for them,

I'm also concerned that they do it in a safe way. I want to play my part in helping them." Mrs. Monshi nodded in agreement.

All of these providers agreed that their services were underutilized, and that there was a need to reach out to the youth population. Dr. Mehran noted that radio and television are good vehicles for reaching out to today's youth, and that sex educators can use these means to reach their target populations. She also stressed the need to build up the peer education component of sex education, and she indicated her willingness to join a coalition to train young peer educators. Dr. Roozbakhsh and several of the other staff members of the triangular clinics lamented that young people did not use their services regularly. They believe that there is a need to do more outreach so that young people are more aware of the resources available to them through venues such as the clinics or the counseling and drop-in centers. All of the providers and counselors I spoke with indicated a gap between themselves and the population they are trying to serve, and they clamored for more information about how to close this gap.

It is of no small significance that harm reduction centers (and centers just for women) have been legalized and constructed and are supported (to varying degrees) by the government. The efforts of many activists, doctors, and health outreach workers must not go unnoticed and are significant when considering the ways in which civil society has changed in Tehran. Although the providers still complain of a disconnection between themselves and the youth who concern them, the efforts of the providers to create a health infrastructure to address changing youth needs, and the ways in which the government has supported providers in creating this infrastructure, are significant changes and evidence of shifts in attitudes taking place in Tehran today.

The Physicians: Gynecologists and Mental Health Workers

Many of the gynecologists I encountered were reluctant to speak with me because, as some colleagues explained to me, they preferred to keep a low profile due to the sensitive nature of their work. Many doctors' offices had been randomly shut down during the 1980s; thus many physicians remained fearful of losing their jobs by being exposed in any way.

Several of them asked me to leave their office or lose their phone number or denied the fact that they were gynecologists when I asked if I could interview them. Fortunately, however, two gynecologists (one male and one female) not only agreed to be interviewed but also spoke very candidly. The first one, Dr. Sadeghi, a man in his late fifties, has been performing illegal abortions for more than twenty years. "I'm a doctor who does a lot of abortions, it's true. Some people call me the abortion doctor. I've been doing this so long that it seems even the mullahs [clerics] trust me," he said by way of introduction. Several of my informants had referred me to Dr. Sadeghi, who had performed abortions on them. I had heard he was lively, open, and honest, and his introduction only confirmed these rumors. "As you know, Khānum, we don't have a handle on our nation's youth, especially on their health," he explained, closing the door to his office tightly to make sure no sound would escape. "Our kids are in trouble. Sex is happening behind closed doors, fourteen-year-olds are coming in here asking for abortions, third-year medical students are coming back for multiple abortions because they can't stop sleeping with their married professors, and AIDS and infections are on the rise. I don't think there is any place in the world—well, at least any place in the Muslim world—where the abortion rate is so high." When I asked him what percentage of his patients who came in requesting abortions were unmarried, he responded, "More than 60 percent! No, actually, I would say even 70 percent are unmarried. But the ones that come to me, they are the lucky ones," he said, looking down at me over his spectacles.

Out of every one hundred women who need an abortion, only five end up on a doctor's table at some point. Most of them, sadly, are scared, so they try to handle this problem on their own. As you know—well, I don't know whether you do or don't know—but there are these injections sold on the black market at Nasser Khosrow Avenue. They are injections intended for animals, filled with chemicals, and they aren't more than ten toumans (meaning ten thousand toumans or US$11). They use these dangerous drugs for self-aborting and then have many problems. Many of them try to deal with these problems on their own and end up sick for life. Some get over their fears and go to the hospital or come to see me. The really brave ones—well, and the ones who can afford it—come to me to begin with. But sadly I am not doing enough abortions compared to those that are needed.

I then asked Dr. Sadeghi why he thought the abortion rate was so high among young adults in urban Iran. He was quick to answer this question, as though it was a common topic of discussion. "Simple: the kids here are going crazy, you know? They are all—I would say 90 percent of them are confused and angry, so they turn to sex. It's a tough life here for young people," he explained, taking off his glasses and wiping sweat from his brow. "Take my daughter here," he said, pointing to a framed picture of a young woman on his desk. "She is sixteen, and I feel for her. The kids here are suffocated, they have no freedoms, no dancing, no movies, no fun. It's like you can't keep a teenage girl locked up like a caged animal. The other day, you know, she likes to wear Bermuda shorts, and they arrest her for it all the time. Now she has to take pills to calm her nerves! At the age of sixteen! She is on antidepressants, and she isn't the only one; a lot of them are too!" Dr. Sadeghi was getting very upset talking about his daughter. "It's just so sad. Perhaps we should talk about something else?" he asked me. "Well," I began, trying to come up with a question to take us in a different direction. "What I'm wondering is, if these kids are having so much sex, why don't they just use condoms or birth control pills? This might help them, right?" He again shook his head. "There is a climate of fear in this country, Khānum. Kids are scared even of their own parents. They are afraid that one day their parents may find their pills or condoms, and then it's over." "But aren't they more afraid of getting pregnant or at least of no longer being a virgin?" I asked. "With the virginity thing," he said, "well, first of all, I am here to report to you that I do at least eight hymen reconstructions a week. Now, but for those who aren't getting them, a lot of them don't realize that their future husbands will realize that they aren't virgins. They think, oh well, I'll deal with it then," he explained. I asked him to expand on this, so he responded:

Well, I'll tell you, a lot of them don't really know what they are doing, and a lot of them have friends who say, "Don't worry, they'll never know." And then some of them, the parents who are wanting a certain girl as their future daughter-in-law, will bring them to me, or one of my colleagues, and ask us to certify that they are virgins. Now, I'm telling you, my colleagues and I, regardless of whether these women are really virgins or not, we tell the parents they are. Then, for the women who aren't virgins—which is most of them—I take them aside and tell them what to do on their wedding night so blood is shed on the sheet. I have a lot of very religious families come in here, so I know how it is. I tell the women that the night of the wedding they should put a capsule of goats blood—sometimes I give these to them myself; they sell them at the black market in Nasser Khosrow—in their vaginas and then it will bleed. Other times I tell the women to grab a razor blade and squeeze between their thighs on the night of the wedding so that fresh droplets of their blood come onto the sheet. No one will ever know, I tell them.

I was very surprised to hear that the doctors were often so helpful to the young people and commended him for his actions. "And they trust you? The young people, I mean. They trust you to do abortions and to help them with virginity issues?" I asked incredulously. "Sometimes, because I'm their doctor, they have no choice but to trust me, but a lot of them don't. I can't tell you how many of my patients come in here and give me incorrect names and information. But what can we do? They need a service and we provide it," he said. Dr. Sadeghi added that he thought trust was a big problem among the youth population and believed that many of them in fact do not trust their doctors. "We need to lessen this climate of fear and distrust," he concluded, emphasizing that a lot of young people are uncomfortable with the idea of seeing a gynecologist, even for a checkup.

A month after interviewing Dr. Sadeghi, I decided to seek out a female gynecologist to interview in order to assess if female doctors had different viewpoints or experiences. After contacting six female gynecologists and receiving five firm negative responses, I had the opportunity to interview Dr. Poursartip, a female gynecologist who practices in the lower part of town. Dr. Poursartip was a younger woman, probably in her early forties, who did not wear a chādor or a maghna'e. In fact, her head was loosely covered with a violet headscarf to match her pink lab coat, and tufts of bottle-bleached blonde hair fell out of her hejāb. She was soft-spoken but friendly and invited me to have tea with her in her office. She echoed many of Dr. Sadeghi's sentiments, agreeing that most of the patients who came in for abortions were unmarried and under the age of twenty-five. "I would bet that most people in your sample age are having sex, and that a lot of them have faced unwanted pregnancies," she said while pouring me a cup of tea. "As you know, many of them try to take care of these themselves, and sadly we see them only after a lot of harm has come to them. It's a sad state of affairs." She sighed. I then asked her what the rate of STIs was in her patients. "It's not low," she responded. "HPV and herpes are the highest, but we also have a lot of gonorrhea. But the kids don't really come to us with those things unless it's very bad. Usually, if they think they may have an STI, I think they go to a clinic. But again, there is no regular testing, and a lot of kids think they are their own doctors. But it makes me sad because I know that a lot of the women don't come in here because they are scared." When I asked her what she thought the kids were scared of, she responded, "Parents. They are afraid their parents might find out, but this is a real problem. Some parents are now more sympathetic to their children and are open to talking about issues related to sex with them; but some of them, the kids I mean, especially the ones I see, can't go to their parents with their issues, but they also don't trust their doctors. This is something we, as parents, as adults, as caring members of society, need to work on." Dr. Poursartip seemed very frustrated that many young people were not utilizing many of her services until it was too late. "And this fear and confusion leads only to the potential of mental health problems," she said. "I'm telling you, these kids are not well in their heads. They are all on medicines. My office is relatively quiet, you see; but go to a psychiatrist's office and you'll see, there is a line out the door." She sighed again. I took her advice and began to seek out mental health care providers.

It is interesting that the number of self-help books and the public dialogue about mental health have increased dramatically in the last decade.[2] Today there are increasing numbers of mental health care providers, and most of them are quite busy every day. "It's amazing to me," said Soodabeh, a thirty-five-year-old mother of two. "But you know that mental health problems and depression have become more socially acceptable in Iran now than they were twenty years ago. When I was younger, it was shameful to admit seeing a psychiatrist or psychologist; but today they have them in schools, can you believe it? My son, who is only twelve years old, met with a psychologist at school to make sure that he is OK! What an amazing change! And what a great one. I wish it was this way when I was young!" Nine other parents with whom I spoke expressed similar sentiments and told me that their children were all reading self-help books (that their parents had purchased for them). Four parents told me they were taking their children to a psychotherapist. All nine of these parents emphasized that they felt that discussing mental health problems openly had become socially acceptable only in the last five years, and they felt that this open dialogue was helping young people work out many of the potential mental health issues that accompanied growing up in what they saw as a "challenging environment."

"It's hard for young people here," said Mina, a professor of psychology at Tehran University and mother of a daughter and a son (ages 22 and 25 respectively). "They have to have two identities: *bāten* [an inner personality that manifests in private] and *zaher* [an outer personality or persona projected in public]. And these two identities come together to produce potential mental health issues. But the kids actually aren't depressed," she quickly added. "They have zāher/bāten issues, but they don't affect them mentally, for two reasons: first, because they can talk about them due to this new climate of social acceptability of mental health issues; and second, because they are working to change the divide so that the personality they have in public matches the personality they have at home or inside." When I interviewed her two children (as well as thirty other young adults) specifically about having to have one personality at home and another personality on the streets, they all said it didn't really affect them in terms of their mental well-being. "We're fine," said Amir Ali, Mina's son. "Yes, we have to behave a different way at school or at work; we have to say we don't drink or hang out with women, and the women have to say they are virgins or something, while at home we do what we want and talk about our beliefs openly. But that doesn't mean we are depressed. We really are fine; it's just a part of our lives here." His sister, Nina, nodded in agreement. Fifteen other young people with whom I spoke expressed similar sentiments, indicating that having to project different identities at home and at school or at work isn't the source of their frustration or unhappiness. "People think that we are *bihoviyat* [without identity] or that we have all this depression because of the whole zāher/bāten thing," began twenty-five-year-old filmmaker Reza. "But that's not true. We are unhappy with our environment, yes. Unhappy with the regime, with the failing economy, which means that

educated people don't have jobs and are bored all day long; but we're
not depressed, and we are actually trying to *do* something about our
unhappiness; we are trying to change the system, be the same person
outside as inside."

During the summer of 2007 I had the opportunity to interview seven
mental health care providers, including psychotherapists, psychiatrists,
and social workers. I had heard (in documentaries and journalistic pieces)
that depression was quite high among the youth in Tehran, and I could
understand why. A failing economy, no jobs or opportunities, and heavy
restrictions on socializing could be challenging; but after talking to
many of my informants as well as to mental health providers about this
issue, it seemed that, in their limited experience, this was not the case
at all. Rather, these providers seemed to think that depression was more
prevalent among the parents of the young people I was interested in than
in the youth themselves. "The young people you are talking about, do
I think they're depressed? Well, not more than the ones in the United
States," explained Dr. Hekmat, a female psychotherapist in the northern part of Tehran. "Some young people are depressed, sure; but most
of them come in with relationship problems or family problems. Or else
they are just bored and frustrated that they can't find jobs. But no, depressed, no. Also, the fact that so many people come and see me and the
fact that my colleagues and I are so busy, I think that is helping to keep
depression down, because they talk out their problems."

The psychiatrists and social workers with whom I spoke did seem
very busy and barely had time to tell me that they just couldn't see me
or do an interview this month. After much persistence I was able to persuade two psychiatrists (who also considered themselves social workers)
to speak with me about their views on Tehran's youth. One of the women
I interviewed, Mrs. Arminpour, was also the head of a youth drop-in
and runaway shelter with offices located mainly in the poorer parts of
town. Her clientele was made up mostly of young people from the poorer classes and volunteers from the university, who served to train and
educate potential peer educators. Her center provides basic services to
young people, including housing, medical attention, and education. The
peer educators and counselors work with the young people who frequent
the center, both runaways and those who come seeking food, medical

attention, counseling, and education. The centers, all converted offices, now have dormitories and classrooms in which the young people can spend time. They are brightly decorated with pictures and posters, and cheerful young university students provide arts and crafts, cooking, and also family planning seminars for interested youth.

According to Mrs. Arminpour, many of the young people of the lower and middle classes come to the center seeking advice about sexual health because they feel they cannot discuss these questions with their parents. "A lot of the problem is that these kids are unemployed and lonely, so they go after sexual relations because in intimacy they can lose themselves. They have no other fun, nothing to do, so their lives revolve around these intimacies, which is fine with me, except then they sometimes end up with unwanted children or diseases." She guided me through her center and showed me the various classrooms and recreational areas where young people of all ages were congregating. "They can't behave like other young people, and many of them feel they cannot *dard-e-del* [speak from the heart] with their parents, so they really rely on these partners and intimate relationships. Then, when these relationships fall through, they come to us if they have problems. But that is what most of their mental health concerns focus on: relationships. Otherwise they are more concerned with getting meals and, for some of the women, contraception." She pulled out her office drawer to show me bags of condoms and birth control pills.

During the summers of 2004 and 2005, I spoke with another psychiatrist, Mrs. Rahimi, who echoed many of Mrs. Aminpour's statements. Similar to many of the other providers I spoke with, Mrs. Rahimi is also a parent and became interested in working with young people through her experiences with her own children. She is now one of the most popular psychiatrist-social workers at Tehran University, and as Dr. Poursartip predicted, has a long line of people waiting to see her at all times. Mrs. Rahimi also emphasized the damage that trust issues had caused for the young people she works with. "These kids need to feel calmness and trust in their families," she said. "And now some of them do, and I think that's important in keeping young people healthy. But the ones that don't end up in my office; that's why good parenting is so important. But because they don't get this at home, they go elsewhere looking for this peace. Like their partners or other kids their age." With her soft voice and empathetic manner, I could see why Mrs. Rahimi was so popular among the students at the university. She always had a smile on her face and there was a kindness to her manner and demeanor. "I also think the kids here lie too much; they have become used to it, and psychologically this affects them," she said. "The kids have been made so many empty promises by the Islamic Republic, and have been forced into lying by their parents or the contradictions in their environment, and they themselves are now always lying. This is a problem and creates emotional tension, but not depression. Plus, they are coming to see us, so that's a step in the right direction. They are reading all the popular self-help books and listening to all these talk shows on radio and television, so this helps too." I asked Mrs. Rahimi why she thought young Tehranis lied so much. "Because they have been living lies their whole lives, especially the children of the revolution," she answered. She then described a scenario that was corroborated by other parents and informants with whom I spoke:

It's because the kids are taught to lie and have had to lead a dual life since the Islamic Republic took over. When these children are young, they are at home and their mothers say to them, "Darling, when you go to school, don't tell the kids that your mommy drinks or that she wears makeup at home. Just tell them that all your mommy does is pray." Well, this confuses the kid who learns from an early age that private and public demeanor must be different. But that's why they are acting out now. They are starting this cultural revolution, trying to wear lots of makeup and have their sex out in the street where everyone can see them, because they are done with the lies. This is their revolution! And they will go far!

The exact reasons behind the shift in parents' and health care providers' attitudes toward changing youth behaviors are not clear. Perhaps young people have pushed so hard to change the sexual and social culture that their efforts have affected the adults and larger society around them. Perhaps the limited number of parents and health care providers I interviewed happen to all be concerned about the well-being of the future of the country and are now adapting to the changes in young people's behavior as a way to ensure their future and health. Or perhaps as time has passed, people have simply become more open to changes in the sexual culture. Whatever the exact reasons are, the ways in which parents and other adults throughout the health and educational infrastructure are changing and seeking to help the youth as they enact changes in sexual and social behavior serve as important landmarks of change in social and sexual attitudes. The creation of drop-in centers for youth, triangular clinics, harm-reduction services, and the myriad mental health care options that are available to young people (such as social workers in the schools and subsidized psychotherapy and psychiatry) all show ways in which there has been an important shift in knowledge, attitudes, and practices. Although young people are still struggling with the many changes they are enacting, the changing adult perspectives are an important indicator of a larger societal and infrastructural shift.

I RAN'S SEXUAL REVOLUTION is taking place at a crucial point in Iran's history and is being enacted by
young adults against the backdrop of a theocratic regime. Today, most
of Iran's population is young and educated, has a lot of free time (due to
unemployment and lack of proper recreational activities), and is frustrated with a regime that seeks to legislate their personal lives while
simultaneously creating an environment in which a significant portion
of the population has limited employment opportunities. The combination of a downward-spiraling economy, large numbers of young people,
a repressive regime that is overly focused on social and sexual issues,
and access to a globalizing youth culture have created an environment
that is ripe for a sexual revolution. Young people are speaking back to
a regime under which they feel suffocated. Years of playing tug-of-war
with the regime have furthered young people's resolve to push for social
change. Many young adults do not care about the opinions of the religious leaders, nor do they fear the legal punishments or sanctions that
could be placed on their behavior by the regime or by their parents.
Young people indicate that they are fed up with the regime, and numb
to potential punishments, such as detainment or lashings, which occur
far less frequently now than they did fifteen years ago.

The focus of this book has been the intersection of sexuality and
politics in postrevolutionary Iran, and the resultant changes in attitudes and behaviors that this intersection has caused. Although I have
been working with a small group of people, and although my work has
been ethnographic and qualitative, I believe that many of the changes

described by my informants, their parents, and the many educators and health care providers who work with them are significant and have far-reaching potential. While I do not wish to make generalizations about the people I studied or about Tehrani or Iranian youth in general, I believe that the common themes expressed by many of my informants are important to examine in the context of a changing Iran. I have described, examined, and analyzed different ways that political dissatisfaction can be manifested, while also highlighting the ways in which the state has changed to adjust to its transforming youth. In the absence of an option to overtly dissent, the sexual and social revolution described by my informants has become a substitution or creative alternative to overt political dissent and has resulted in a shift in attitudes about sexuality and the body. Sexual and social behaviors have taken on significance in the Iranian sociopolitical climate, and changes have occurred as a result of this alternative form of protest. These changes, although not always recognized by activists, advocates, and scholars, have affected the current regime, as well as the society as a whole, as evidenced in part by the creation of an infrastructure to address new risk behavior among youth and foster more open discussion between youth and parents, which could signal cultural and political changes taking place in Tehran. In concluding, I ask the reader to think about this tension and the complicated relationship between sexuality and politics in postrevolutionary Iran, and I hope we can speculate together about the future of this young population: Where are they headed?

Expanding Notions of Dissent

Does political behavior always have to be verbal? Is dissent expressed only overtly? How can private behaviors express desires for political change? How can sexuality be seen as a political move? How can fashion be seen as politics? These are just some of the questions regarding dissent and political engagement and how sexuality and politics intersect that are raised by the information presented in this book. Although some may not see nonverbal communication (such as style of dress or association) as political, I argue that these things have become politicized, for at least two reasons: (1) because the machinery of the state has been enlisted to regulate morality, social behaviors such as fashion, and sexuality in extreme ways (and thus any deviations from state moral codes becomes dissent); and (2) because the current regime in Iran came to power under the platform of moral values; that is, one of the mandates of the Islamic Republic and the goals of Islamification was to address problems of morality. Therefore, when a large portion of the population (the young people) is enacting a counterrevolution by creating its own moral values, the very fabric of the regime and what it stands for are threatened.

Some elements of this social and sexual revolution are clearly public, although these aspects are often nonverbal. Although some scholars may argue that political protest requires speech, I argue that instead of mass street demonstrations with loud chanting (which is construed as political in other countries), walking the streets of Tehran in styles of dress that defy Islamic codes, or holding hands with a person to whom one is not married, could be viewed as a large nonverbal demonstration occurring everyday in Tehran's busy city streets.

Other aspects of the social and sexual revolution are more private. Some may ask the question about private sexual behaviors and how these could be construed as political dissent. Some might argue that sexual nonconformity could not be considered political behavior because it is not always public and does not take the form of overt, organized political dissent. Others would say that the regime does not see what it does not wish to and thus cannot be threatened by private acts of transgressive sexuality. Dissent takes different forms in different political and social climates. For this reason, it is important to highlight a few things about the Iranian situation: (1) nothing that occurs in Iran is completely private, to the extent that morality police can (and do) come into private homes and arrest people engaging in "immoral" acts; (2) when young women are arrested for various "moral crimes," including partying, drinking, and dancing, they are taken to jail and sometimes given virginity tests (therefore their private sexual choices are made public); and (3) because being caught engaging in transgressive sexual behavior potentially brings punishment from the state, the stakes of engaging in this behavior are high.

The first two points speak to the question of privacy and whether the behaviors I have described could be seen as sexual revolt if they are private. It is important to note that many of the choices that young people make and the behaviors they engage in *are* public (that is, enacted in public venues, for example, wearing fashion and makeup on the streets or engaging in intimate acts in public places such as parks or cars or squares). Those behaviors that are viewed as private (parties, dancing, and sexual encounters that occur in the home) are only semiprivate because they *could* be (though are not always) supervised and publicized at any time by the morality police, parents, or neighbors. Although young people are not always punished for their "immoral behaviors" (which indicates that the state is embodying the attitude shift), the fact that they could be makes their behaviors significant.

The third point speaks to the question of the legitimacy of the regime and the moral values platform on which the regime has claimed power. Indeed, both the state and many of the young people themselves view changes in sexual and social behavior and attitudes as an integral part of delegitimizing the power of the regime—which claims to have brought moral values to the Islamic Republic—over social behaviors. It is also important to note that the legitimacy of the regime is being shaken and questioned by the young people, making clear that the regime has not won the hearts and minds of a large portion of its population. Additionally, it is important that the regime is not able to control the revolutionary behavior of, for example, fashion or young adult behavior, because changes in fashion and rejection of Islamic dress codes (such as the decision of young women to expose their feet and ankles) occur on such a large scale that policing large numbers of people is impossible (picture arresting half a million women in sandals!). Iran's demographic shift in favor of large numbers of educated, unemployed youth presents the dwindling numbers of komite with their greatest challenge yet: being outnumbered by youth and supporters of young adults. Additionally, some of the behavior is so subtle that the state is unsure about the need to police it, and some of the behavior does still occur in private, regardless of occasional invasions by members of the morality police.

Perhaps it is this inability to police large numbers of people that has led to the state adjusting its behavior and moral standards, or perhaps the young people have succeeded in changing the conversation. Either way, young people interact with the state and members of the morality police in a very different way today than they did twenty years ago. Today young people in Tehran are seen talking back to members of the morality police who are trying to arrest them, and passersby come to the aid of the youth, sometimes by physically assaulting members of the morality police and telling them to leave the youth alone. The fear of the state that once may have existed does still exist on a certain level and among certain parts of the population, but it has greatly lessened in the last ten years, according to my informants, who now say they aren't afraid of the morality police at all. When I ask them why this has happened, they point to a shift in viewpoints and how things are talked about that the sexual revolution has brought about, and they describe the majority of Tehran's population as restless youth or sympathetic adults who are all tired of the repression of the regime and ready to respond and stand up for their rights. Young people are increasingly asserting their agency and citizenship relative to the state.

The question is also raised of whether or not young people would continue this behavior if regime change were to occur. In other words, would young people continue to engage in these sexual and social behaviors if it were not against the backdrop of a theocratic regime? And if these behaviors were to continue, would they still be seen as dissent? Would the movement still be called a sexual revolution? Many of my informants say they participate in the sexual revolution to enact social change, some youth indicate that their goal is to change the conversation, and still others say they engage in these behaviors for personal pleasure. Therefore, it is not clear whether young people would continue their push for sexual and social change if the current regime were to be replaced with a regime that is less repressive; however, I believe that many young people would remain vested in changing the conversation on sexuality at the cultural (if no longer political) level.

Changes Resulting from the Sexual Revolution

Without question, these young adults have succeeded in capturing the attention of members of the regime and in bringing about change. Former president and recent presidential candidate Rafsanjani's stance on social and moral codes of conduct illustrate ways in which young people have affected conservative politicians and legislators in power. As described in Chapter 5, when Rafsanjani (a member of the conservative rather than reform movement) was president, he insisted on cracking down on young people who defied Islamic moral values. The decision to punish lipstick-wearing young women by using a razor to slash their lips or arresting women who showed any hair beneath their headscarves came during Rafsanjani's presidency in the mid-1990s. During the last election in 2005, however, Rafsanjani had made such a turnaround in his views that he was paying young people who had a certain style (makeup and colorful headscarves for young women, and long hair and accessories for young men) to campaign for him. Rafsanjani even went so far as to construct his campaign headquarters in popular young adult hangout spots and install a disco ball and an expensive sound system. He presented himself as a friend of the young people and even created and distributed CDs for his campaign that were set to techno music, the very type of music he had previously frowned upon during his presidency. Rafsanjani was now appearing in commercials with young women who wore lipstick and "bad Islamic dress," and showing himself driving around with other "defiant" young people playing loud, illegal music. Although not emulated by all members of the conservative party, Rafsanjani's transformation is evidence of the ways in which some members of the regime have been affected by the social revolution mobilized by many of these young adults. Although it is possible that Rafsanjani was just using the young people in order to get elected, he has demonstrated his commitment to loosening social restrictions beyond the campaign through his actions in the Iranian Parliament.

Young Tehranis use the language of sexual revolution when describing their own behavior, attitudes, and ideas. What can be seen in the information and stories presented in this book is that there has been a change in sexual culture among Iranian young people in urban areas. For example, young adults are now seen engaging in romantic acts with members of the opposite sex in public spaces. There have also been shifts in how sexuality is talked about in present-day Iran, and many of these changes have been politicized. Through discussions in schools, underground music, and popular Web sites maintained by young Iranians, young adults throughout the country are calling for a more open dialogue about issues pertaining to sexuality. Additionally, according to many of my colleagues at various academic institutions in Iran, students at universities throughout the country have been lobbying for the addition of sex education courses in their schools. It is clear that young people are striving to create the space in which to publicize dialogue about sexuality and accommodate a changing sexual culture. As noted in Chapter 7, many of the adults who interact with youth (including parents, teachers, and health care providers) are also seeking to address these needs and promote an infrastructure where these conversations can take place and the young people's changing needs can be met. The Iranian sexual revolution has brought about change by providing a context for young people to express their dissent, and in the process they are succeeding in reclaiming their agency.

There are limits to the change that sexual and social revolutions can achieve, both in terms of how people view sexuality and in terms of changing governance. This sexual revolution still has not changed many cultural norms, such as the pressure to get married, and marriage to a member of the opposite sex is still held as a necessary goal in life, even though in the last couple of years several of the young women with whom I spoke no longer saw this as their primary goal and indicated their preference for remaining single. Premarital sex is still policed, female subordination continues to be demanded, and no public socializing between men that might construe homosexuality is permitted. Finally, the sexual and social revolution of young Iranians has not and will not achieve regime change overnight. One needs only to look to Iran's neighbor to the north, the former Soviet Union, or even to the Czech Republic's "Velvet Revolution," to realize that so-called "soft" revolutions (which is how Iran's social and sexual revolution could be described) can result in the collapse of a state due to lack of governmental legitimacy.[1] I argue that this Iranian counterrevolution of values is striving to destroy the legitimacy of the regime (which has reaffirmed conservative values) in order to slowly bring about regime change.

Where This Is Headed

When writing about Iran, people often want a prediction: where is the country headed, what will happen to the young people, and will the regime be toppled? It is of course impossible to make predictions such as these on the basis of an ethnographic study of a small number of people in Tehran. In this book I have tried to analyze the complexity of social, political, economic, and sexual dynamics within the Islamic Republic. I have attempted to show how the social and sexual culture of Tehran is changing by pointing to behavioral, attitudinal, and theoretical shifts throughout the city. It is difficult, however, to make specific predictions about the regime or the future of the young adult movement, or about Iran in general at this highly sensitive moment in its history.

Nonetheless, it is important to reemphasize (as I tried to do in the introduction) that the regime currently in power is by no means monolithic. The reform and conservative parties in Iran have different goals, with the reformists aggressively lobbying for social change and an opening up of the country (although I also do not mean to assert that members of either party are uniform in their beliefs). Although conservatives generally agree on the need for tighter control, there are disagreements within the conservative movement itself, and different clerics often take opposing views. The different approaches taken by candidates during the election of summer 2005 highlight these differences. Although seven of the presidential candidates were from the conservative party, their views and methods of campaigning showed the discrepancies in their beliefs, policies, and ideas about Iran's future. While Rafsanjani presented himself as an open visionary (trying to make himself appear similar to former President Khatami) and Qalibauf called for a renewed economic dialogue with the West, campaigning with Western-style photographs taken by European photographers, Ahmadinejad talked about closing Iran's doors to the West completely.

Clerics, whether in the conservative or reform party, frequently disagree on many social, political, economic, and moral issues. This may in part explain the fluidity in many of Iran's policies depending on shifts in power (within the Parliament, in the Ministries, and among the heads of the morality police). Many clerics are sympathetic to the calls of the young dissidents, and some have even called for more open dialogue about issues of interest to the young people. This openness can also be seen in the way various clerics approach the issue of Islamic dress. Although some clerics feel that young people should be able to dress as they please as long as they follow Islamic codes while praying or at the mosque, other clerics call for the arrest of young people and the banning of new styles of fashion and young adult congregation (such as the ever popular coffee shops that have sprung up in Tehran).

Tehran and Iran have changed dramatically since the revolution of 1979, but more specifically in the last ten years. In 1996, the young people who now make up the bulk of the population were coming of age and only beginning their call for social change. In 1997, when Khatami, the favored young adult candidate, was elected, the social revolution gained momentum, and students and young people began to push for change. Today, colorful hejābs and māntos that are fashionable and "un-Islamic" are the majority rather than the black headscarves and heavy trench coats that dominated female wardrobes in the early 1990s. Young people now drive nicer cars, coffee shops have sprung up on every corner, and young people can be seen walking around parks, malls, and city squares hand-in-hand.

Today, AIDS posters have replaced many Islamist slogans, and advertisements for cars, furniture, and clothing have replaced billboards featuring mostly martyrs and soldiers. Needle exchange has been legalized, and free drop-in centers for young people have been established. Young ministers of health and education continue to campaign for sex education in schools, and continue their attempts to reach out to young people, remaining a force for change within government structures.

Although the image of Iran in the Western press is constantly changing, young Iranians are pushing for more social, economic, and political changes, and they are lobbying for a new type of regime from within. Tehrani young people continue to test the limits of social control by moving forward with the social and sexual revolution, and they have succeeded in changing much of the conversation around sexuality in Tehran among their peers, family members, and members of the health and service-providing infrastructure.

Iran has changed physically, economically, and socially. These changes have been gradual, but many of the changes in the social environment and in social and sexual attitudes and practices can and must be attributed to the young adults and their yearning for social change within their own country.

What Does the Future Hold?

Since my return to the United States from my last visit to Iran in 2007, I have struggled with many lingering questions—questions that I hope will be addressed someday. I wonder if the sexual revolution will live on as these young people grow up and change. I question whether these young people would still be enacting a sexual revolution if the regime were to change. If some of the repression was dissolved, would young people still resist in this way? Would talk about sexual matters still take center stage? Would there be a change in how sex is talked about? Would young adults continue to engage in sexual behaviors that put them at risk both physically and mentally? Will their efforts to attain sex education and risk-reduction resources be successful? And then I wonder what will happen if things do not change? What will become of the nation's youth?

Reference Matter

Acknowledgments

T HE RESEARCH FOR THIS BOOK would not have been possible without the financial support of the following fellowships: the Woodrow Wilson Women's Health Fellowship, the Cordier Fellowship, the National Development and Research Institute behavioral science training fellowship, the Institute for Social and Economic Research and Policy fellowship program, the Mellon fellowship, and the Pomona College Faculty Research Grant.

Many friends and professional colleagues helped me in this endeavor through informal readings, writing groups, and support during this process. I would first and foremost like to thank my mentor and friend Carole Vance, without whose enduring support, inspiration, and belief in me this book would not have been possible. She read countless drafts of my work, and supported me from the beginning; I can't thank her enough. I would also like to thank the many professors who worked with me and provided vital feedback, including Lila Abu-Lughod, Lynn Freedman, Shahla Haeri, and Rebecca Young. The following people read many drafts of chapters and provided helpful commentaries and support: Beth Filiano, Alicia Peters, Ernesto Vasquez, Farzaneh Hemmasi, Victoria Cain, Julia Heck, and Karin Zitzewitz. I am also grateful to Erin Runions, April Mayes, Tomas Summers-Sandoval, Kevin Jones, and Zayn Kassam, who helped me in the final stages of the book. Additionally, I wish to acknowledge our departmental assistant at Pomona College, Gail Orozco, who was always a great help in preparing the manuscript, as well as Joan Dempsey, who provided exceptional editorial feedback on my final draft.

I would like to thank Lilynaaz Rahnema, Daniel Yousef Tehrani, Lila Nazemian, and Semira Nikou, whose support and assistance were vital while I was in Iran. Many people provided support in numerous forms during my time in Tehran, and they are too many to name. A few of these people are the Owsia family, the Shahvalli family, the Adel family, the Mahjouri family, and the Mahdavi family. I would additionally like to extend heartfelt gratitude toward my editor, Kate Wahl, for taking a chance on my manuscript and for being such a joy to work with. I would also like to thank the anonymous reviewers, and Bill Beeman and Sally Guttmacher, for providing helpful feedback about the manuscript, as well as the staff at Stanford University Press, especially Puja Sangar, Mariana Raykov, and Joa Suorez, for helping me produce and promote the book.

I would also like to thank the people closest to me, who through their love and support made this a more endurable and even enjoyable process. I would like to thank my husband, Ahmad Kiarostami, for his assistance, support, and encouragement, and for being my lifeline and my strength. I would like to thank Ghazal Badiozamani, Ladan Akbarnia, Mary Boyington, and Jeff Waller for being my biggest supporters from the beginning. Additionally, I would like to thank my family: my brothers, Paymohn and Paasha, for their love, support, wisdom, guidance, and many hugs and kisses; and my parents, Mahmood and Fereshteh, who walked every step of this journey with me. I could not have done this without you. Finally, I wish to acknowledge my wonderful informants, who opened their hearts to me and without whose stories this story could not have been written.

Notes

Prologue

1. Giddens 1993: 1.

2. For an in-depth discussion of the significance of "opening-up" in a country, see Farrer 2002.

3. The word *informants* is an anthropological term used to refer to people with whom an anthropologist spoke or interacted, or whom the anthropologist interviewed for the purposes of the study; literally, those who "informed" the study.

4. The word *hejāb* is used to refer to women's Islamic dress in general but can also refer to proper veiling attire, and specifically to the headscarf. *Mānto*, derived from the French word for *coat, monteau*, refers to the approved outer coat for women in the Islamic Republic; it is supposed to hide body shape and skin.

5. For further discussion of self-induced abortions, see Chapter 7.

6. Living in "uptown" neighborhoods in Tehran denotes upper class while being from "downtown" can indicate lower socioeconomic status, as is discussed in the next chapter.

7. Varzi 2006: 41.

8. Varzi 2006: 133.

9. Throughout this text, the word *Islamist* is used to refer to Muslim authorities who believe that *sharia* (Islamic law) should be the instrument used to govern society. It refers to those individuals who view Islam as political ideology.

10. Esposito and Ramazani 2001; *Economist* 2007.

11. Joseph and Najmabadi 2005.

12. Basmenji 2006; Amuzegar 2004. As scholars such as Jahangir Amuzegar have noted, however, "statistics on Iran's employment and unemployment are the flimsiest, least reliable and most contested of all basic indicators" (Amuzegar 2004). I believe that many of the statistical figures on Iran, including those on health, marriage status, and population and family planning, are also flawed, which makes it difficult to provide exact baseline statistics for the reader. "The principal sources of data are either out of reach, limited or largely conjectural. Iran's total population itself is based on conflicting *estimates*. And estimated figures for any given year vary between those of the UN

Secretariat, Iran's Statistics Center, other local authorities, and foreign organizations—
often with a 10 percent margin of difference" (Amuzegar 2004).

    13. Hebdige 1979.

Chapter 1

    1. Throughout the text, the word *Islamist* is used to refer to Muslim authorities
who believe that sharia should be the instrument used to govern society. It refers to
those individuals who view Islam as political ideology.

    2. Abrahimian 1982.

    3. *Khabarnāme* blog, February 6, 2004; printed in Alavi 2005: 45. This comment
is presented in the blog as a statement of opinion rather than as fact because it is not
clear how many people were killed during the first few days of the revolution; the author of the blog is making a point about the large-scale violence that occurred during
the revolution.

    4. Moghadam 2003.

    5. Esposito and Ramazani 2001.

    6. Moghadam 2003.

    7. Haeri 1990.

    8. Basmenji 2006.

    9. Holy month of fasting.

    10. Holy month of mourning.

    11. Hirsch 2003.

    12. Giddens 1991.

    13. R. H. Khomeini, statement to public gathering in what is now Imam Khomeini
Square, March 21, 1980. Archived in Khomeini's Mausoleum.

    14. Adelkhah 2004.

    15. Due to the sensitive nature of the topic, a random sampling scheme was not
possible; thus I relied on chain, referral, or snowball sampling (asking informants to
refer me to other informants), targeted sampling (looking for informants in particular
venues), and theoretical sampling (sampling where one theorizes one's sample will be
located). Also, due to the ethnographic nature of the study (that is, that there was only
one ethnographer), I was able to interview only 105 young people throughout my study.
I attempted to sample from most of the neighborhoods in Tehran, but often members
of the lower classes did not wish to speak to me. Therefore, much of my data on lower
class youth are based on observation of and stories from the few members of the lower
class who would speak to me. In general, youth who considered themselves leaders of
the sexual revolution came from the middle and upper classes.

    16. As Roxanne Varzi notes, the term *secular youths* requires closer examination
and definition, because simple dichotomies (such as religious / secular, urban / rural,
and cosmopolitan / traditional) do not translate well in Iran. The term can be defined
as "youth from a wide background—those who may be practicing Muslims, Christians,
Bahais, Jews, or Zoroastrians; those who are believers in these religious but not practicing; and those who are agnostic or atheist but who also have in common the belief
that religion is a private practice that should not be condoned, enforced, or abhorred

by public policy. In other words, the main characteristic of secular youths is not that they are religious but that they do not want public law to be interpreted through religious edicts" (Varzi 2006: 12). For this reason I refer to them throughout the text as members of the nonreligious middle class.

17. I spent a significant amount of time conducting participant observation in lower class parts of town as well as in Shiraz, Esfahan, and Mashad. It is on the basis of these observations that I make this assertion.

18. This effect is exemplified by the sexual revolution that took place in the United States in the 1960s; it began among a small group of middle class young people in Greenwich Village in New York City and then spread throughout the country.

19. The city of Tehran has a gridlike layout, and socioeconomic status is often inferred from neighborhood of residence. Living uptown denotes upper class, while living in the southern parts of town or downtown denotes lower class.

20. Azad University has a number of campuses around the country. The campus in Rudehen is located in a village-like suburb of Tehran, about twenty miles outside the city.

21. The word used for someone of a lower class, *pāyin shahri* means "someone from the lower part of town."

22. Alavi 2005: 15.

23. Excerpt from Sheer Blog, October 2003; this blog no longer exists.

Chapter 2

1. Afary 2006.

2. *Bazari* have been defined by Roxanne Varzi and others as "merchants in the bāzār, who belong to the more religiously conservative groups" (Varzi 2006: 20).

3. This campus of Azad University is located near the peak of Damavand Mountain, about a two-hour drive outside of Tehran. Although Asana wanted to attend university closer to the city, she was accepted only at this particular campus of Azad University to study urban planning.

4. Today many of the guards, especially in private universities, no longer harass the young women. This is both evidence of the success of the young people in carving out social freedoms for themselves and an indicator of the ways in which the state is attempting to change to integrate its youth.

5. In Iran there are different kinds of taxi services. One kind is commonly referred to as *āzhāns*. These taxis are summoned by telephone only and will not pick up other passengers. To use a shared public taxi, however, you wave down a cab going in the direction you want, regardless of whether there are other people in it. There may be two, three, or sometimes four other passengers in the cab, and each person gets out wherever he or she chooses. It is interesting that in a country where there are separate elevators for men and women, and where male and female cousins are discouraged from sleeping in the same bed, it is appropriate for women to squeeze into the back of a Paykan or Peugeot with three or four men who are total strangers and have either their arms around you or their knees under you. This practice seems totally contradictory to Islamic rules, yet there is very little commentary on this phenomenon.

6. Such a rack is common in many households throughout Tehran.

7. Keddie and Richard 2003.

8. Due to class tensions, some people have referred to this neighborhood as the place where the nouveau riche (the newly monied) settle.

9. In Tehran, if one is of a certain socioeconomic class—namely middle or upper middle—it is not uncommon to hire day laborers to assist with cooking and cleaning. These laborers often live with the families for whom they work; others work for the day and are shared by extended families or by friends occupying the same building. Employing these laborers was often a sign of having attained higher socioeconomic status.

10. Interpretation of Iranian Statistical Center findings as quoted in http://www.payvand.com/news/03/jul/1001.html

11. Amuzegar 2004.

12. Adelkhah 2004: 19.

13. http://www.factbook.net

14. http://www.friendster.com; http://www.orkut.com

15. Alavi 2005.

16. *Sighe* allows a young man and woman to get married for an amount of time—between one hour and ninety-nine years—specified at the beginning of the contract. These marriages are often performed at a mosque, with a cleric present, and including some kind of transaction in which the man gives goods or money to the woman. A man can have up to ninety-nine temporary wives, but a woman can be married to only one man at a time.

17. Many religious leaders now have their own Web sites and blogs, where they write about the importance of using the Internet in ways that are in accordance with Islam. Apparently sighe.net was once in accordance with Islam, but it perhaps fell out of favor when the leaders realized that people were not taking it seriously.

18. The three major reasons cited for not engaging in sighe were as follows: (1) the first time one wants to have a temporary marriage one needs parental consent, which is often difficult to acquire because many parents look down on temporary marriage for their children and instead encourage them to make a permanent marriage; (2) temporary marriage was recently stigmatized as a form of legal prostitution; and (3) women who have not yet been permanently married are hesitant about sighe because they worry it will hurt their eligibility and opportunity for a "better," permanent marriage down the road.

19. http://www.wired.com

20. Nevertheless, many of the young Iranians with whom I spoke indicated that they consistently preferred Iranian music to Western pop.

21. This may be a polite way of saying that I do not attend to my appearance enough, do not wear enough makeup, and do not style my hair unless for a special occasion. My informants seemed to think this made me "sporty" or gave me an "athletic" look.

22. In most cities in Iran, opium and heroin are cheaper than chewing gum or cigarettes, and opiates are much more readily available than alcohol. When doing my weekly shopping at the food stand I was often offered opium as dessert. Additionally, there are many opium dens in the lower-income parts of town, and opiate dealers target

mostly lower-middle- and lower-class youth. Upper-class young people tend to prefer cocaine, *shisheh* (slang for crack or crystal), or marijuana.

23. Varzi 2006: 158.

Chapter 3

1. Quoted in Hebdige 1979: 100.

2. At the entrance to the airport there are separate rooms for men and women in which travelers' bags are searched and where bodies and outward appearance are simultaneously checked to ensure that proper Islamic dress and comportment are maintained.

3. A car recently available in Iran.

4. Varzi 2006: 145.

5. Shavarini 2006: 189.

6. Shavarini 2006: 197.

7. Hebdige 1979, Peiss 1986.

8. Moghadam 2003: 98.

9. Moghadam 2003: 98.

10. Literally, "westoxication" or "weststruckness." A criticism was leveled against people who seemed infatuated with the West and sought to emulate it, thereby losing or loosening their Iranian identity. For further discussion of this term, see Al-Ahmad 1962.

11. Moghadam 2003: 98.

12. Posted in an anonymous blog, July 5, 2005.

13. From the Wikipedia definition of Subcultures, http://en.wikipedia.org/wiki/Subcultures. Also draws heavily on Gelder 2007.

14. Varzi 2006: 138.

15. Women who work at government agencies or universities must wear *chādor* or *maghna'e*, as do students when they attend class at public universities.

16. *Jun* is a Persian term of endearment. It is also used to refer informally to elders.

17. Straight hair is highly desirable in Tehran, where many of the women have naturally curly or wavy hair.

18. Varzi 2006: 142.

19. Moaveni 2005: 203.

20. "Kill me, but make me beautiful" is the literal translation of this popular Persian idiom, which refers to the fact that Iranian women are willing to undergo pain and high prices for their beauty.

21. Varzi 2006: 173.

Chapter 4

1. Historically, before the 1960s, and continuing in some families even today, Persian parents encourage arranged marriages in which the couple meet perhaps for the first time the day of their engagement or the day the man's parents come to the

woman's house to ask for her hand (referred to as the *khastegari*). According to my informants, as well as some parents with whom I spoke, premarital contact is sometimes heavily regulated by parents, by the regime, and by Islamic law (depending on the community).

2. Currently, young men and women in Iran who are not related or not married are not supposed to be seen in the company of one another in public. However, as with many other social issues in Iran, the limits of this rule are being pushed and tested as young people go on dates in parks, restaurants, and movie theaters in the hope that they will not be caught, and in recent years they have been getting away with it more and more.

3. Hourani 1983.

4. http://www.metimes.com

5. Although homosexuality emerged as a theme throughout my time in Iran, it is a complex topic that requires in-depth discussion including historical framing and analysis of homosexuality in Islam and in Iran during the last several centuries. For further reading about homosexuality in Iran, please refer to Najmabadi 2005.

6. This notion builds on Pierre Bourdieu's idea of marriage as social capital. For an in-depth discussion of this concept, see Bourdieu 1986.

7. Haeri 1990.

8. This is admittedly a high number and may speak to my sampling scheme. Perhaps the married women who frequented the parties, salons, and gyms (which were predominantly singles scenes) were more interested in finding other sexual partners and in playing the role of being single. Additionally, most of these women are, according to them, unhappily married.

9. Loose translation; the idiom also refers to being lazy and lounging around the house.

Chapter 5

1. According to Hebdige (1979), young adult culture often represents a response to a particular set of circumstances. The group or subculture encompasses tradition, language, and style that provide power to those alienated from the dominant culture. In other words, this group and their resistance may represent a conflict between two groups. The dominant group (the Islamist regime) controls the discourse surrounding meanings and ideas about life objects and concepts (Hebdige, 1979). They also control all intellectual media and all material forces. Therefore, young Tehranis are told that how they should think about and perceive things is truly how the dominant group thinks and perceives things; young people's thoughts and perceptions are hegemonic, that is, constructed of dominant majority attitudes (Hebdige, 1979). Young Tehrani resistance is an attempt to take control of the discourse and to alter the meaning of certain societal behaviors and how those behaviors are perceived and understood. The group encompasses a tradition, language, and style that provide the alienated group with a sense of power and identity. According to Hebdige (1979), to understand young adult cultures, the researcher must recognize that they emerge within particular political, social, and economic contexts, and they create an ideology that shapes the development of a style, a choice of lifestyle, and sometimes an outlook on the world.

2. Varzi 2006: 147.

3. *Meydoon* is a common name for street corners where young people hang out.

4. See https://www.cia.gov/library/publications/the-world-factbook/index .html

5. Young people of the same age group in the United States, such as many of the students I teach, are not as avid consumers of news and often do not know, nor care, about global events.

6. The Council of Guardians is a council of jurists appointed by both the Supreme Leader and the *Majlis*. It holds most of the legal power in Iran. The Council also interprets the Constitution and is the legal arm of the Majlis.

7. When young people are caught for social crimes or for crimes against morality, they are sent to holding or detention centers, which they refer to as *jail* although they are not actually prisons. Young people are held in these centers for a night or two and often released after being fined or lashed. If it is their first offense and the activity was minor (such as socializing with the opposite sex or dancing), the young people are often set free within a day or two, and sometimes their arrest is not written in the public record or on their identification card. Sometimes, however, depending on the season of the harassment (that is, whether or not they were caught near a religious holiday), the nature of the offense (such as drinking or drug use, or committing political acts that displeased the regime), or the number of the offense (such as if it is a person's third or more time being detained), they might be transferred to an actual jail and detained for longer or placed in solitary confinement. When they are sent to the larger jails, it is indicated on their record and identification card, which can make attaining employment (already a challenge for most Tehrani youth) very difficult. These arrest records are reviewed periodically and can make attaining any position in the government or in government-controlled ministries or organizations nearly impossible.

8. *Maha-ra-tu jeebesh gozasht*, a Persian idiom meaning "being controlling."

9. Iran is on the lunar calendar, with different months and years. Mehr 6 corresponds to September 27.

Chapter 6

1. One of the biggest challenges in assessing sex education, abortion and contraception rates, and transmission of HIV and other sexually transmitted infections (STIs) is the paucity of research conducted on these sensitive issues in Iran. There are no formal research organizations within Tehran systematically recording contraceptive use or HIV and STI transmission among unmarried young adults, because premarital sex is both illegal and considered a social taboo. Thus I had to rely on often conflicting statistics from the United Nations, the Ministries of Health and Education, and the Center for Disease Management in Tehran, which often provide figures based on limited research in specific towns or parts of towns. Due to the sensitivity of high-risk behavior, many people who would be at risk for health problems constitute a "hidden population" that may be reluctant to participate in a study conducted by the government or that might not trust the researchers and thus would not provide honest answers. Therefore, the accuracy of data collected by government statistical

centers has been questioned by members of the international community such as the United Nations and Human Rights Watch. Similarly, laws and regulations about abortion and contraception, although broadly based on sharia, are often open to diverse interpretations based on whether members of the parliament and lawmakers follow conservative or reformist interpretations of Islam. An extensive amount of research was conducted to try to ascertain baseline and basic statistical data to speak to sex education, contraceptive usage, abortion rates, and STI and HIV rates. United Nations agencies had only estimates, and archival work in the country produced a limited number of studies in Persian. Given the researcher's weak literacy in Persian, translations from friends and colleagues were often relied on for reading these studies. The small amount of baseline data that I was able to accumulate, including the history of sex education in Iran as well as legal codes pertaining to abortion and treatment, is presented throughout this chapter.

2. Francoeur and Noonan 2004.

3. Francoeur and Noonan 2004: 191.

4. Afary 2006.

5. http://www.who.int

6. Center for Disease Management, Ministry of Health and Medical Education 2004).

7. http://www.who.int, http://www.unaids.org

8. In Iran it is permissible to register as a drug addict, and the harm-reduction program approved in 2003 provides methadone treatment and needle exchange for registered drug users. The two million figure is based on numbers of Iranians attending needle-exchange and harm-reduction clinics. It is also important to note that one reason drug use is so high in Iran is because of the country's close proximity to Afghanistan, a major opium-producing nation. Because Iran is used as a route for drug trafficking, opium and heroin are extremely affordable and in most parts of the country cost less than cigarettes or chewing gum. Additionally, these opiates are more available, and more affordable, to young people than alcohol. Thus many people choose to use opiates as a substitution for alcohol.

9. Based on a survey of street drug users combined with data on needle exchanges throughout the country.

10. Center for Disease Management 2004.

11. Abbasi-Shavazi 2001.

12. Abbasi-Shavazi 2001.

13. Aghajānian and Merhyar 1999.

14. Abbasi-Shavazi 2001.

15. Encouragement by the government to have more children in order to further populate the nation with Iranian citizens.

16. Abbasi-Shavazi 2001.

17. Abbasi-Shavazi 2001.

18. Abbasi-Shavazi 2001.

19. Abbasi-Shavazi, Mchryar, Jones, and McDonald 2001.

20. Boonstra 2001.

21. Abbasi-Shavazi, Mchryar, Jones, and McDonald 2001: 4.

22. Boonstra 2001.

23. Aghajānian and Mehryar 1999.

24. Aghajānian and Mehryar 1999.

25. National Report on Population, IRI 1994.

26. Aghajānian and Mehryar 1999.

27. Roudi-Fahimi 2000.

28. Roudi-Fahimi 2000.

29. Ahmadi and Iranmahboob 2005.

30. Bearman and Burns 1998.

31. United Nations Department of Economic and Social Affairs (DESA). http://www.un.org/esa/desa

32. DESA. http://www.un.org/esa/desa

33. DESA. http://www.un.org/esa/desa

34. Harrison 2005.

35. Lifesite 2005; http://www.lifesite.net/ldn/2005/may/05050909.html

Chapter 7

1. Harm reduction services, or "meeting people where they are at," include offering the public information and resources to lower the risk in high-risk behavior. Some examples of harm reduction include providing injection drug users with clean needles or safe injection rooms, offering safer cigarettes, and providing sexually active people with condoms and contraception.

2. Adelkhah 2004.

Chapter 8

1. For further discussion of the Velvet Revolution, see Kukral 1997.

Works Cited

Books and Periodicals

Abbasi-Shavazi, M. J. 2001, November. "The Fertility Revolution in Iran." *Population and Societies*, 373: 1-4.

Abbasi-Shavazi, M. J., A. Mchryar, G. Jones, and P. McDonald. 2001. "Revolution, War, and Modernization: Population Policy and Fertility Change in Iran." *Journal of Population Research*, 19(1): 25-46.

Abrahamian, E. 1982. *Iran Between Two Revolutions*. Princeton Studies on the Near East. Princeton, N.J.: Princeton University Press.

Adelkhah, F. 2004. *Being Modern in Iran*. New York: Columbia University Press.

Aghajānian, A., and A. H. Merhyar. 1999, June. "Fertility, Contraceptive Use, and Family Planning Program Activity in the Islamic Republic of Iran." *International Family Planning Perspectives* 25(2): 98-102.

Ahmadi, A., and J. Iranmahboob. 2005, July 18–23. "Unmet Need for Family Planning in Iran." Paper presented at Twenty-Fifth International Union for the Scientific Study of Population International Population Conference, Tours, France. Paris: IUSSP.

Alavi, N. 2005. *We Are Iran: The Persian Blogs*. Brooklyn: Soft Skull Press.

Al-Ahmad, J. 1962. *Gharb-zadagi [Weststruckness]*. Tehran: Azad Press.

Amuzegar, J. 2004, October 11. "Iran's Unemployment Crisis." *Middle East Economic Survey* 47(41). http://iranvajahan.net/cgi-bin/news .pl?l=en&y=2004&m=10&d=15&a=5

Basmenji, K. 2006. *Tehran Blues: Youth Culture in Iran*. Tehran: Saqi Books.

Bearman, P., and L. Burns. 1998. "Adolescents, Health, and School: Early Analyses from the National Longitudinal Study of Adolescent Health." *NASSP Bulletin* 82(601): 1-12.

Boonstra, H. 2001, December. "The Guttmacher Report on Public Policy." *Islam, Women, and Family Planning: A Primer* 4(6): 4-7.

Bourdieu, P. 1986. "The Forms of Capital." In J. G. Richardson (ed.), *Handbook of Theory and Research for the Sociology of Education*. New York: Greenwood Press. (Originally published 1983, in French.)

Center for Disease Management, Ministry of Health and Medical Education. 2004, December. *AIDS/HIV Surveillance Report*. Tehran, Iran: CDM.

Central Intelligence Agency. 2008. *World Factbook*. https://www.cia.gov/library/publications/the-world-factbook/index.html

Economist, The. 2007, July 19. "Khomeini's Children." http://www.economist.com/surveys/displaystory.cfm?story_id=9466776

Esposito, J. L., and R. K. Ramazani. 2001. *Iran at the Crossroads*. New York: Palgrave.

Farrer, J. 2002. *Opening Up: Youth, Sex Culture, and Market Reform in Shanghai*. Chicago: University of Chicago Press.

Francoeur, R., and R. Noonan. 2004. *International Encyclopedia of Sexuality*. New York: Continuum International.

Gelder, Ken. 2007. *Subcultures: Cultural Histories and Social Practice*. London: Routledge.

Giddens, A. 1991. *Modernity and Self-Identity: Self and Society in the Late Modern Age*. Stanford, Calif.: Stanford University Press.

Giddens, A. 1993. *The Transformation of Intimacy*. Stanford, Calif.: Stanford University Press.

Haeri, S. 1990. *Law of Desire: Temporary Marriage in Shi'i Iran*. Syracuse, N.Y.: Syracuse University Press.

Harrison, F. 2005. "Iran Liberalises Laws on Abortion." BBC News. http://news.bbc.co.uk/2/hi/middle_east/4436445.stm. Retrieved May 12, 2006.

Hebdige, D. 1979. *Subculture: The Meaning of Style*. London: Routledge.

Hirsch, J. S. 2003. *A Courtship After Marriage: Sexuality and Love in Mexican Transnational Families*. Berkeley: University of California Press.

Hourani, A. 1983. *Arabic Thought in the Liberal Age 1798–1939*. Cambridge, U.K.: Cambridge University Press.

Joseph, S., and A. Najmabadi. 2005. *Encyclopedia of Women and Islamic Cultures*. Boston: Brill Academic Publishers.

Keddie, N. R., and Y. Richard. 2003. *Modern Iran: Roots and Results of Revolution*. New Haven, Conn.: Yale University Press.

Kukral, M. 1997. *Theater of Revolution*. New York: Columbia University Press.

Moaveni, A. 2005. *Lipstick Jihad: A Memoir of Growing Up Iranian in America and American in Iran*. New York: Public Affairs.

Moghadam, V. 2003. *Modernizing Women: Gender and Social Change in the Middle East*. 2nd edition. Boulder, Colo.: L. Rienner.

Najmabadi, A. 2005. *Women with Mustaches and Men Without Beards: Gender and Sexual Anxieties of Iranian Modernity.* Berkeley: University of California Press.

Peiss, K. L. 1986. *Cheap Amusements: Working Women and Leisure in Turn-of-the-Century New York.* Philadelphia: Temple University Press.

Roudi-Fahimi, F. 2000. "Iran's Family Planning Program: Responding to a Nation's Needs." MENA Policy Brief. Washington, D.C.: Population Reference Bureau.

Shavarini, Mitra K. 2006, May. "Wearing the Veil to College: The Paradox of Higher Education in the Lives of Iranian Women." *International Journal of Middle East Studies* 38(2): 189–211.

Varzi, R. 2006. *Warring Souls: Youth, Media, and Martyrdom in Post-Revolution Iran.* Durham, N.C.: Duke University Press.

Lectures

Afary, Janet. "Iran's Sexual Revolution." Pomona College, November 2006.

Web Sites

United Nations AIDS Organization: http://www.unaids.org

United Nations Department of Economic and Social Affairs: http://www.un.org/esa/desa

World Health Organization: http://www.who.int

Index

Page numbers in italics indicate illustrations.

on condom use, 241, 243; on cybersex, 171; dating, 135–45; delaying marriage for financial reasons, 151; focus on appearance by, 120; Islamic dress for, 110; learning to understand women, 141–43; long hair on, 20, 110, 124, 125, 129–30, 274, 303; lower-class men emulate middle-class, 118–19; neckties, 56; premarital sex, 172; punishment for un-Islamic dress, 129–30; as status objects to women, 144, 162–63; stylish, 113, *113*, *114*; talking with their mothers about sex, 275; vasectomies, 239; on virginity, 146–48, 152–54; women judge by appearance, 125–26; women wear Islamic dress to fend off, 34–35

menstruation, 220, 221, 275
mental health providers, 292–97
methadone, 285, 286, 287, 320n8
methodology of this study, 23–25
Moatamedi, M. R., 238
Moein, Mostafa, 193
Moghaddam, Val, 107
morality: state regulation of, 20, 299–300. *See also* Islamic values
morality police (*komite*), 3; Ahmadinejad on increasing power of, 17; airport morality attendants, 104; antagonism toward, 128; arrest as regular occurrence for youth, 22, 197, 202; attacks on, 210, 302; author's experience of raid by, 4–5; avoid following, 211; bloggers harassed by, 79; bribing, 48, 83, 213; "caught" stories, 195–215; change in response of, 6–7, 123, 124, 132–34, 200, 214–15; class and behavior of, 203, 213–14; conservative dress of, 118; consumer culture suppressed by, 23; control desired by, 129; crackdown cycles of, 56, 93, 111, 209–10; and dating, 138; diversity among, 215; dwindling numbers of, 301; at election time, 87; feared less than in past, 102, 214–15, 301–2; flirting with, 6, 7, 208; green suits of, 12, 205; marriage as protection mechanism against, 63, 160–61; mountainside cafes for avoiding, 74; neckties opposed by, 56; outdriving, 174; outwitting to wear makeup to school, 37, 49, 127; pants' lengths measured by, 130–31; parents bribe, 48, 83; parents defend their children against, 273, 274, 275–76; parties raided by, 23, 81, 82, 83, 85, 86, 96, 214; patrol the streets looking for violators, 18; people look over their shoulders for, 14; privacy invaded by, 300, 301; strategies for deal-

ing with, 212–13; women given harder time by, 67, 70
morning-after pill, 218, 249, 250
Mossadegh, Mohammad, 15
mountain areas, 73–74, 82
music: approved by Islamic Republic, 13; at coffee shops, 45; downloading from Internet, 80, 81; as increasingly tolerated, 44; Islamic lifestyle prohibits, 18, 90–91; at parties, 82, 85, 89, 97, 99; Persian pop, 89, 316n20; playing in cars, 76, 197; popular diasporic, 11, 13, 51, 63; techno, 85, 89, 96, 181, 193, 277, 303

nail polish, 110, 116, 122, 123, 124, 129, 131–32, 187, 277
National Birth Control Policy, 238–40
neckties, 56
needle-exchange programs, 229, 286, 287, 306, 320n8
newspapers, 14, 192
nose jobs, 33, 54, 57, 120–21

open-toed shoes, 20, 29, 30, 110, 123, 127, 130, 131
opiates: availability of, 316n22; heroin, 99, 316n22, 320n8; at lower-class parties, 97; methadone maintenance, 285, 286, 287, 320n8; opium, 60, 99, 185, 316n22, 320n8
opium, 60, 99, 185, 316n22, 320n8
oral contraceptives: morning-after pill, 218, 249, 250; self-administered, 218, 249–50. *See also* birth-control pills
orgies (group sex), 91–92, 180–82
Orkut, 77, 170
outercourse, 172

Pahlavi, Mohammad Reza Shah, 15–16, 107–8
pants: capri pants, 105, 125, 128, 130, 210, 211; long pants for men, 110; morality police measure length of, 130–31; rolled-up, 20, 130; shorts, 20, 63, 110, 290
parents, 269–79; on arrests of their children, 195; attend parties with their children, 276; called by morality police, 200, 204, 276; categories of, 269; dating becomes accepted by, 136, 144–45, 274–75; in denial about their children's behavior, 270–73; enact behavior of their children, 270, 276–77; interviews for this study, 25; lying to, 50, 270–71, 272; on marrying well, 162; as open to change among youth, 47–48, 123–24, 268–69, 270, 273–76, 292, 296–97; parties hosted by,